The United States 1783

Lake Huron

St. Lawrence River

Lake Champlain

Lake Ontario

N.H.

MASS.
Boston

Fort Niagara

NEW YORK

1.
Albany
(see inset)

Providence

Lake Erie

2.

CONN.

R.I.

3.

New Haven

Ohio Country

PENNSYLVANIA

4.
Elizabethtown

New York City

Fort Necessity

Cumberland

Philadelphia

Princeton
Trenton

12.

13.

Charles Town

Mason-Dixon Line

Baltimore

3.

NEW JERSEY

GW

6.

DELAWARE

GW

11.

5.

Alexandria
(see inset)

MARYLAND

Charlottesville

7.

George Washington's western lands

GW

10.

9.

8.

Richmond

Yorktown

VIRGINIA

Williamsburg

Norfolk

1763 Proclamation Line

NORTH CAROLINA

SOUTH CAROLINA

ATLANTIC OCEAN

GEORGIA

Charleston

Key

1) Mohawk River
2) Hudson River
3) Delaware River
4) Susquehanna River
5) Potomac River
6) Shenandoah River
7) Rappahannock River
8) York River
9) James River
10) Great Kanawha River
11) Little Kanawha River
12) Miami River
13) Monongahela River

Spanish Florida

0   100   200
Scale of Miles

PATRIOTISM
& PROFIT

PATRIOTISM & PROFIT

Washington, Hamilton, Schuyler &
the Rivalry for America's Capital City

SUSAN NAGEL

PEGASUS BOOKS
NEW YORK LONDON

PATRIOTISM & PROFIT

Pegasus Books, Ltd.
148 West 37th Street, 13th Floor
New York, NY 10018

First Pegasus Books cloth edition October 2021

Interior design by Maria Torres

ISBN: 978-1-64313-708-7

10 9 8 7 6 5 4 3 2 1

Printed in the United States of America
Distributed by Simon & Schuster
www.pegasusbooks.com

For Hadley

There is a tide in the affairs of men,
Which, taken at the flood, leads on to fortune;
Omitted, all the voyage of their life
Is bound in shallows and in miseries.
On such a full sea are we now afloat;
And we must take the current when it serves,
Or lose our ventures.

[BRUTUS TO CASSIUS, *JULIUS CAESAR*, ACT 4, SCENE 3]

CONTENTS

A NOTE ON SPELLING

As scholar Jeremy Gregory has written, "Eighteenth-century spelling was notoriously idiosyncratic," and nowhere more so than in the colonies, where diverging American spelling had yet to be cataloged and standardized. (Noah Webster, an incidental character in this narrative, performed much of that heroic work in his *An American Dictionary of the English Language,* 1828.) The spelling of American place names, especially those names transliterated from unwritten Native American languages, could be especially changeable; Potomac, for example, derives from an Algonquian word for a tribe settled along its banks, first recorded by Captain John Smith as Patawomeck in 1612. Its spelling remained unsettled for more than two centuries. When quoting from eighteenth-century letters, journals, diaries, and other contemporaneous accounts, I have preserved the writers' original spelling, abbreviations, and punctuation. Thus, the reader will encounter Potowmack, Potomack, and Patowmac, among other adaptations.

It Did Not Happen
in the Room

ON MARCH 20, 1790. THOMAS Jefferson ferried across the Hudson River to New York City. It was the first day of spring, an auspicious day to join George Washington's cabinet as secretary of state. After having lived luxuriously in Paris for five years while serving as Minister to France, Jefferson was affronted that his best housing option in lower Manhattan was unfashionable 57 Maiden Lane, which he was forced to lease from a grocer. Jefferson's seeming unpreparedness is surprising: he most assuredly knew beforehand that the city was teeming with politicians. The American Congress had been convening in New York City for over five years and operating there under the brand-new Constitution for more than a year. Jefferson also claimed that until his arrival he was supposedly unaware of any ugly bickering going on between the representatives of the northern and southern states. This, too, was disingenuous, as Jefferson had been in frequent correspondence with James Madison and others.

The young nation to which Jefferson had returned in 1790 was in danger of being torn asunder over two divisive issues: a permanent location for the new nation's capital city and Alexander Hamilton's program for the federal assumption of wartime debts. We know many of Jefferson's thoughts about his life in New York City and his time of federal service there because he chronicled and published them. Jefferson asserted that he felt compelled to negotiate détente, so he invited leaders of the two factions to a dinner party. Again, according to Jefferson's account, it was at this June 20, 1790, gathering where he, Jefferson, masterfully mediated the hard-won agreement that would reunify the country: the seat of government would remove to a swamp on the Potomac River to please the southerners in exchange for the necessary votes for Hamilton's plan, which would satisfy the north. Jefferson recounted this version of the dinner party three times: in his own papers in 1792, in a September 9, 1792, letter to George Washington, and in his memoirs published in a collection called the *Anas*.

Jefferson's narrative has been engraved in our nation's lore as the Compromise of 1790 or the Dinner Table Bargain, and has been called one of the most pivotal and important moments in American history. Even Lin-Manuel Miranda's hip-hop dramatization, *Hamilton: An American Musical*, venerates the celebrated soirée in the song, "The Room Where It Happens." Sung by Aaron Burr, who would murder Hamilton in a duel, and who was excluded from Jefferson's dinner, Burr not only aches to be a player but also with great relish accuses Alexander Hamilton for posterity of "sell[ing] New York down the river." That damning charge was Jefferson's intent. Miranda, however, gets it right in his refrain, "Thomas claims."

Thomas Jefferson was merely a bit player in the drama now known as the Compromise of 1790. The protagonists engaged in the battle that would separate our financial capital from the political seat of power were close friends and rivals, President George Washington and New York Senator Philip Schuyler, whose parallel dreams, analogous visions, and similar skills provoked an intense, decades-long rivalry and protracted crusade for the location of the new empire city. Alexander Hamilton, son-in-law to Schuyler and surrogate son to George Washington, was helplessly caught in the middle. By the time of the now fabled dinner party at Jefferson's seedy quarters, Jefferson was openly seething with jealousy about the familial closeness between the president and his young protégé, Secretary of the Treasury Alexander Hamilton. Neither the funding bill nor the location of the permanent capital city of the American empire was settled at the summer solstice dinner party. The issues were protracted, as evinced in even Jefferson's own letters.

The true story that resulted in the dual passage of the so-called Assumption Bill and the Residence Act of July 1790 is indeed about "selling down the river"—it is, in fact, about two rivers, three men, only one of whom—Hamilton—was at this legendary dinner party, and unchecked greed. *Patriotism and Profit: Washington, Hamilton, Schuyler & the Rivalry for America's Capital City* is a timely companion to urgent current-day conversation and campaign rhetoric about draining the swamp. The story contains analogous themes that resonate today and will expose the roots of and reasons for some of our nation's most pressing problems.

The financial and geopolitical wrangling among the European settlers on the North American continent had gone on long before the War of Independence. Before planes, trains, trucks, and cars, the only way to transport quantities of goods and people was via water. From the very moment when Captains John Smith and Henry Hudson sailed into Chesapeake Bay and into New York Harbor, respectively, in the early seventeenth century, a geomagnetic impulse to reach the Pacific Ocean via interior water routes pulsed in the blood of those daring to cross the Atlantic Ocean.

Some 175 year later, the Founding Fathers of the United States of America, acknowledging that they were birthing an empire, believed that it was essential for the seat of that empire—the new nation's capital city—to connect the interior of North America with a coastal port along the Atlantic Ocean. In Philip Schuyler's vision, New York City was the natural capital of the new empire. George Washington, however, was intent on depriving Schuyler of that trophy. Washington's lifelong obsession was to establish the capital of the new republic in Alexandria, Virginia, some eight miles from his Mount Vernon plantation.

New York, with Philip Schuyler in the lead, and Virginia—George Washington, the guiding force—were openly at war for the capital city. New York City's harbor could transport goods and people from the ocean up the Hudson River to the Mohawk River along the Oneida Carry to the Great Lakes, down the Ohio and Mississippi Rivers, or from the Hudson River north to Canada through Lake Champlain and again to the Great Lakes and the Atlantic Ocean via the St. Lawrence River. Virginians argued that the tidewater Potomac River provided the same opportunity into the interior of North America.

Schuyler and Washington both proposed canal systems, long before the War of Independence, that would expand the flow of humanity and product from thirteen coastal colonies, now states, toward the Pacific Ocean. Forging a continental empire was a noble and patriotic enterprise. Nevertheless, both men were also landlords and commercial innovators, and these schemes would also enrich them immeasurably. New York Senator Philip Schuyler owned an enormous swath of fertile land from New York Harbor, which sat at the confluence of three rivers: the East River, the Hudson River and the Raritan River, which connects the Hudson River with the Delaware River. Schuyler's properties along the Hudson River went for many miles north along the river valleys toward Canada; he also had tens of thousands of acres along the Mohawk River westward toward the Great Lakes. President George Washington, a life-long tidewater Virginian, also had amassed significant parcels of real estate housing farms, taverns, stills, and mills, along the Potomac and her tributaries out west toward the Ohio Valley. To hedge his bets, Washington also bought land along the Mohawk Valley in upstate New York.

Patriotism and Profit: Washington, Hamilton, Schuyler & the Rivalry for America's Capital City is not a muckraking exercise to discredit our Founding Fathers. The true story will teach the reader to understand our nation's founders in a larger and hitherto unexamined context. In 1790, old habits died hard: the Founding Fathers, though enlightened and progressive brilliant thinkers, had been born into the European tradition of tribute. George Washington himself had expressed the belief that the country owed him his empire city on the Potomac River, and he did not have to explain himself to anybody. Most of the members of all three branches of the fledgling government of the United States were significant landowners; many of them were real estate and financial speculators; many also owned government-issued certificates repurchased from impoverished soldiers, who had been forced to sell. These same politicians were also the ones who would vote on how much the federal government was going to repay bondholders and at what interest, as well as on the location of the permanent capital city of the American empire. It was not until 1978, two hundred years after the ratification of the U.S. Constitution, that the Congress enacted the Ethics in Government Act, mandating financial disclosure from our public servants.

There were many steps made by our Founding Fathers in the other two branches of government that today would result in investigation, censure, and even prosecution. The vice president's wife, Abigail Adams, held war certificates. Her husband's authority in government could have impact on her investment. The financial windfall by family members of government officials with inside information and influence is one of the most topical subjects of the twenty-first century. In 1789, the new nation's first chief executive, President George Washington, simultaneously served as president of—and the largest single shareholder in—the Potomac River Canal Company, whose purpose was to profit from the development of the Potomac River. Today, he would have been forced to place his holdings into a blind trust. Although the Emoluments Clause, which precludes a president of the United States from personally profiting from his office, had been set in place in the US Constitution, no action by the Congress was ever taken against Washington.

In the Judicial branch, the very first chief justice of the United States, John Jay, presided over a case in 1791 called *Van Staphorst v. Maryland*. The case involved a longstanding dispute between the state of Maryland and Dutch bankers. Jay's late brother-in-law, Matthew Ridley, had brokered the deal. Jay's own previous participation as an arbitrator in the case presented a problematic conflict as well. Another brother-in-law planted newspaper articles implying that Jay was privately benefiting from his office. One can only imagine the outcry if this situation had occurred today.

Patriotism and Profit: Washington, Hamilton, Schuyler & the Rivalry for America's Capital City will reveal, as did Miranda's musical, that our Founding Fathers were flawed human beings, just like we are. They were avaricious, passionate, and also visionary. They loved, hated, sacrificed, and aspired. Their caveats remain our concerns, and, sometimes, despite their roles as public servants, their other obligations—as lawyers, farmers, doctors, and devoted sons and husbands—sometimes placed them in direct conflict with the very constitution they fought so hard to pass.

The first real estate developer president of the United States was not Donald Trump, but the first president of the United States. Until Donald Trump, George Washington was the most successful property speculator president

of the United States. *Patriotism and Profit: Washington, Hamilton, Schuyler &*
the Rivalry for the America's Capital City will explore how George Washington
successfully masterminded the real estate deal of the millennium and by doing
so abused the power of his position in order to enrich himself. George Washington borrowed, leveraged, misled, coerced, and otherwise cheated his way
to creating the nation's capital city.

Scrupulous study of the facts through personal letters and diaries of over
twenty of our Founding Mothers and Fathers, contemporaneous publications,
and official government records have evoked provocative questions germane
to our own current zeitgeist: Does writing history to lionize flawed men inevitably lead to the toppling of their monuments? What do we do when a real
estate developer president of the United States violates Article II, Section 1,
Clause 7—the Presidential Emoluments Clause—of the US Constitution?
How do we respond when the president of the United States is involved in a
conspiracy or nefariously colludes with others for personal gain? If the physical swamp that was drained to construct the capital city was the creation of a
morass of ethically questionable engineers, and the "shining city on a hill"—
a symbol of the pinnacle of our finest values—is really just a house built on sand
by foolish men, for how long will it—and does it deserve to—endure? Why
was it so important to our Founding Fathers to keep the seat of government
paradoxically politically independent from the very supervision it domiciles?

So much of *Patriotism and Profit: Washington, Hamilton, Schuyler & the*
Rivalry for America's Capital City will provide answers to current headlines. For
example, on Friday, June 26, 2020, the United States House of Representatives
passed HR 51 completely on partisan lines. The bill first appeared in the House
on March 8, 2019, following the Senate's May 2017 failed Washington, DC,
Admission Act. Both bills, favored by Democrats, propose to create a fifty-first
state of the District of Columbia. HR 51 cites its authority as Article IV,
Section 3, Clause 1 of the U.S. Constitution that stipulates that an annexed
territory may be granted statehood through an act of Congress. Although the
House of Representatives passed the bill on Thursday, April 22, 2021, this is
going to be a hotly contested ongoing issue. Conferring statehood on the federal District of Columbia actually requires a multistep demanding procedure.

Accession for Washington, DC, would not only necessitate approval from the state of Maryland, the original land grantor, but also would require a constitutional amendment. The constitutional amendment can occur only one of two ways: either both the House of Representatives and the US Senate pass the bill with a two-thirds vote, or all fifty state legislatures pass the bill with a two-thirds vote. It will not be easy.

The historicity offered in *Patriotism and Profit: Washington, Hamilton, Schuyler & the Rivalry for the America's Capital City* will illuminate why and how the current Washington, DC, Admission Act flouts the intent not only of the framers but also of the capital's creator—George Washington—who were all resolved that the seat of government paradoxically must be kept apart from the very government it houses. The reasons can be traced to an episode that occurred on June 21, 1783, echoes of which were reiterated forcefully in the 1788 *Federalist Papers* number 43, in the 1789 passage of the Constitution (Article I, Section 8, Clause 17), and again in the Residence Act of 1790.

Behind the politics lies a fascinating personal tension and dynamic in the interactions among George Washington, Philip Schuyler, and Alexander Hamilton, all three alpha males, combatting for their places in history.

PART I

COLONIAL RIVALS

CHAPTER 1

The Race for a New World Capital of Empire

THE "OFFICIAL" NARRATIVE OF THE thousand-year-old panoramic struggle for the capital city of the New World empire appears in a painstakingly curated assemblage of art in the Rotunda of United States Capitol Building. Visitors to the Capitol can perch on a balcony some 152 feet in the air from the floor of the Rotunda and peer above into an oculus. Girdling the circumference of the vault is a continuous series of paintings and trompe l'oeil friezes that illustrate a varnished version of the epic story. Soaring even sixty-seven feet higher at the apex of the dome, a 4,664-square-foot allegorical fresco called the *Apotheosis of Washington* crowns the cupola. The ceiling mural, painted sixty-six years after George Washington's death, depicts the nation's first president, flanked by two female figures representing Liberty and Victory, ascending toward heaven. Washington and the rest of his exalted cluster are encircled by group-ings of Roman gods and goddesses meant to symbolize war, science, the sea, commerce, agriculture, and mechanics; Washington is deified, and United States exceptionalism is divinely ordained.

Positioned near George Washington in the tableau is Vulcan, the god of fire, who is standing at his anvil, foot atop a cannon, boldly affirming that success and progress were predestined for the United States. Vulcan's important

placement is undoubtedly owing to his contribution to the location of the
capital city itself: the providential invention in 1770 of the rubber eraser,
which would lay the foundation for the 1839 innovation of vulcanized rubber,
would play a significant role in the fate of where the federal government of the
American empire would reside.

The story of the rise of every great empire begins with the founding of its
capital city. This origin mythology explains the rise to greatness and reveals the
values of its civilization. In the Judeo-Christian Bible's book of Genesis, Cain,
who has murdered his brother, flees to Nod, east of Eden, gets married somewhere along the way, and then builds "a city . . . the name of the city after the
name of his son—Enoch." Noah's sons allegedly traveled the earth establishing
post-flood seats of empire. Biblical patriarch Isaiah claims to have created
Jerusalem. In Revelation, the perfect seat of the eternal empire is revealed to
be laid out in a square.

Classical mythology includes figures like the Sumerian Gilgamesh, Alexander the Great, and Theseus, who all created seats of empire. The *Aeneid,*
which begins, *"dum conderet urbem"*—"until he should found a city"—echoes
in the fourth *Eclogue,* that this new empire city will create a new world order:
"Magnus ab integro saeclorum nascitur ordo." Romulus and Remus fought each
other in about 753 B.C.E., according to lore, for the privilege of choosing the
location of Rome: Romulus preferred Palatine Hill, Remus selected Aventine.
Romulus kills his brother, and the matter is settled. To perpetuate imperial
propaganda, the Roman calendar actually points to the beginning of its empire
as *"Ab urbe condita"*—"from the founding of the city."

Through the collaboration of professionals from varying fields and diverse
scientific methods like DNA testing, carbon dating, and chemical deconstruc-
tion, ancient physical and organic matter can be accurately identified. There
is now concrete proof of the physical presence of western Europeans in the
New World as long ago as the early Middle Ages. There have been mysterious
tales that spoke of transatlantic journeys but all had been dismissed as folk-
lore. One such Irish "immram," known as the "Voyage of Saint Brendan the
Abbot," details the perilous voyage of a group of monks who went to sea in
a primitive leather-hulled boat called a "currah." Their leader, Brendan, who

really did live c. 484–577 C.E., and his fellow friars arrived at a faraway "Isle of the Blessed." For nearly 1,500 years, there was conjecture that this distant Promised Land of Saints was North America but it was thought impossible for such a crude vessel to sail across the Atlantic Ocean. In the 1970s, however, British explorer Timothy Severin crafted a replica of St. Brendan's boat and successfully completed the trip, proving that the voyage was indeed feasible. More recently, a group of scientists and linguistic experts have uncovered petroglyphs on rocks in West Virginia that they authenticated as sixth-century C.E. Ogam (Old Irish) carvings.

European yearnings for a New World empire can again be traced to the year 1000 C.E. when, led by the sun, the stars, and a shard of light-polarizing crystal for cloudy days, a group of brutal hyperborean Vikings made their own foray to North America. The king of Norway had dispatched "Lucky" Leif Erikson into uncharted waters to find and convert heathens. Erikson's Norwegian-born father, Erik the Red, and his grandfather were on the run from murder charges, and, while he was a reluctant convert, he was an eager and daring voyager. His exploits were chronicled by many, among them his contemporary Adam of Bremen, and in the "Greenlanders Saga." According to both, Erikson journeyed to a place called "Vinland," where he established a Christian settlement. The ambiguous location and the mysterious evaporation of the European society at "Vinland" continue to tantalize. Some have asserted that "Vinland" was, in reality, the island of Newfoundland. A Viking settlement, named "L'Anse aux Meadows" by the French, has been excavated there, but there is no irrefutable proof that it was the site of Erikson's New World society. More recently, archaeologist Erik Wahlgren and Icelandic climate expert Pall Bergthorsson have separately concluded that based upon the descriptions of fish, flora, fauna, and the climate described in the saga, "Vinland" was most probably located around New York Harbor and the Hudson River.

When Erikson's New World Viking colony was established at the dawn of the eleventh century, London was still an insignificant, small commercial town. Sixty-six years later, in 1066 C.E., King William of Normandy, whose great-great-great-grandfather was a Viking raider named Rollo, conquered England. The island of Britain would remain in turmoil for another hundred years. According to a medieval romance, Prince Madog ab Owain Gwynedd, one of nineteen children of the king of Wales, could not tolerate the violence. Madog took one hundred traveling companions and went in search of a new world where he could live the rest of his life in serenity. It is alleged that the group arrived in North America in 1170 C.E. and established a new city. Although there is no extant authentic contemporaneous chronicle, two poems, one by a Welshman and one by a Flemish poet, that were written within fifty years of Madog's escape do survive. Both make reference to the "splendid" prince of peace.

No archaeological evidence has been found of Madog's "paradise" of "love and music," which is said to have been located everywhere from present-day Louisville to Mexico, but a story was passed on for generations that the Welsh émigrés met and married the Native Americans. In the eighteenth century, there were a handful of reports from European immigrants to North America that Welsh-speaking tribes were living in Tennessee and along the Missouri River. Called the Mandans, this tribe fished from boats known as coracles, which were similar to those still found in Wales today; the Mandans had also constructed villages with streets and squares, a pattern unknown to other pre-Columbian Natives.

Some 250 years after Madog and companions allegedly found their utopian oasis in the New World, thousands of miles to the east the Ottomans forcibly gained control of Constantinople—the capital city that bridged two Old World continents. The fierce Turkish military cut off the Silk Road from European contact, coercing the Europeans to find another route to China. The Portuguese began sailing south, west, and north to reach the East. They sailed the coast of Africa, establishing trading posts, and around the continent to India and Asia. Lisbon soon became the premier metropolis in Europe. The Portuguese success prompted the Spanish to enter the exploration fray. Territorial discovery was a lawless pursuit, and the booty remained in the hands of the strongest.

Italian-born Christopher Columbus petitioned the king of Portugal to support a voyage but was declined. Columbus next approached the king of Spain. While waiting for an answer, Columbus dispatched his brother, Bartholomew, to King Henry VII of England with the same proposal. By the time

Bartholomew returned to Spain with an agreement from Henry, Christopher Columbus had already received patronage from the Castilians. In 1492, nearly one thousand years after Saint Brendan was alleged to have found his city of goodness, Columbus stumbled upon the Caribbean islands. The game immediately changed, and the race for a New World empire city accelerated.

The Portuguese not only regretted their rebuff but they also now felt their supremacy over the seas threatened. When Columbus established two settlements on the island of Hispaniola in Central America, the Portuguese protested. The menace of war now loomed between the two Catholic countries so Pope Alexander VI stepped in to mediate. His solution was nothing short of the wisdom of King Solomon. The pope drew a vertical line some two thousand miles west of the Cape Verde islands: all new discoveries west of that line would belong to Spain, and, those east of that demarcation would belong to Portugal. He signed two papal bulls, and it was so—for the moment. The treaties were subsequently amended, and the Portuguese began seeding Brazil with Jews escaping the Spanish Inquisition.

King Henry VII of England, completely ignoring the pope, launched a navigation of his own. Henry granted Italian-born Giovanni Caboto (John Cabot) a petition to sail to North America in 1496. Cabot's first voyage was unsuccessful but on a subsequent voyage in 1497, he arrived in Newfoundland, which he—and King Henry VII—claimed for England. Newfoundland had been populated by Beothuk Natives for over a thousand years. Every spring, the Beothuk would paint their bodies and their houses a bright red color, which custom gave rise to the "red man" designation for American Indigenous peoples among the British. While the island was the first foothold for the English in North America, no effort to settle the island would be attempted for another hundred years. Christopher Columbus learned of Cabot's discovery from an anonymous "John Day" letter written by a Bristol merchant acquainted with both Cabot and himself. Cabot would be among many to challenge Columbus.

Columbus's brother, Bartholomew, established his own settlement on Hispaniola and proclaimed it the official capital city. Christopher Columbus's son, Diego Colón (the Hispanized version of Columbus), arrived at his uncle's capital and, asserting hereditary rights over the islands that his father discovered,

Diego began prolonged legal battles for autonomous rule. First, he battled with King Ferdinand and next, his successor, Holy Roman Emperor Charles V. Diego's crusade for New World autonomy was in fact the first American Revolution. His palace, called Alcázar de Colón, still stands today in Santo Domingo, which remains the oldest continuously inhabited European-settled capital in the New World.

Diego Colón's capital city was the first major commercial city in New Spain and served as a magnet for rascals. The Founding Fathers of Central America gathered their forces in Santo Domingo among a rogue's gallery of men who had exiled themselves from the Old World. Explorers like Vasco Núñez de Balboa, Hernán Cortés, Diego Velázquez de Cuéllar, and Juan Ponce de León became collectively known as "conquistadores." They were more feared than pirates. Armor-suited warrior messengers, these men delivered a stream of bloody coups d'états. Their sadism, confirmed by eyewitness accounts, became collectively known as the terrifying "Black Legend." Some "conquistadores" would tie up entire Native villages, murder selected members of the Indigenous community, and then force them to eat one another. Other "conquistadores" favored roasting men alive like pigs over a fire. Still others preferred disemboweling their own countrymen and even their own family members, all for four fifths of whatever could be extracted from the New World. The king of Spain, whose swelling coffers were reaping his royal one-fifth, the "quinto real," turned a blind eye to the barbarity; hence, the "Golden Age" of Spain began under a cloud of darkness.

In the Capitol Building Rotunda, all traces of the murder and mayhem perpetrated by the conquistadores have been whitewashed—erased from cultural memory—in the trompe l'oeil tableaux that memorialize these men and their voyages. Instead, the audacity of champions is celebrated. There is no illustration of how Velázquez de Cuéllar tamed the Taíno Natives on Cuba by burning their chieftain alive when he refused to accept Christ. Neither is there a depiction of Francisco Hernández de Córdoba's massacre of the Natives on the Yucatan Peninsula. Córdoba, who sailed with three ships and one hundred men through a very rough storm, arrived safely there, saw Mayan stone buildings, believed that the structures were the work of Muslims, and named the place El Oran Cairo (Cabo Catoche), which means "Little Cairo." As a good Catholic Spaniard, he promptly supervised the genocide of the local "Muslims."

The Rotunda frieze does narrate a cartoonish and cringeworthy version of the exploits of Hernán Cortés, who is seen entering a sacred Aztec temple, hailed as a god by Moctezuma II. That moment of harmony captured by an artist is pure fantasy. Hernán Cortés founded a city on the coast of Mexico, which was situated at the mouth of a river. He named it "Villahermosa"— "Beautiful Town." To his surprise, two Spaniards appeared. These two men had been among fifteen survivors of a shipwreck a few years earlier; the other thirteen had either been sacrificed or worked to death by the Mayans. One of the men who stood before Cortés had gone native: he now called himself "Cacique." "Cacique" had learned Mayan, had married a Mayan princess with whom he had three children, and had become a chieftain. Mayor of his own city called Chetumal, "Cacique" told Cortés to leave. The men fought, and ultimately Cortés abandoned the town, dragging the other Spaniard with him to serve as interpreter. Cortés also helped himself to a Native mistress named "La Malinche."

"La Malinche" gave Cortés valuable information. She informed him that the Aztec emperor, Moctezuma II, possessed vast quantities of gold at an inland city, known as Tenochtitlan. Tenochtitlan had served as the capital of the Aztec empire since 1325. Cortés immediately hatched a plan to gain control over the fortune and the capital city. First, he scuttled his own vessels to prevent his crewmembers from escaping. Next, he declared himself ruler, denounced any other authority, and marshaled his own army to capture Tenochtitlan.

En route to Tenochtitlan, Cortés found that a rival Spanish army had developed a parallel plan, and he found himself in combat with his own countrymen. Cortés would often affirm that his worst opponent was not the Indigenous Aztec but his fellow Spaniards. Cortés was merciless in battle, even beheading former friends. After slaughtering his own brethren, Cortés went on to crush the Aztecs. The Aztecs, who fought with primitive spike-covered clubs, were no match for Cortés, whose army was equipped with weapons of metal. Cortés's appearance before Moctezuma II was not as a friend as depicted in the Capitol Building Rotunda mural but as a vanquishing warrior. Cortés, enjoying his triumph, even renamed the two-hundred-year-old seat of Aztec power Mexico City. He then went on to inflict a wider path of destruction, adding Honduras to his plunder.

A figure that looms large among the Eurocentric origin stories of New World Latin America is Vasco Núñez de Balboa. Balboa is rightfully hailed in official history as the founder of the Colombian city Santa María la Antigua del Darién, which boasts the double distinction of being the first capital city on the mainland of South America and having the first democratically elected government in the New World. Carefully censored from the story, however, was the fact that the Hispanic pioneers were so afraid of Balboa's brutality that when they voted, they elected him "co-mayor," limiting his power. Balboa's incandescent ambition burned much brighter than serving as co-mayor of one town. On September 29, 1513, he became the first European to reach the Pacific Ocean through the Isthmus of Panama, for which he is also famous. Dramatically raising his sword, and with great fervor, he saluted the Pacific Ocean, opening the channel through which Spanish galleons could transport trunks of gold from the west coast of South America across the Isthmus of Panama and back to Spain. What is less often relayed is that owing to the number of men who died along the route, it became known as the "Camino de Cruces," the "Path of Crosses."

Another of the men lurking about the port on Hispaniola was Juan Ponce de León. On one of his runs, Ponce de León spied what he thought was an island. It was Florida. He stepped on shore, perhaps the first European man to set foot on continental North America since "Lucky" Leif Erikson's arrival some five hundred years before (if, as scientists currently believe, the Vikings had landed and established "Vinland" around New York Harbor). The exact location of Ponce de León's arrival on mainland North America remains unknown; it is generally believed, however, that, despite popular lore, he did not alight at what today is the city of St. Augustine, which was founded fifty-two years later, in 1565, by Pedro Menéndez on August 28, the feast day of St. Augustine.

In the 1520s, Mexico City, Santo Domingo, and Havana were all competing to be the premier New World capital. These nascent cities were the physical, palpable representations of the dreams of fearless men who were desperate to sculpt New World fiefdoms. Panama City, founded by *converso* Pedro Arias Dávila, also became a contender. Dávila's daughter would marry Hernando de Soto, who led the first European cavalcade into the interior of North America and arrived at the Mississippi River, an event also commemorated in the United States Capitol Building Rotunda.

The conquistadores were given free rein to ruthlessly manage their New World cities because Holy Roman Emperor Charles V was burdened with Old World matters like the Ottomans to the east and Protestants to the north. In 1525, the Emperor's formidable counterparts included his uncle-by-marriage King Henry VIII of England, Ottoman Emperor Suleyman I ("the Magnificent"), Medici Pope Clement VII, and Venetian Doge Andrea Gritti. Charles received both uplifting news that year when the Spanish army captured and humiliated his longtime nemesis, King Francis I of France, in the Battle of Pavia, as well as distressing information that Francis was striking at Spain's new domains.

Charles V had dispatched a convoy led by Portuguese-born Estêvão Gomes into the colder waters of the Atlantic Ocean. Gomes sailed from Nova Scotia down the coastline of Maine, into New York Harbor, up the Hudson River, which he named the "San Antonio," and south to Florida. When the Holy Roman Emperor learned that a French fleet captained by a Florentine sailor named Giovanni da Verrazzano had narrowly preceded Gomes into New York Bay, the monarch was livid. The French remained undaunted, and persevered with their own program of exploration. On behalf of the king of France, Jacques Cartier would map the Gulf of Saint Lawrence, which joined the Atlantic Ocean to the Great Lakes. Within ten years, the French would gain a sturdy foothold in North America and establish Quebec.

Maritime warfare became bigger business. Among the maneuvers employed to deter antagonists were impressment and the dissemination of disinformation, which included elaborately drawn and widely circulated fake maps. The bona fide atlases were kept in vaults, and cartographers became very valuable people. They were sometimes held for ransom or detained by officials of various sovereigns until they spilled knowledge. Mapmaker Diego Ribeiro was able to delineate an accurate outline of the entire east coast of North America

based on Estêvão Gomes's voyage. Ribeiro's chart became the template for the
"Padrón Real," the official but secret master map used by Spanish royal envoys.
The map was so crucial to exploration that nearly a full century later, when
Englishman Henry Hudson sailed to the New World for the Dutch, he would
depend on this same diagram. The Gomes-Ribeiro chart was so valuable that
Hudson, upon his return voyage, was captured and remanded by the English,
who forcibly seized his logbook.

Good cartographers, surveyors, and topographers would translate virgin
territory into visual design so that cities could rise. Surveying and appraising
his New World cities became an obsession with Spanish King Philip II, who
ascended the throne in 1556 after the death of his father, Charles V. Philip,
in contrast with his father's laissez-faire position, decided to micromanage his
empire, as he became in clear danger of losing it.

Philip faced Old World domain problems in 1579, when the seven provinces
that comprised the Protestant northern Netherlands declared their independence from the Holy Roman Empire. Two years later, the seven regions joined
together, forming a republic. A democratically elected states-general, comprised
of representatives called "stadholders," would convene in The Hague, to be the
confederation's new seat of government. The newly elected government established two quasi-governmental international trading corporations, the Dutch
East India Company and the Dutch West India Company, which would offer
shares to the general public in multiple cities. The legislature next determined
that, while it was to reside in The Hague, they would take a pioneering step to
remove the stock market to Rotterdam initially and then to Amsterdam: this
was an innovative move because until that point in time it was the only time in
European history when the seat of government of a nation would be separated
from its commercial capital.[1] The geographic importance of all of the seven
provinces of the northern Netherlands, along three of Europe's most important
rivers, made it collectively a financial powerhouse, with each of the seven dis-
tricts sharing in decision-making as well as in the success of the confederation.

The upstart and progressive stadholder-led management quickly organized
a healthy financial ship of state, which funded a very impressive navy. Philip's
former subjects, now his commercial adversaries, joined in the race for the

development of a New World capital city. Guided by the "majesty of the multitude," a term later coined by American Revolutionary spokesperson Thomas
Paine, the republic formed in the Netherlands was an indisputable triumph,
providing inspiration for those unhappy with autocratic rule. John Adams later
admitted that, vis-à-vis the organization of the United States of America, "the
origins of the two Republics are so much alike that the history of one seems
but a transcript from that of the other."

The Dutch rebellion did not go unnoticed in Philip's New World cities, where
settlers also clamored for political autonomy. A second generation of New World
citizens saw no reason why they should be subject to authority that was located
thousands of miles away. Fueling revolution were some of the sons and grandsons
of those legendary conquistadores, who were asserting their rights to govern the
lands seized by their forebears. For the Spanish monarch, it was history repeating
itself: three generations of the same family feuds every way he turned.

King Philip II also faced direct attack by the British, whose buccaneers known
as the "sea dogs" began assaulting his New World dominions. By the second
half of the sixteenth century, about 240,000 Europeans had disembarked at
New Spain's ports, and American silver provided about one fifth of Spain's total
budget. Philip enjoyed not only these riches but also the benefits belonging to
his wife (and cousin), Queen Mary I of England. After Mary's death, however,
her half sister, Elizabeth, ascended the throne, and she hated Philip. The feeling
was mutual. Philip was a key player in the "Ridolfi plot" to assassinate his
sister-in-law, and she, in turn, issued "letters of marque," which actually licensed
English privateers to attack and plunder foreign—Spanish—ships.

Philip wanted to contain dissatisfaction in his New World cities. He distributed extensive questionnaires called "*relaciones geográficas*" to become expert;
and, from the massive El Escorial palace outside Madrid, he published his
famous and expansive "*Ordenanzas,*" the first New World arcology manifesto
envisaged by an Old World European. These Royal Ordinances amounted to well
over one hundred decrees on how every single inch of urban space was to be
arranged. Philip's commands were exacting and revolutionary. He insisted first
and foremost that his cities should be designed "without doing hurt to the
Indians and natives":

its plazas, streets, and building lots laid out exactly, beginning with the main plaza. From thence the streets, gates, and principal roads, shall be laid out . . . The main plaza whence a beginning is to be made, if the town is situated on the seacoast, should be made at the landing place of the port . . . From the plaza shall run four main streets, one from the middle of each side . . . As for the temple of the cathedral, if the town is situated on the coast, it shall be built in part so that it may be seen on leaving the sea . . . if those towns which are laid out away from the port and inland be built if possible on the shores of a navigable river . . .

King Philip specified that "the choice of a plaza shall be made with reference to the growth" expected, that there should be plenty of space made available for this anticipated expansion, and he isolated grime-producing industries to ensure long-term fresh water for the city's increasing population. Philip was not only a man in search of contented subjects but also a hopeful visionary. He promoted the gentrification of his New World capital cities, believing that high culture would implant there as a glowing reflection of the European Renaissance.

Conversely, arts and letters in late-sixteenth-century Europe, which set a benchmark of excellence for centuries to come, demonstrated a zeitgeist penetrated by imaginings of the New World. Since the early Renaissance, the voyages of sailors, warriors, and pilgrims in *Africa*, *The Canterbury Tales*, and the *Decameron* by Petrarch, Chaucer, and Boccaccio, respectively, had been filled with tales of great cities of the ancient world. It was extremely convenient for the designs of Queen Elizabeth I of England that five different versions of the Madog myth appeared in the 1580s. The thousand-year-old story about the quest for a New World city full of goodness enjoyed tremendous popularity, sparking widespread opinion in England that the British right to New World territories had existed even before John Cabot's discoveries—and, even more significantly to Queen Elizabeth, long before the Spanish had laid claim. Popular endorsement sparked Queen Elizabeth to intensify her aggression against King Philip so that England could enjoy New World hegemony.

One of Elizabeth's henchmen, an adventurer named Sir Francis Drake, added yet another chapter to the British epic narrative, buoying an English origin myth in order to glaze England with legitimate primacy in the Western Hemisphere. According to the British version of the founding of the west coast of North America, Drake disembarked in San Francisco, claimed the territory "New Albion," nailed a sixpence to a post, and inscribed the Queen's name above the coin so that the Indigenous peoples could worship her. No one questioned the fact that the Natives probably did not read English. Drake also undertook another mission—to destroy every Spanish capital in the Western Hemisphere. He devastated Santo Domingo on Hispaniola, Cartagena in Colombia, and Santiago in Chile.

Queen Elizabeth relentlessly antagonized King Philip. In the early 1570s, a group of Spanish Jesuit priests had established a settlement on the bank of a 440-mile waterway near the mouth of the Chesapeake Bay. Known as the Powhatan River at that time, after the tribal confederation living in the region, the river was the major lifeline for nearly 5,000 Native people, providing transportation and rich mineral deposits for farming. The Christian settlement was short-lived because the Powhatans murdered the clerics. The Spanish navy arrived to exact revenge but did not rebuild a community there. British fleets, smelling blood in the water, began circling the bay and river, vowing to succeed where the Spanish had failed. In 1586, Queen Elizabeth I further goaded Philip II when she granted a charter to Sir Walter Raleigh for the settlement of British citizens where the ill-fated Spanish Jesuits had encamped. The queen's actions were gutsy and dangerous but two years later, in 1588, when the British navy annihilated the heretofore-invincible Spanish Armada, her boldness paid off, easing the way for the British colonization of the Americas.

Although Raleigh never set foot in the New World, a group of Englishmen and women journeyed there on his behalf. They carved a settlement in the "Virginia" wilderness. The "Lost Colony of Roanoke" vanished inexplicably, and, in a story that is eerily parallel to the mysterious extinction of the colonists of Leif Erikson's Vinland, both legends herald the birth of the first European baby to be born in North America—Snorri, the Viking boy, and Virginia Dare, the little English girl—and conclude with a haunting assertion that each child had survived and was living amongst "savages."

British Renaissance authors embraced the idea of a new romance, which would reflect the ideas and ideals of their own age. It was widely believed that William Shakespeare patterned his character Miranda in *The Tempest* after Virginia Dare. He was fascinated by the New World, and although he never left the island of Britain, his works are filled with maritime allusions and faraway settings. Shakespeare referred to the west "Indies" and "America" multiple times in plays like *As You Like It, Henry VIII, The Comedy of Errors, The Merry Wives of Windsor*, and *The Merchant of Venice*. Edmund Spenser's *Fairie Queene* also contains homage to the New World:

And daily how through hardy enterprise
Many great Regions are discovered,
Which to late age were never mentioned.
Who ever heard of th' Indian Peru?
Or who in venturous vessel measured
The Amazon huge river, now found trew? [sic]
Or fruitfullest Virginia who did ever vew? [sic]

Christopher Marlowe, whose many dramas focused on the foundation stories of capital cities, made his artistic debut with *Dido, Queen of Carthage*. In *Tamburlaine the Great*, about a conqueror who created an empire, he wrote, "So from the East unto the furthest West / Shall Tamburlaine extend his puissant arm . . . from Persepolis to Mexico," and in *Doctor Faustus*, "I'll have them fly to India for gold, / Ransack the Ocean for orient pearl, / And search all corners of the new-found world / For pleasant fruits and princely delicates." These beautiful words inspired the British, as did the 1590 publication of *A Briefe and True Report of the New Found Land of Virginia* by Thomas Harriot, which extolled the beauties and opportunities along the Chesapeake Bay and James River.

The British therefore remained undeterred by Raleigh's failed attempt at colonization. In fact, it was quite the opposite: the English now began to compete amongst themselves to establish a New World capital city.

CHAPTER 2

The British Quest for New World Dominance

BECAUSE THE SPANISH HAD FORBIDDEN unmarried women from jour-
neying to New Spain, ladies played very little part in the foundation stories
of the New World in their lore. The notable exception was for Native women
like La Malinche, who bore bastard children that were derisively called "mes-
tizos," half-breeds. When the British began to arrive in North America, they
came with wives, sisters, daughters, and female servants. Despite the death
of Queen Elizabeth I, the impact of her nearly half-century matriarchal rule
over the British people provided an ethnogenesis for the American spirit. She
was "Virginia," the "Virgin Queen." New World British foundation stories,
which include a significant feminine presence, are romantic and chivalrous.
The British national psyche craved and created New World origin stories unlike
those of the machismo Spanish conquistadores. The figure of Virginia Dare,
who allegedly lived on peacefully among the natives and roamed freely about,
frolicking in natural surroundings, would now be supplemented by additional
female characters in the annals of the British New World epic tale of the race
to establish an empire city.

Female figures in geopolitical mythology, like Europa, were endowed
with status as potent symbols for the promise of fecundity. Where the Jesuit

encampment had been scorched, new life abounded: as promised, the British established their first North American capital, called Jamestown, along the Powhatan River, which they re-christened the James River, both after their monarch. The Jamestown foundation fable transformed an "Indian Princess" named Pocahontas into a woman with extraordinary goddess-like powers. What the Nile River in Egypt was to the ancient world, as the "cradle of civilization," the James River became to the birthplace of the United States, and Pocahontas, the American Anuket.

According to the now-famous story, the royal daughter of Chief Powhatan defied her father and rescued British captain John Smith. Creating the impression that Pocahontas found British men irresistible, this tale was given further credence when Pocahontas actually did fall in love with and marry British merchant John Rolfe. The narrative thread of this dynamic story of the origin of Virginia's first capital includes the assertion that it was John Rolfe who had introduced a strain of Caribbean tobacco to Virginia, which launched the colony's single largest agricultural crop. Pocahontas was, therefore, not only responsible for saving the lives of the British community in Virginia, she was also the mother of Virginia's most abundant harvest as well as Virginia's first recorded biracial child, Thomas Rolfe.

The story of the life of Pocahontas transformed as it was passed on from generation to generation and as the American identity diverged from that of the British. The facts are that Pocahontas traveled to England, changed her name to Rebecca, lived for a short while among "civilized society," and perished not long after her arrival. The narrative evolved reflecting a variance between imperialist and colonial expatriate. The English took credit for taming the savage; the Americans blamed the British for Pocahontas's death, which was caused by exposure to diseases unknown to the North American Natives. The British excused John Rolfe for abandoning their son in favor of seeking his fortune. The Americans distrusted John Rolfe's motives, suspecting him of racism. For the British, Pocahontas's story ends with her death. For the Americans, the next chapter is as important: Thomas Rolfe, who grew up in England, returned to Virginia as an adult, and, claiming to be equally proud of both of his heritages, was known to maintain friendly relations with both European émigrés as well as with his mother's tribe.

Thomas Rolfe reflected a Jamestown that was becoming multicultural: in 1608, John Smith had recruited a group of craftsmen from Poland, Armenia, Slovakia, and Germany to Jamestown. Although the artisans had been welcomed for their skills, they were precluded from voting, and, thus, held the first organized strike in British America in 1619. The British-born town leaders acquiesced to the protestors, realizing that disallowing other ethnic groups from participating in local decision-making would discourage immigration. It was bad publicity for Jamestown. That same year, in 1619, a group of Africans were forcibly brought to the James River tobacco farms but were not permitted any participation in the administration of Jamestown.

The farms in Jamestown were quickly becoming plantations, as there was an abundant yield of the crop that Rolfe Senior had brought to the colony. In order to keep prices high, the king issued a proclamation on June 29, 1620, "for restraint of the disordered trading of tobacco." King James I, now an emperor, displayed inconsistent behavior toward his colonies: he was at once controlling, as demonstrated by his decision to closely regulate produce, and at the same time he recognized that those bound for Jamestown desired a great deal of self-governance, which he permitted when, in 1621, he granted the Jamestonians their own House of Burgesses.

While the Anglo-Americans were experiencing new freedoms, Europeans were engulfed in protracted religious wars that levied destruction against one another during the Thirty Years' War. Protestant sects even quarreled with one another, causing a whirlpool of migration among the northern countries.

In 1620, a ship called the *Mayflower*, which was carrying a sect of Protestant Separatists bound for Jamestown, was diverted by difficult winds. There were 101 passengers on board when on November 11, 41 men signed an agreement for a majority-rule government upon their arrival in the New World. Their accord, known as the Mayflower Compact, provided a paradigm for New England theocracies to come. The Puritans, alternatively called the Pilgrims, as they had drifted between England and the Netherlands and ultimately to the New World, suffered great hardship their first winter in Massachusetts. The autumn of 1621, however, had yielded an abundant harvest. According to the story that has been handed down since the nineteenth century, the very

first Thanksgiving occurred when, grateful to God for their crops, the Separatists spontaneously invited the local natives to join them in a feast. That lovely
story of British benevolence contributed greatly to the foundation mythology
of America that bestowed the best of Christian virtue, charity, and cooperation
on its national character.

In truth, the Pilgrims had celebrated an official Thanksgiving Day long before
their arrival at Plymouth Rock. Thanksgiving had been a well-established holiday
in Leiden, Holland, since the 1570s, where many among the group who jour-
neyed aboard the *Mayflower* had resided during their peripatetic wanderings.
The first Thanksgiving Day known to the Separatists took place during the reign
of Queen Elizabeth I when the Dutch were struggling for independence from
Spain. Aided and abetted by Queen Elizabeth I, a Flemish fleet known as the
Sea Beggars wrested a coastal town called Den Briel away from the Spanish.
Infuriated, the Spanish warriors retaliated, surrounding the town of Leiden.
While the city lay under siege, many of its citizens were starving. According
to military sources, a seductive spy—a Catholic woman—named Magdalena
Moons passed secrets from the Spanish to the Sea Beggars, who rescued Leiden.
Town leaders, grateful for their unlikely deliverance, declared a day of thanks-
giving on October 3, which was celebrated not only by locals but also by the
English Protestants who had settled there. Thus, the conventional American
Thanksgiving story, which was fashioned to fit a desired mythological narrative
that has become sacred, was actually rooted in violent revolution.

In addition to mirroring the Jamestown foundation story of taming the
heathen with teamwork, Plymouth Colony contributed its own spunky and
prolific founding mother, Priscilla Mullins, to their British North American
foundation narrative. Priscilla, about seventeen years old when she traveled
aboard the *Mayflower* with her parents, was proposed to by a Mr. John Alden on
behalf of his friend, Miles Standish. In response to Mr. Alden's advocacy, Priscilla
famously answered the go-between, "Why don't you speak for yourself, John?"
John and Priscilla married and had ten children, populating Plymouth Colony.

The British had hoped that their settlements would eclipse the Spanish-held
New World capital cities to become the more important trading ports in the
Western Hemisphere, but pockets of competing French, Dutch, and Swedish

settlements began to dot the North American shoreline. The Dutch West India Company claimed an area north of Virginia that they named New Nether-lands, which today would comprise most of New York, New Jersey, and parts of Delaware and Pennsylvania. The island that the Indigenous tribes called "Manhattan" was renamed "New Amsterdam," which, like Jamestown, was settled for the purpose of doing business. The founding myth in which New Yorkers take great pride is the story that salutes Manhattan's first savvy real estate deal: according to that tale, the Dutch wrested away the island of Man-hattan from the tribes for $24. The Dutch who settled in the New World were agog at the rivers teeming with fish, the seemingly endless amounts of tillable land, and the roaming fauna for eating and skinning. Many of the details they reported back to the Old World parallel the natural environment recorded in the "Vinland" legend.

The industrious Dutch were not going to allow their assets to vanish into thin air. In order to make its New World venture profitable, the Dutch West India Company established the "Patroonship" program, open to anyone of any nationality. The incentive was that in exchange for financing the transportation and settlement of colonists, a "patroon" would be given an enormous tract of land along with the authority to settle all legal cases except for capital ones. In essence, a democratically elected government and a publicly held corporation were jointly establishing a feudal system in North America. This seemingly simple business experiment would actually cause a ripple of consequences for generations to come.

Another wave of Protestant Separatists emigrated from England to North America when King James I died in 1625 and his son, anti-Calvinist King Charles I, ascended the throne. This next group, which established the Mas-sachusetts Bay Colony, engendered its own origin myth that had its source aboard the *Arabella*. In a statement that would reverberate throughout the history of the United States and become a guiding tenet, a wealthy lawyer named John Winthrop addressed his fellow passengers, cautioning them that although they were off to test their fortunes, they were also religious pilgrims. Like Adam and Eve, who had been expelled from the Garden of Eden, like Abraham told by God to leave his home and family, like Noah, who was tossed on the seas, like Moses, who wandered the desert, like Mary, Joseph, and Jesus, they were God's chosen people in exile. Winthrop advised that once his ship-mates disembarked in North America it would be their obligation to create a New World city of righteousness: "for wee must Consider that wee shall be as a Citty upon a Hill, the eies [sic] of all people are uppon us."

Winthrop's words were familiar to his audience. His devout friends were familiar with Jesus's "Sermon on the Mount" from the parable of Salt and Light. In Matthew 5:14, Jesus preaches, "You are the light of the world. A city that is set on a hill cannot be hidden." Another lesson that had implanted in Christian tradition came from *The City of God,* a book that was written in the early fifth century by Algerian-born St. Augustine of Hippo. In the book, St. Augustine taught a theology of the search for a spiritual home, which he found in the church. For twelve centuries, *The City of God* inspired a myriad of pilgrimages. Christians had two powerful mandates to create a New World city of the righteous.

It seemed that the New World might just be a haven from the religious wars that had been monopolizing Europe. The Anglicans, Calvinists, Separatists, Jews, and Quakers all found homes in early North American colonies, as did controversial female evangelists like Anne Hutchinson and Anabaptist Lady Deborah Moody. In 1632, King Charles I of England granted a land patent of Maryland to Cecil Calvert, Baron of Baltimore, who opened his territory to Catholics. The Marylanders proudly established their capital, St. Mary's City, claiming it to be the first ecumenical capital in the British American colonies. St. Mary's was located on the mouth of the Potomac River, where it meets the Chesapeake Bay. Sadly, when Civil War broke out in England, the religious wars of the Old World spilled into the lives of those who had migrated to the New World to escape persecution, polluting the cities in North America.

The first battles on North American soil between British citizens occurred along the Chesapeake when Anglicans, Puritans, and Catholics went to war in the mid-seventeenth century. The Virginians, who had settled along the James, and more recently the York and Potomac Rivers, practiced the Anglican faith. When the Virginia Anglicans invaded Catholic Maryland, attacking St. Mary's City, Catholics were forced to move their capital city farther upstream on the

Chesapeake and away from shared waters. This new settlement was named Annapolis, after Lord Baltimore's deceased wife, Anne Arundel. Neither was New Amsterdam immune from infighting amongst the European settlers: a stockade was erected at the north of town to protect the settlement from English invasion. The barrier was later fortified with earth, and the path that ran along it would become known as "Wall Street."

Up to the mid-seventeenth century, Jamestown and the Massachusetts Bay and Plymouth Colonies, which had amalgamated into Boston, had become the two most active colonial cities in British North America. Manhattan Island and Albany, advantageously located upstream on the Hudson River, and the budding towns along the Delaware and Susquehanna Rivers were under Dutch control until 1664, when they were ceded to England. At that time, England also gained the Swedish-controlled outpost that was located in the vicinity of what today includes Philadelphia and the Wilmington, Delaware, area, where over 600 Swedes, Finns, Dutch, and Germans had gathered to build a New World city. Prolonged warring among the European nations in the second half of the seventeenth century as well as internal political turmoil in England resulted in a dizzying array of unreliable territorial land grants.

A cogent chronology of the overlapping patents, urban development, and path to self-rule in British America was assembled in 1781 by Thomas Jefferson in his *Notes on the State of Virginia*. In his outline, it is apparent that, as more cities like Charleston and Philadelphia rose, the constant friction and bickering among the different colonies intensified. Each citizenry vied with the other to dominate trade and to become the most important seaport capital of the New World.

More and more, the North American populace resented interfering proclamations that emanated from England. Well-documented in Jefferson's history is the narrative of elected local assemblies and community councils, a record that colonists demanded rights and rewards for their achievements. The colonists asserted a position that their cousins back in England were not the sowers of budding Boston, Charleston, Philadelphia, or New York.

Lively debates have always referred to Enlightenment thought on the subject of the nature of government as a great influence of the American Revolution.

Descartes, Locke, and Spinoza did indeed encourage reflection on liberty, and a multitude of books like *Leviathan* by Thomas Hobbes, *Utopia* by Thomas More, and *The Commonwealth of Oceana* by James Harrington presented fabulist versions of differing societies, which provoked energetic contemporaneous discussions. Harrington was provocative when he claimed that ancient Israel was the first republic, as it "consisted of the Senate, the people, and the magistracy."

Another of Harrington's statements, that "government is no other than the soul of a nation or a city," offers a glimpse into an equally important conversation to the seventeenth century. Driven in no small way by the intense competition for a New World capital city, reflection on the nature and the role of the city prompted continued and ongoing analysis. The translation of Giovanni Botero's *On the Causes of the Greatness and Magnificence of Cities* was such a success when it was published in London in 1606 that Sir Walter Raleigh plagiarized and condensed the work, renaming his own version *Observations Concerning the Causes of the Magnificency and Opulence of Cities*. Botero's thoughtful study offered insight into the phenomena of urban living. He considered the reasons for which people come together in cities: both pleasurable and profitable, these include for defense, for community, and for cultural enrichment. In addition, Botero dissected the geography of the evolution of the great cities of history. First, early cities were assembled on mountain peaks, which provided the safest locations for towns; however, he commented that while those hilltop sites are "noble," proximity to water was much more indispensable to the great capital city of empire of the seventeenth century. Also crucial to any city is money and "vendible merchandise." The city provides endless delights: architecture, entertainment, and a home for artisans, who derive their living from patronage. Using ancient Rome as an example, Botero reminded his audience that social life there offered, "sword players, the hunting of wild beasts . . . plays . . . pomp." Religion and schools also bind people to a city, and the city "must be the center of the apparatus of justice administration." Historically, Old World city-states like Eridu, Rome, Sparta, Athens, Carthage, and Venice all transformed into influential capitals of mighty empires.

From the very moment when charter-bearing aspirational voyagers arrived in the Americas, they demonstrated confidence in a mandate to create and define their own New World capital cities. As each town in North America began to develop, each polis took on its own unique spirit based on geography, demographics, and local industry and production; the values, concerns, and attitudes of its population are reflected in the themes of foundation stories: Tidewater Virginia mythology is about race and agriculture; New York City's most famous tale demonstrates pride in commerce; Boston lore is about rectitude. The opportunity to create a novus ordo seclorum—a new world order—made it possible for any one of them—Jamestown, New York, Boston, or Annapolis—to become the capital city of a New World empire. Despite the differences in the motivation behind the founding of each one of these hubs, squabbling new Americans would learn that they would have to cooperate for each of their urban centers to survive.

CHAPTER 3

Parallel Lives: George Washington and Philip Schuyler

WHETHER, AS IN THE CASE of New York or Jamestown, a colony had been established for commercial purposes, or, as in the case of St. Mary's and Massachusetts, had been founded for religious freedom, each of the New World hamlets had established their respective urban myths by the mid-seventeenth century. As the colonies became more successful, a particular relationship for each of the settlements with Britain became apparent according to the nature of those very beginnings: Virginia may have had a House of Burgesses, which had given settlers the appearance of autonomy, but as a "crown colony," their autonomy was consistently and persistently eroded by the British so that profit would be directed back to England. The colonies in New England, on the other hand, which operated under a corporate charter, had more administrative leeway. Maryland and Carolina (there was not yet a north-south division) were considered "proprietary," under the owner-management of an individual or small group of people. By the early eighteenth century, each colony was so distinct that, indeed, it could have been considered a separate country, and in many cases, a man would refer with chauvinism to Virginia or New York as his "country."

The competition for the capital city of the embryonic United States can be traced, with homage to the great biographer Plutarch, through the parallel lives of contemporaries George Washington, a Virginian born on February 22, 1732, and New Yorker Philip Schuyler, born on November 20, 1733. Alexander Hamilton, the young man they would both embrace as a son, and who would be unhappily caught between the warring titans, was a generation younger.

Both Schuyler and Washington foresaw a continental North American empire carved by waterways and canal systems whose source began at the port, the coastal harbor, in his own "country" and would flow alongside his lands. Both Schuyler and Washington were fourth-generation Americans whose ancestors had amassed significant lands in New York and Virginia respectively. Although the War of Independence would lead to the unification of the states, the contention for the location of the city of empire was sectional. Four of the thirteen colonies had deepwater coastal ports that sat at the mouth of a corridor river. The rivalry between New York and Virginia—between Philip Schuyler and George Washington—was a predictable clash.

Both colonies continued the Old World principle of primogeniture, wherein the eldest son would inherit any titles and the bulk of his father's estate whilst his younger siblings were legated minor allotments. Both Philip Schuyler and George Washington lost their fathers when quite young and were raised by single widowed mothers. With unexpected inheritances, Schuyler and Washington were made aware early on of the power of landowners. They would make most of life's decisions with that as their primary consideration. Schuyler and Washington, both obsessed with acquiring more and more property that would enhance in value, marched into the Seven Years' War to protect their real estate holdings and to participate in the dream of British expansion, which, of course, meant more land. They would marry women of property and enter politics to shape legislation about property disputes and navigation.

Both men were exceedingly practical about their property—George Washington always carried a compass to chart topography and Schuyler a ledger and drafting equipment. They were also visionary entrepreneurial innovators who ran commercial conglomerates. They supervised concerns that tested new planting, construction, animal husbandry, milling, mining, distilling, and transportation methods. They were also both westward-looking dreamers. Washington set up a tobacco enterprise on his Shenandoah land, a distillery at Mount Vernon, at least one mill in the Ohio Valley, and leased to other distillers and millers; Schuyler, whose tenant farmers paid him in currency and produce, began the first flax mill in North America and owned a timber mill, a wheat mill, a retail store, and a shipping business to send all that he owned downriver to New York City for domestic and international export.

Washington and Schuyler's parallel lives become tangent when they met in person for the first time at the Second Continental Congress in 1775. Each had known about the other for years, and when the Continental Congress marshalled an army that spring, Washington and Schuyler rode side by side from Philadelphia into battle. They were brothers in combat, best of friends, political allies, ideological twins, and ambitious adversaries. The root of the fierce dispute between the two men implanted near two different rivers—the Potomac and the Hudson.

Philip Schuyler was born a member of all four very rich Dutch patroon New York clans named Schuyler, van Rensselaer, van Cortlandt, and Livingston (a Scott transplanted to the Netherlands), whose millions of acres of property abutted New York harbor, the Hudson River, and its tributaries north and west. These four families customarily married each other and bequeathed parcels of land amongst their children to keep properties intact. As the eldest son of Johannes Schuyler Jr. and Cornelia van Cortlandt, whose family had been ennobled in Europe as the Dukes of Courland, the seigneurs of a duchy that changed hands frequently, Philip Schuyler, was, at birth, the heir to at least two great fortunes. Johannes owned sizeable property in Albany, land along the Mohawk River, and part of the 168,000-acre Saratoga Patent. Along with substantial real estate in New York City, Cornelia owned a generous portion of the 62,000-acre Claverack Manor on the Hudson River. Their son, Philip, was born in Albany, New York, and lived amongst the four families' various estates in New York City, along the Hudson, in Albany, and farther upstate in Saratoga. Johannes died on the eve of Philip's eighth birthday, which placed Cornelia van Cortlandt Schuyler as trustee of her son's farms and family trade concerns until his twenty-first birthday.

The Schuyler, van Rensselaer, van Cortlandt, and Livingston land barons came into frequent contact with members of the Iroquois Confederacy. Philip even learned to speak Mohawk. French soldiers, based in Canada along her maritime borders with New York State, waged ongoing diplomatic and insurgent campaigns to provoke upheaval in the northern British colonies. When Philip was twelve, his childless uncle, who owned approximately 15 percent of the 168,000 Saratoga Patent acres, was murdered by marauding French soldiers and their Native American accomplices at the outset of King George's War. Young Philip, his heir, added those 25,000 acres to his father's portion of the patent, becoming the majority owner of that entire county.

Partially for his safety and also to prepare him to head an important family, Philip left to attend school in New Rochelle, a town just north of New York City that had been settled by exiled French Huguenots. His tutor, the Reverend Stouppe, would also teach the future first chief justice of the United States Supreme Court, Philip Schuyler's second cousin John Jay, a decade later. Under Stouppe's guidance, Schuyler perfected his French, which supplemented his fluency in English, Dutch, and Mohawk, learned practical math skills, which he would later put to good use to measure canal locks and study sinking funds, studied advances in agriculture, and performed science experiments. It was an empirical education intended for the international businessman that Philip was expected to become.

Philip's social life, which revolved around the clans, was not, however, provincial. William Livingston, the future governor of New Jersey, and Judge Robert R. Livingston, were among several elder male cousins who stepped in as father figures. As a teenager, Philip mingled amongst the highest echelons of New York society based along the Hudson River. He was also regularly invited to formal balls at the court of the royal governor in New York City. In the early 1750s, New York City, whose population was about 13,000—2,000 of whom were African Americans—was already the "melting pot" which it would become famously known to be. In addition to the Dutch Reformed and Episcopal churches, there were German Lutheran and Moravian congregations, Jewish synagogues, and Quaker meeting houses.

Philip Schuyler enjoyed the sophisticated fun and pleasures that rich young men could afford: dances at the assembly hall on Broad Street, horse races and gambling salons, where he was mostly a spectator, and the company of fashionable young ladies. On September 21, 1753, Philip wrote an Albany friend, Abraham Ten Broeck, from New York City that he and his cousin Philip Livingston had escorted a group of pretty girls to the theater on Nassau Street. It was the first time that a theatrical company had come to New York City. Though the girls were charming and delightful, for Philip Schuyler, they all paled in comparison with "sweet Kitty V.R."—Catherine van Rensselaer—whom Schuyler was openly courting. Ten Broeck was instructed to send regards to "sweet Kitty." The message, of course, was loud and clear to all of the young gentlemen in his circle: Philip Schuyler planned to marry Catherine van Rensselaer, and they were all to back off.

Schuyler had every reason to be confident in his marriage prospects. Washington less so, and, before the time George Washington reached the age of majority, he had already been rejected by at least one Virginia belle. Washington was born with neither Schuyler's impeccable pedigree nor his inheritance. At a time when rarified Virginia society clustered around its colonial capital (since 1699), Williamsburg, the elegant plantations of the prominent families dotted the James and York Rivers. George's great-grandfather, John Washington, the first of the family to arrive in the New World, was priced out of those more expensive locations, amassing instead less valuable and more rural properties further north along the Potomac and Rappahannock Rivers. John Washington's most substantial parcel of land was some 5,000 acres at Hunting Creek near the Potomac, not considered prime.

John Washington bequeathed the Hunting Creek property to John Jr., his son. John Jr.'s second son, Augustine, was George Washington's father. As a second son, Augustine was not John Jr.'s principal beneficiary, again, according to the tradition of primogeniture. George Washington was also not a firstborn son. He was the eldest son of his father's second wife, Mary, and was, therefore, at least third behind his two elder half brothers, Lawrence and Augustine Jr., for any bequest. George Washington was born in a twenty-four-square-foot cabin near Popes Creek, a Potomac River offshoot, in Westmoreland County. When little George was three years old, Augustine Washington moved the family to Epsewasson Farm, situated on the John Washington Hunting Creek property. In 1738, five-year-old George moved again to Ferry Farm, a 260-acre parcel of land located on Bridges Creek adjacent to the Rappahannock River in Westmoreland County. That was where he would spend most of his childhood in a very modest house.

Augustine Washington felt it was his duty to send all of his sons to the Appleby School, his alma mater, in the wilds of Cumbria in northwest England. Lawrence and Augustine Jr. followed in their father's footsteps but after Augustine Sr. died when George was eleven, there was not enough money to send young George abroad. George Washington was, therefore, deprived of the formal British education and the London gentleman's polish he had anticipated. Eldest surviving brother Lawrence Washington inherited the Hunting Creek farm, Epsewasson, that had been part of his great-grandfather's legacy, as well as an interest in an iron works and a mill. Lawrence renamed Epsewasson "Mount Vernon" in honor of Admiral Edward Vernon, under whose command he served in Cartagena.

Augustine was able to set aside the much smaller Ferry Farm on Bridges Creek for George as well as a half-interest, shared with George's brother, Samuel, of a property on Deep Run. George's mother, Mary, was bequeathed the right to live and farm on the Bridges Creek property for five years and the responsibility of managing George's interests until he reached the age of majority (she would later refuse to leave Ferry Farm and fought with George to retain control of his inheritance). Ferry Farm provided insufficient income for the family, according to Mary, so she sent her eldest son, George, to work. Her stepson, Lawrence, suggest a naval career; Mary rejected that idea. Instead, fourteen-year-old George became a land surveyor and real estate appraiser. When he was fifteen, George, now his family's main breadwinner, measured and mapped tidal property at the mouth of the Potomac River to feed his mother and five siblings.

Lawrence Washington tried to help his father's second family. When he married Anne Fairfax, he used his new family connection to profit young George. Anne's father, Colonel William Fairfax, was a member of the Virginia planter class and served as agent for his cousin, Thomas, Lord Fairfax. Lord Fairfax owned 5.2 million acres of the Northern Neck of Virginia and along the Shenandoah Valley. In March 1748, Colonel Fairfax hired sixteen-year-old

George to chart some of the family's western properties. It was the first time that George had journeyed away from coastal Virginia. As he rode out past the Blue Ridge Mountains, he was awed by the majesty of the lush and expansive rolling terrain. Engrossed by his assignment, George very much enjoyed returning on several occasions over the next three years to the Shenandoah Valley in the employ of the Fairfax family and familiarized himself with its meandering and lush wilderness. In 1750, eighteen-year-old Washington used some of his earnings to purchase 1,459 acres on Bullskin Creek, a tributary of the Shenandoah River in Frederick County. Over the next two years, he increased his holdings there to 2,314 acres and, on March 8, 1753, purchased an additional 240 acres of Frederick County land on the Potomac River.

As the population of the thirteen British colonies grew, settlements in Virginia spread up the Chesapeake toward its northern tributaries and northwest along the Potomac River. Lawrence Washington, as a new member of the Fairfax family, was appointed a trustee of the developing Potomac port at a town that would be named Alexandria, a hopeful nod to the legendary ancient Egyptian Hellenic port city that boasted a famous lighthouse and was the commercial, intellectual, and cultural capital of the Ptolemaic empire. Lawrence Washington arranged for his brother, George, to get hired as a member of the crew that would lay out the grid for the embryonic Virginia seaside town. George was only seventeen in 1749, when he was offering his professional opinion on the foundations of houses to be constructed in the emerging metropolis. The Fairfax and Lee families would build stately brick city mansions, situated some half an acre back from the street, bordered by intricate brick mosaic walls that enclosed elegantly designed, vibrant gardens. Visitors to Alexandria, Virginia, today can see George Washington's house, which stands in stark contrast: it is a tiny, rickety wood structure that adjoins the road. George's reduced and déclassé circumstances did not prevent him from community leadership; he was an active, early, and enthusiastic promoter of the advancement of Alexandria, Virginia.

In July of that same year, Colonel Fairfax appointed George the official surveyor of Culpeper County on the Northern Neck of Virginia, where Lord Fairfax owned his millions of acres. George accepted the post, a great honor for one so young, but resigned less than a year later because he was longing to return to the Shenandoah Valley. He yearned for a fortune and, observing the Fairfax family, among other very rich Virginia land-owning dynasties, Washington determined to earn that money through the acquisition of land. He could not afford much of it along the pricey Chesapeake estuary but he could try to accumulate some less expensive western properties that he hoped would appreciate. Washington, throughout his life, was frequently indiscreet and direct about his burning desire for material ease, freely confessing "want."

George's brother Lawrence also turned his gaze westward for riches. His marriage to Anne Fairfax greatly elevated his status and bestowed upon him a credibility as a young *homme d'affaires* to watch. Along with a group of some very rich Virginians, Lawrence had secured a grant of half a million acres from King George in "Ohio Country" between the Monongahela and Kanawha Rivers. Their new company, the Ohio Company of Virginia, attracted investors, among them a smattering of Lees and Mercers, George Mason, and the newly arrived Virginia royal governor, Robert Dinwiddie. Now among the royal governor's inner circle and married to a Fairfax, Lawrence Washington was on the path that his younger half brother George greatly hoped to emulate.

Lawrence Washington became gravely ill with tuberculosis. He traveled to the springs in western Virginia and to England for a cure. Not improving, Lawrence decided to travel to the tropical Caribbean island of Barbados. He invited his younger half brother George to accompany him. The trip to Barbados would be George Washington's only trip abroad in his entire life. While on the island of Barbados, George contracted a mild case of smallpox, and Lawrence's condition worsened. In 1752, Lawrence Washington died prematurely at the age of thirty-four. He left behind his wife, Anne Fairfax Washington, and a daughter. Within a year after Lawrence's death, his daughter, heiress to his estate, also died. Twenty-two-year-old George Washington became the new legatee of the Mount Vernon plantation, which he would possess outright ten years later upon the death of Anne Fairfax Washington, whose husband had bequeathed her the rights of the plantation's lifetime residency. Thus, by the age of majority, George Washington owned Ferry Farm, the Bullskin Creek parcel, and could list the Mount Vernon estate, to which he would add acreage by gobbling up adjacent farms, among his assets.

Before his death, Lawrence Washington had put in a request to Governor Dinwiddie for his brother, George, to receive a commission in the Virginia militia. Out of respect for his late friend Lawrence, Governor Dinwiddie expedited George Washington's appointment. Now, at twenty-years-old, George Washington was captain in the Virginia military. With absolutely no prior military experience, George Washington found himself in the role of training squads of men.

By the early 1750s, the population in the British North American colonies had risen to some 1.2 million settlers. The French had been antagonizing settlers north along the New York–Canadian border; they had been interfering with British trade at the mouth of the Mississippi River and had been constructing forts along the Ohio River. Philip Schuyler took several reconnaissance forays into the wilderness to assess French and Native American activity. Under the guise of his own trading businesses wherein he used the timber from his own lands to make boats in which he could travel on streams and rivers, Schuyler met with French traders and Native Americans. The tribesmen were so impressed by his skills, the effort he made to learn their languages, his fierce rawhide costume, and his reciprocal hospitality to members of the Native families that they assumed his name, Schuyler, as a badge of honor. There are living today in upstate New York descendants of the Oneida chiefs who still bear the last name Schuyler. His geniality, however, belied his worry. In September 1753, Schuyler wrote his friend, Abraham Ten Broeck, "I believe we shall have a war again with the French . . . soon."

Philip Schuyler, like his coeval, George Washington, could survey, measure, chop, construct, and kill. Schuyler and Washington both possessed exceptional skills and the ability to gather and gauge intelligence that would prove invaluable: there was indeed a growing alliance between the Native Americans and the French, who were strategically erecting fortifications to contain the British and stifle the dreams of British-American colonial expansion. When Virginia Royal Governor Dinwiddie received that intelligence in the fall of 1753, he summoned George Washington to Williamsburg. Dinwiddie handed Washington a letter with instructions: Washington was ordered to travel to Fort Le Boeuf, positioned in the "Ohio Country" near Lake Erie, and tell the French to get off British—and Ohio Company—land. Dinwiddie further charged Washington with keeping a detailed account of the whole adventure: to note the topography, the French forts, the Native and French forces and munitions. Washington had been west of the Blue Ridge Mountains but never west of the Allegheny Mountains into "Ohio Country," and jumped at the chance to explore more of the frontier.

From different starting points, both men, Philip Schuyler and George Washington, would see the shores of Lake Erie, not a small feat for anyone in 1753, even more unusual for civilized men of property. That journey toward the interior of the continent was dangerous and lacked any conveniences. For Schuyler, it meant heading out along the Mohawk River. George Washington's trip began in Alexandria. From the town he had helped design, he would sail on the Potomac toward the falls at Georgetown, whose obstacles required dis-embarkation. He would then proceed by land to Fort Cumberland on a road that had been opened by the Ohio Company in 1748. It was then a rough trek north through western Pennsylvania along the Monongahela and Allegheny Rivers toward the Great Lakes. Although the land around those rivers belonged to Pennsylvania, the Quakers in Philadelphia refused to take up arms. It fell to Virginia, which also claimed the Ohio Valley, to secure the border.

On December 11, 1753, young Lieutenant Colonel Washington arrived near Lake Erie at the French Fort Le Boeuf and handed Dinwiddie's message to the fort's newly arrived commander, Jacques Legardeur de Saint-Pierre. Saint-Pierre was a member of a prominent French-Canadian family, who, in addition to soldiering for many years, had been tasked by his French superiors to follow the rivers of North America until he could link the Pacific Ocean with the Atlantic. Saint-Pierre rejected Dinwiddie's directive but Washington liked him anyway.

Washington's 1753 report to Governor Dinwiddie was a detailed account of the untamed wilderness and the savagery of the Native Americans, whose butchery he witnessed firsthand. Washington described with vividness mounds of dead bodies of European settlers and their children who had been scalped and eviscerated. Dinwiddie read the document and presented it to the House of Burgesses, after which it was published in colonial newspapers and, in 1754, in England and Scotland, making twenty-two-year-old George Washington a transatlantic, canoe-traveling, buckskin-wearing, derring-do celebrity.

British outrage at the trespassers, as well as the governor's own investments in the Ohio Company, prompted Dinwiddie to bolster the British presence in the Ohio Valley. On February 19, 1754, Dinwiddie issued a proclamation "for encouraging men to enlist in his Majesty's service for the defence [sic] and security of this colony." The declaration offered all volunteers who joined in the effort to build a fort "on the River Ohio, at the Fork of Monongahela . . . over and above their pay" a piece of a 200,000-acre parcel of land in that fertile valley. As an enlisted officer, Washington followed orders. As the senior-ranking officer, he dreamed of a rather large slice of that territorial pie.

Washington and his ragtag militia, largely corralled and induced along the way, arrived at the Forks of the Ohio only to discover that the French had already hunkered down in their own fort, named Duquesne in honor of the governor general of Canada, the Marquis Du Quesne. Precluded from constructing a British fort at Dinwiddie's already-occupied designated location, Washington selected another area, the Great Meadows, on which to construct his supply depot and battlements. He named it Fort Necessity.

The French and their tribal allies repeatedly antagonized Washington's soldiers. Washington returned the favor with the help of a Mingo chief named Tanacharison. During a skirmish initiated by Washington, his men captured a French-Canadian soldier named de Jumonville, whom Washington treated properly as a prisoner of war. Tanacharison, however, hurled a tomahawk through the skull of de Jumonville, prompting justified outrage from the French. Washington knew there would be reprisals.

Between May and early July Washington's men widened and extended the roads from the Allegheny Mountains toward Fort Duquesne along the rivers. He logged every possible route, including centuries-old Native American trails, that could serve as a corridor from the Potomac to the Ohio River. Whether it was over the Alleghanies to the Youghiogheny River or westward from the Great and Little Kanhawa Rivers, it was George Washington's painstaking maps of the Virginia, Maryland, and Pennsylvania footpaths, forests, mountains, valleys, rivers, streams, and creeks that would educate future troops and guide pioneers for decades to come.

On July 3, 1754, the French attacked Fort Necessity, as Washington had expected. Among the fighters was commander Jacques Legardeur de Saint-Pierre. Fort Necessity was destroyed, most of the Virginians were killed, and George Washington, forced to surrender, was routed. Depending on which version of the two-month series of fire exchange one found credible, George Washington became either a hero or a notorious disgrace. It had been his order to fire on Fort Duquesne in May; it was under his command that de Jumonville had been butchered. These two events purportedly caused the outbreak of the Seven Years' War.

Washington redeployed his energy. Even more determined that the British Americans, more importantly, the Virginians, were going to own the Ohio Valley, Washington took a strategic next step. While he had not proved to be a first-rate soldier, no one discounted his surveying skills. In a report to House of Burgess member Charles Carter in August 1754, Washington submitted a detailed account of a post-battle journey on the upper Potomac. The purpose of this report was to demonstrate how the Potomac River could be rendered navigable for the people of Virginia and the benefits of such an undertaking. Washington's letter to Carter was the very first recorded proposal to establish a canal system on the Potomac River that would connect Virginia, not Pennsylvania, to the Ohio River. A very abridged assessment describes how removing rocks, diverting water, and scooping river bottom for increased depth was required:

> From the mouth of Paterson's Creek to the beg [sic] of Shannon-doah [sic] Falls there is no other obstacle than the shallowness of the Water to prevent Craft from passing . . . the first of which is tolerably clear of Rocks but shallow yet may be much amended by digging a Channel . . . & what adds much to the difficulty is the bottom being exceeding Rocky occasions a Rippling so prodigious that none but boats or late Canoes Can pass . . . The Seneca Fall is easily pass'd [sic] in two places . . . but further it is not possible . . . I have given you an acct [sic] of the Conveniences and inconveniences that attend

the Navigation of Potomack [sic] . . . I may further say . . . the most
expeditious way to the Country.

While Washington was meandering the Potomac, his trouncing by the
French had caused a ripple effect among the other British colonies. In mid-
July, representatives from seven of the thirteen British colonies arrived in
Albany, New York, to discuss the growing tensions at the northern border
with Canada. The Albany Convention, the first intercolonial meeting of British
North American provinces, would serve as the model for later congresses. At
the conference, Benjamin Franklin proposed the formation of an armed confederation among the thirteen British colonies. The Albany Plan of Union,
presented by Franklin, was a prescient call to establish a unified British North
America. Twenty-year-old Philip Schuyler had more to lose than most if the
British colonies could not defend their northern border. Four months after this
historic assembly, Philip Schuyler would turn twenty-one and would inherit
an enormous aggregate of properties in northern New York. As Franklin's
proposal was not implemented, Philip Schuyler raised and paid for his own
army to protect his own lands.

The commotion that Washington had caused embarrassed Virginia Governor Dinwiddie, who resolved that he had no further use for George Washington, soldier. Washington, incredulous, as he sincerely believed that he was
owed a promotion for fighting as an underdog, resigned after being passed over
for advancement. Echoing a complaint expressed by his late brother Lawrence,
Washington decided that American soldiers were being treated like second-class
citizens: they were receiving less pay and preferment than their British-born
and -trained counterparts.

Without George Washington, Dinwiddie proceeded to beef up his army. In
London, the British Parliament appointed Scottish-born major general Edward
Braddock as the new North American commander in chief. Braddock sailed
to North America, disembarking in Virginia in February 1755. Familiar with
Washington's report and the young Virginian's experiences in the backwoods,
Braddock persuaded Washington to join his staff as aide-de-camp, an honor
for any soldier.

George Washington, accompanied by Major General Braddock and his army, returned a third time to the Ohio Valley. Braddock traveled with so much gear and so many comforts that the road had to be widened. It would later be named the Braddock Road in his honor. All the way, Washington tried to explain to the classically trained soldier that in North America guerilla warfare would be more successful than the European-style meticulous line formations. Braddock ignored Washington, who, so far, had only been trounced in battle. When Braddock's forces at last clashed with the French and Native Americans, Braddock and his ornately outfitted and perfectly queued soldiers were slaughtered. As the highest-ranking officer to survive, George Washington was in command. Once again, Washington's fortunes would veer by an unexpected inheritance.

With the increased incentive of gaining an even larger portion of the promised lands, George Washington feverishly organized a larger, structured, statewide Virginia regiment. His men went through intense drilling and armament practice, and received handsome new uniforms that Washington personally designed. Given more authority and a freer rein, Washington, the American Iphicrates, implemented an innovative methodology for his European-trained troops so that they would be prepared to fight in the irregular warfare of the North American wilderness.

As Washington readied his men for combat in the Ohio Valley, General William Shirley, the royal governor of Massachusetts, stepped into Braddock's former role as the British North American commander in chief. Shirley put a program in place to gut the French presence along the northern waterways. Protection of Lakes Ontario and Erie, the St. Lawrence River, Lake Champlain, and the Hudson River required a multiprong offensive. Parliament and King George, advised that the French incursions were serious, increased the expenditures for war in North America.

In Albany, New York, Philip Schuyler received two letters from New York Governor James De Lancey. The first, dated May 5, 1755, appealed to Schuyler to raise one of eight companies, financed by His Majesty, for an attack against the French and their Native allies. Schuyler was tasked to assist in building and securing forts in upstate New York along the Canadian border. Schuyler recruited one hundred men. On the 14 of June, a second letter arrived in which De Lancey offered Schuyler a commission as captain of his unit. Schuyler and his regiment were to report to Major General William Johnson.

It was midsummer 1755 when Johnson, General Phineas Lyman of New England, and Commander in Chief Shirley all arrived at the Schuyler property in Saratoga known as the Flatts to mobilize their armies. The expeditions would fan out in the north from Acadia to Fort Niagara on Lake Ontario. At that rendezvous were a number of other men who would make history, including Ephraim Williams, who wrote his will that day, bequeathing the money for Williams College, and Israel Putnam, whose exploits, including great bravado at Bunker Hill, would make him a folk hero.

Philip Schuyler was there as well. He and his men rode with Johnson northward toward Lac du Saint Sacrement, which Johnson renamed Lake George to assert dominion of the British king. Johnson tasked the troops with constructing a battlement they would name Fort William Henry at the southern end of Lake George. Their ultimate goals, however, were to capture and decimate the French forts Carillon, later Fort Ticonderoga, and Saint Frédéric at Crown Point, some fifteen miles farther north. Both forts, near Lake Champlain at the New York and Vermont borders, loomed as constant taunts. To the northeast of those French battlements, in Nova Scotia, some 15,000 British soldiers waited menacingly at Fort Edward to begin the cleanse and removal of the French population.

Johnson's regiment was traveling northward at the same time that French General Baron Dieskau, was repositioning his three thousand soldiers, among whom were hundreds of Native Americans, first to Crown Point and then south to the Hudson River. Dieskau divided his troops in half, dispatching some to Fort Lyman—which would later also be named Fort Edward—on the Hudson River, and the other half to Ticonderoga on the southern shore of Lake George, not far from where Johnson's men were encamped. On September 8, 1755, Dieskau received intelligence that Johnson's men were going to attack. Dieskau ordered his men to ambush the British. Placed in charge of the Native American soldiers, Jacques Legardeur de Saint-Pierre, the officer to whom George Washington had delivered Governor Dinwiddie's message at Fort Le Boeuf nearly two years earlier, was mortally wounded. Both Johnson and Dieskau were wounded. Dieskau, taken prisoner, was removed to Johnson's medical tent. When, in a chilling echo of the de Jumonville situation the previous year, a Native American appeared and angrily proposed that he scalp, eat, and smoke Dieskau, Johnson quickly ordered the evacuation of the French general and his wounded. Johnson sought someone who could speak French to the general and his aide-de-camp, Bernier. Philip Schuyler was chosen to lead the cortege of French prisoners to Albany. On October 5, after Schuyler had returned to battle, Bernier wrote him on behalf of his commander that both men had greatly appreciated Schuyler's hospitality, assuring Schuyler that both his mother and his wife displayed every politeness to the enemy.

Nine days after the September 8, 1755, Battle of Lake George, Philip Schuyler married his "sweet Kitty," Catherine van Rensselaer. Both Philip and Catherine were descendants of Philip Pieterse Schuyler, founder of that dynasty. The van Rensselaers were a fabulously rich family that had lived uniquely as feudal lords, with all those rights and privileges, on their nearly one million acres on both sides along the Hudson River. As the new husband of a young van Rensselaer bride, Philip was now in control of her properties as well.

George Washington did not fare as well in his hunt for a bride. In February 1756, only three months before the formal declaration of war, Washington stopped in New York city en route to a meeting with General Shirley in New England. While in New York City, Washington was introduced to his friend's sister-in-law, Mary Philipse. Known as "Charming Polly," Mary Philipse was heiress to one-third of the Highland, or Philipse, Patent, another enormous Hudson River estate. Her father, Frederick Philipse, was the second Lord of the Manor. He owned toll roads, bridges, and a thriving slave-trade business. Washington proposed to Polly but she declined his offer. Two years later, she would marry another British soldier, Colonel Roger Morris. The couple would live in New York City and build Mount Morris, their country home, in, ironically, a section of northern Manhattan known today as Washington Heights.

Also in February 1756, five months after their wedding, Catherine and Philip Schuyler celebrated the birth of their first child, Angelica. The following year, when their second daughter, Elizabeth "Betsey,"[1] was born, her future husband, the illegitimate son of a woman who had been jailed for adultery, was two years and seven months old. Destined for greatness and a place in history, Alexander Hamilton would escape obscurity and his native Nevis, a remote island in the Caribbean. Hamilton would become a game-changing figure, intersecting the parallel lives of George Washington, his mentor and father figure, and his father-in-law, Philip Schuyler, on a trajectory to greatness.

Philip and Catherine were blessed with a growing and spirited family, which they steeped in Dutch tradition. Progressive in their view that their daughters should be given the same education as their sons, the Schuyler sisters became legendary: the eldest, Angelica, would dazzle some of the world's most brilliant men with her beauty and cleverness; Elizabeth, called "Betsey," would marry Alexander Hamilton; a younger daughter, Margarita "Peggy" would marry cousin Stephen van Rensselaer III, perennially listed as amongst the ten richest men in the history of the United States. The van Rensselaer properties, twenty-four miles east and west of the Hudson River, housed some 80,000 tenants. Peggy's husband, the eldest son of the deceased ninth patroon, also received his inheritance at the age of twenty-one. In honor of his very well-educated wife, Stephen van Rensselaer III became one of the pioneer proponents of higher education for women.

Philip Schuyler, promoted to the rank of major, was intent on protecting his dynastic lands. Major Schuyler fought in the north with Lord Jeffrey Amherst, who was victorious in gaining Canadian territory for the British. In 1758, Major George Washington returned to the Ohio Valley for the third time as part of the Forbes Expedition. General John Forbes decided to settle his headquarters in Carlisle, Pennsylvania, and preferred to attempt an attack on Fort Duquesne via the construction of a new road directly west through Pennsylvania. Washington, intent on keeping Braddock's Virginia road the main thoroughfare, protested. Though he claimed that his reasons were strictly military, in fact, his complaints to the royal government in his own state reveal his partisan interests. The Braddock Road, already well-defined, would make Virginia the main thoroughfare to the west. Washington was further angered by the Pennsylvanians who believed that, according to their own royal charter,

Alexandria belonged to them. Washington's pleas were ignored but he accompanied the troops toward Fort Duquesne anyway. This time, the British and British-American armies were more fortunate. As they approached the area, they were intercepted by a small band of French fighters, who revealed that there was only a skeleton force stationed at Fort Duquesne. Of course, Forbes and his men were wary of the intelligence. When they attacked Fort Duquesne, they found an abandoned battlement, deserted by the small group afraid of being outnumbered and overpowered. Though an easily won battle, it had been a four-and-a-half-year-long struggle for the British to capture the citadel they would rebuild and call Fort Pitt.

Washington was also more successful in his private life, at long last finding a woman with whom he could share his future. Widowed in 1756 with two small children, Martha Dandridge Custis accepted George Washington's offer of marriage. A few months older than Washington, Martha and her first husband, Daniel Parke Custis, were members of the elite planter group of families with rolling properties along the York River. Custis, twenty years older than his wife, possessed some 18,000 acres of the most sought-after Virginia real estate. Upon his death, Martha received her dower share of the twenty-eight square miles, which transferred to George Washington's control. That property would revert, along with the rest of her deceased husband's, to her eldest son, John Parke "Jacky" Custis, after her death. Jacky would marry Eleanor Calvert, granddaughter of Charles Calvert, 5th Baron Baltimore, who inherited the entire "province of Maryland" when he was fifteen years old. Eleanor's inherited land would be transferred to her husband, Jacky, who would die prematurely during the War of Independence.

After years and years of circuitous and unexpected legacies, George Washington, the insignificant younger son of a younger son, was now a newly elected first-time member of the Virginia House of Burgesses for Frederick County on the Northern Neck as well as a twenty-seven-year-old land baron. Both he and Philip Schuyler resigned from their respective regiments to focus on family life and the business of real estate development.

CHAPTER 4

A Chain, a Compass, and a Tomahawk

LONG BEFORE THE SEVEN YEARS' WAR and the 1776 Declaration of Independence, British North Americans, scrambling to create and control the New World's preeminent city, faced challenges on many levels. To create a London or Paris on the North American continent, King George's subjects had to find, clear, and map untrodden roads and waterways—a man-versus-nature Sisyphean battle. Wartime expeditions by surveyors, soldiers, and engineers provided essential information. Micro and macro issues—man versus neighbor, province versus province, British subject versus French subject and Native tribe, and, ultimately, American versus British king and government—crocheted a web of obstacles.

British dominion in North America consisted of a sweep from north to south along the Atlantic coast. A good part of the interior of the continent up through Canada had been claimed in 1608 by the French. Up to the outbreak of the Seven Years' War, only about 10,000 French citizens had immigrated to New France. In comparison, about one-sixth of all British citizenry had emigrated to North America. The British victory expanded her North American border to the Mississippi River, which provided elbow room for her North American citizens, but provincial borders and river rights were still chaotic, and the end of the war did nothing to solve the problem of continued and constant border frictions amongst the British colonies themselves.

British land charters in North America were often ambiguous and overlapping. The shifting political tides in seventeenth-century England—regicide, Cromwell, the Glorious Revolution—caused legal whiplash and settlement upheaval for Americans: those in power an ocean away rewarded favorites with New World terrains that often contradicted or nullified those previously granted. The Penn family of Pennsylvania feuded with the Calvert family of Maryland and the Fairfax family of Virginia over territory along the Potomac and Ohio rivers. In 1730, an actual war, called Cresap's War, broke out between Maryland and Pennsylvania settlers over land near the Susquehanna River. In 1732, the Calvert and Penn families came to an agreement: the Calverts renounced Delaware, and Pennsylvania lost all land fifteen miles south of the southernmost house in Philadelphia. The chancery court approved the truce, adding the suggestion that the two colonies sort out their western lands. In 1767, Charles Mason and Jeremiah Dixon finalized a measurement that would have unforeseeable impact on American history. Their submission became known as the Mason-Dixon Line. Even though Maryland lost about twelve million acres with their proposition, Maryland and Pennsylvania agreed to abide by it. Virginia did not. Virginia also bickered with the Carolina lord proprietors, recipients of yet another royal decree, over their joint boundary demarcation. The colony of New Jersey disputed its border with New York. New York claimed that according to a mid-seventeenth-century patent, its northeastern boundary was the Connecticut River. Connecticut, New Hampshire, and Massachusetts Bay colonies all contested that assertion and emboldened their own citizens to trespass on territory, much of which belonged to the Schuyler and van Rensselaer families.

In addition to intercolonial bickering, there was constant rowing among individual settlers. Private property ownership was often demarked by a chain, a compass, and a tomahawk etching engraved in a tree. If someone claimed that "you missed his mark," in other words, "he got their first," unpleasant, sometimes violent, wrangling and lawsuits would ensue. Land was important not only for agriculture and commercial enterprise but also to meet His Majesty's quitrent requirements. A series of Currency Acts imposed by Great Britain on her North American colonies that banned the establishment of banks made it difficult for the Americans to print money with equal value to the pound sterling, so land was what Americans used as collateral.

American land claimed by England had been inhabited by Indigenous peoples for thousands of years. In an attempt to keep the peace with those Natives, European settlers would negotiate compensatory subagreement "sales." These "sales" were not panaceas because of a fundamental cultural clash between the English and the Native Americans. European contractual property traditions were based along the precepts of the millennium-old Salic law and the 1215 "Articles of the Barons," also known as the Magna Carta. Unfamiliar with these tenets, the Indigenous peoples' ethos was that no one owned Mother Earth; one could only have the right to use it. Accordingly, European Americans would pay the Native tribes for property—swapping weapons, skins, and alcohol—and, when the tribes reappeared for additional trinkets or to use what they perceived to be common hunting grounds, European Americans were confused. One example of this kind of misunderstanding took place on the island of Manhattan. Some fifteen years after Dutch settlers paid the Manhattan tribe for the island, the Natives demanded its return. Puzzled Europeans took up arms against the insistent "Indian givers," and over one thousand colonists and tribesman died before the matter was resolved against the natives.

Europeans were also accustomed to private ownership of waterways. In Europe, people owned bridges, collected tolls, and taxed freight. In George Washington's report from the frontier, part of his purpose was to enlighten the British government as to potential profit in the waterways that connected the coast with the Ohio River. Before Washington's 1753 chart, however, there had been others. Peter Jefferson, for example, father of future president Thomas Jefferson, shared his drawings with neighbors and friends. In 1754, simultaneous with Washington's pamphlet, Lewis Evans published his own essay and map. Evans's thesis confirmed Washington's and Jefferson's assertion that the Potomac River was the gateway to the west. The Potomac River, however, had a rival as the corridor to the interior of North America. As the Reverend James Maury, wrote in 1756 to his uncles in England, "either Hudson's river at New

York or Potomac river in Virginia" would become the major "emporium of all East Indian commodities."[1]

Peter Jefferson died in 1757 when Thomas was thirteen, bequeathing to his son his cherished maps of Virginia, festooned with her abundant rivers, as well as the chauvinistic dream that Virginia would be the focal point of the world. After Peter Jefferson's death, Reverend Maury became Thomas's tutor and reinforced that fixation. Maury also infused the mind of his pupil with classical heroes and thalassocrat empires of antiquity, whose glittering capital cities reflected the empire's finest achievements.

The mythologized sea powers that filled teenage Thomas Jefferson's imagination—ancient China, ancient Egypt, ancient Greece, and the Roman Empire—all sent forth ships to trade and explore. All of them had built canal systems. Medieval Denmark, France, England, and Venice echoed that tradition. In the sixteenth century, the Netherlands became the world's dominant thalassocrat empire. Harnessing water on a scale never before seen, the tiny group of provinces, in total about the size of the state of Maryland, implemented an efficient, productive, hydraulic engineering marvel of waterways and canal systems that traversed and connected her marshy regions. Shipbuilding craftsmanship and outsized investment in expeditions gave her royal and merchant navies unequaled advantage. The Netherlands gained dominions from Southeast Asia to Africa to South and North America. At the turn of the eighteenth century, Czar Peter the Great, intent on creating a modern Russia, lived incognito in Amsterdam to study the inner workings of Dutch water systems. Peter returned to Russia and began the creation of his eponymous metropolis, modeling it after what he had learned. St. Petersburg, the seat of the Romanov dynasty, was built not only as an homage to Peter but also to the success of the Dutchman taming water.

The Dutch West India Company, a Netherlands-based, seafaring global trading conglomerate, was the wellspring of wealth for the New York Dutch American dynasties—the Schuylers, the van Rensselaers, the van Cortlandts, and the Livingstons. Along with the millions of acres conferred by the trading company on the clans, their patents came complete with no taxes for ten years, jurisdiction over colonial lawsuits, and allodial custody over the territory.

Tenant farmers could have no hope to either purchase or trade the lands they tilled. The Dutch clans also enjoyed hegemony over all of the waterways—streams, lakes, and rivers—that abutted their estates; they dictated portage, passage, and fishing.

The Schuylers, the van Rensselaers, the van Cortlandts, and the Livingstons were collectively conscious that they were unlike the Fairfaxes, the Calverts, and the lord proprietors, who had all received their land charters from a monarch. In 1664, the English king added New York to his empire. Determined to follow a laissez-faire policy with the Dutch Americans, the king neither voided nor interfered with the privileges of the clans previously granted. When William and Mary ascended the throne of England in 1689, Dutch-born William reinforced that favor. New York was the only one of the colonies never to have a charter with a British king.

Flowing through the Dutch American clan bloodlines in every successive generation was an atavistic attentiveness to waterways as moneymaking turnpikes. Philip Schuyler, tasked to sort out business for an elderly real estate partner, British quartermaster Colonel John Bradstreet, boarded the *General Wall* for England in February 1761. He and Bradstreet together had invested in land along the Mohawk River (near what today is the city of Utica). With the assistance of a canal system, that river could bring goods and people from New York Harbor up the Hudson River and to the Great Lakes. Schuyler's journey also included the purpose of attending the opening of the forty-one-mile Bridgewater Canal.

Schuyler's journey turned into a very dangerous one. The British and British Americans were still at war with the French. On board the *General Wall*, Schuyler demonstrated such proficient leadership and navigational skills that the dying captain appointed Schuyler his replacement. Soon after Schuyler took the helm, the packet-boat was captured by a French pirate ship, *La Biscayen*. Schuyler's military experience and fluency in French, which he used to negotiate ransom for passengers, saved those on board.

Arrived safely in London, Schuyler was uplifted by an energy he felt in this world capital now at the dawn of a new era. The previous October, King George II had died, and the accession to the throne by his twenty-two-year-old grandson, George III, rejuvenated the nation's mood, divided over the pro-longed wars. Schuyler was buoyant after the very satisfactory meetings he had with members of parliamentary financial committees on Bradstreet's behalf and with a Professor Thomas Brand. He and Brand together schemed to build a settlement in Detroit that was contingent on a British victory.

Schuyler was galvanized for the next leg of his adventure to the northwest of England. Everyone was talking about and writing about the July launch of the 3rd Duke of Bridgewater's canal system. Devised to link the duke's Worsley coal mines with the city of Manchester, the engineering phenom-enon even boasted an aqueduct that was structured over the Irwell River. Schuyler traveled to be there and observed every detail of the Bridgewater project, noting that the canal would cut in half the price of transporting the coal.

His imagination further fired by various visits to flax and hemp mills, Schuyler saw no reason why he could not emulate and even improve on those refineries. The waterpower of the Hudson River could fuel his mills. If the Hudson and Mohawk Rivers could be linked to the Great Lakes or if the Hudson River–Lake Champlain–St. Lawrence River route to both the Great Lakes and the Atlantic Ocean could be pursued, Schuyler could supply the millions of citizens that he foresaw moving to the interior of North America. Conversely, with New York Harbor at the Hudson's mouth downstream and the St. Lawrence emptying into the Atlantic Ocean, Schuyler could bring his products to the world.

Philip Schuyler conveyed his enthusiasm in letters home to his family and friends. When he returned home, he discovered that his excitement had been infectious: Colonel Bradstreet and Kitty van Rensselaer Schuyler had together overseen the enlargement of the Schuyler home in Albany. The elegant hilltop brick Georgian mansion, modestly called "The Pastures," stood imposingly in stark contrast to the modest wooden Dutch-style houses in town. The expansive, sprawling Schuyler estate was the perfect setting for the shimmering sterling silver, gleaming polished furniture, crystalline window panes, and different panels of wall coverings (textured, sheep-flocked wallpaper that resem-bled damask and finely illustrated scenic panels of ancient Roman ruins) that Schuyler had splurged on in England. Kitty Schuyler and Colonel Bradstreet had one more surprise for Philip Schuyler: they had in concert supervised the construction of a new schooner, aptly named *Saratoga*, for Schuyler to haul fish and commodities up and down the Hudson River.

On home soil, Schuyler actively sought to acquire more land. As always, he was strategic. By the beginning of 1762, he closed on a parcel of land along the eastern shore of the Hudson River in Dutchess County. Later that year, his mother died. From her estate, Schuyler inherited an enviable portion of the 86,000-acre van Cortlandt manor and more money, some of which he used to purchase an even bigger percentage of the Saratoga patent in 1763 and another schooner called *Mohawk*. Schuyler initiated the formation of a consortium consisting of clan members, Colonel Bradstreet, and a handful of friends to purchase more land in western and northern New York.

The outcome of the Seven Years' War amputated the French from upper and western New York. The Native Americans, however, could still be a problem, so the syndicate retained Philip Schuyler with full power of attorney to negotiate with the tribal chiefs, who considered Schuyler, at thirty years of age, to be a trusted equal. Schuyler and his associates appeased the tribes and got clear and undisturbed title to tens of thousands of fertile, river-valley acres along the Mohawk. Schuyler also purchased property to the northeast near Fort Edward. It would only take the construction of a small canal to link Lake Champlain to the Hudson River. Schuyler began to draft ideas. While the French were gone and the tribes were at bay, the governor of the province of New Hampshire began to dole out parcels of land west of the Connecticut River that he claimed belonged to New England.

Igniting a problem that could not be extinguished, New Hampshire Governor John Wentworth officially established a town called Bennington (later in Vermont) on the Connecticut River. The New York Assembly disagreed and appointed Schuyler chief negotiator to settle the matter, which became even more dangerous with the establishment of a New Hampshire vigilante group called the Green Mountain Boys. The ongoing dispute would last another twelve years, making Philip Schuyler one of the most hated figures in New England. The New York royal governor protested to King George, who, in 1764, affirmed that the land west of the Connecticut River did indeed belong to the province of New York, which reaffirmed Schuyler's rights against the violent trespassers.

The New England colonies refused to give up the fight and continued to produce and submit to varying legal bodies their own signed charters. The New York Assembly spent most of its time in the mid-1760s defending challenges and drafting heated replies to the assemblies of Massachusetts Bay, New Hampshire, and Connecticut provinces over their ongoing "immoderate claims" to this land. The record of the New York Assembly detailed the historic claims of all parties, which provides a fascinating narration of the settlement of early North America. The New England colonies argued that all Dutch patents were nullified in 1664; the New York Assembly demonstrated that Dutch-born William III, who ascended the English throne in 1689, had not at all annulled New York's original charters. Further, the British monarchs had reaffirmed existing patents along the Connecticut River—to Philip Schuyler's ancestor, Peter Schuyler, dated November 1685; to Killian van Rensselaer, dated November 5, 1685; to Robert Livingston, dated 1684, 1685, and 1686; to Maria van Rensselaer, dated 1688—all of which clearly pre-dated the Massachusetts Bay colony charter of 1691.

Philip Schuyler and George Washington would face similar obstacles in the 1760s that would draw them into politics and war against Britain. Virginians had battled for nine years to gain the Ohio Valley. Unbeknownst to them, they would fight another nine years to gain peaceful dominion over it. Assuming that the war was winding down in their favor, in the early 1760s British Americans began to plan for the moment when they could inhabit and develop the Ohio Valley. George Washington's 1754 letter to Representative Charles Carter did not provide a sophisticated engineering blueprint for developing a Potomac River canal system but, once again, his ability to translate the natural stirred the public: once peace was struck, the Potomac River should be widened, deepened, and cleared. A notice dated February 4, 1762, which appeared a week later in the *Maryland Gazette,* announced that, "The Opening of the River Patowmack [sic], and making it passable . . . will be of the greatest Advantage to Virginia and Maryland . . . it is proposed to solicit the Public for their Contributions, by the Way of Subscription." While the advertisement appeared in an Annapolis newspaper, it stressed that both Virginians—Alexandrians, like George Washington, in particular—and Marylanders should band together: "from Alexandria, or George-Town [sic] [which was in Maryland], to Pittsburgh, will then be short of 90 Miles; whereas the Pennsylvanians (who at present monopolize the very lucrative Skin and Fur Trades) from their nearest Sea Port have at least 300." The article encouraged the project for both public good and private profit. Those with properties along the river and investors in the corporation could receive returns from tolls, travel duties, and the like. Washington's papers reveal that he received queries and requests for his 1754 notes from potential corporate subscribers.

In the advertisement, Alexandria as a focal point was an interesting choice. Although the town was only ten years old, it was booming. The trustees of Alexandria would, in 1762, submit their first application to the General Assembly in Williamsburg for expansion. By the following spring, fifty-eight additional lots had been surveyed and put up for sale. In 1762, the port at Alexandria teemed with Virginia tobacco, grains, fish, and lumber, as well as manufactured goods from England unloaded for customers like gentleman planter George Washington, who placed regular orders with British merchants thanks to his wife's dowry.

Washington was enjoying his life as a now wealthy member of Virginia society and as an esteemed member of the House of Burgesses, where he was appointed to chair that we might name the Veterans' Affairs committee. He was also expanding his Mount Vernon holdings. In January of 1762 he bought 135 acres on the west side of Dogue Run and another 135 acres north of it. Later in the year, he would make another offer to buy land adjacent to that parcel and would buy a 448-acre tract of land along the Leesburg-to-Alexandria main road. Washington kept journals about the price of tobacco, grafting and planting fruit trees, sowing oats, killing hogs, and transferring his steers amongst his properties. In 1763, George Washington became a trustee of the city of Alexandria, and in 1764, he became a member of the House of Burgesses for Fairfax County, the Northern Neck county that abutted the Potomac River. Washington's Mount Vernon now contained five farms. Three years later, he bought another 2,682 acres near the Potomac River from one of the Carter family estates.

In his capacity as a representative on the veterans' committee—and operating under the assumption that he would be awarded among the largest portions of the 200,000 acres decreed by Governor Dinwiddie to the Virginia Regiment— George Washington drafted a "Petition to the King for the Virginia Regiment" in early March 1762. The memorial respectfully asked the new young king to keep the pledge of his forbear's Virginia representative. Washington never got the opportunity to present it to Dinwiddie's successor, Lieutenant Governor Francis Fauquier, because that February Fauquier received instructions from the British Board of Trade prohibiting tramontane settlement. Washington was furious and wrote another plea to His Majesty which, this time, was submitted. This petition to the king was a protest. Attached to it was Virginia Royal Governor Dinwiddie's February 19, 1754, proclamation. To an Englishman that document was an inviolable contract. Washington, as well versed in British real-property law as any member of the British Board of Trade, claimed that Dinwiddie's decree superseded the Trade Board's position that the land was "restrained" for the Native tribes.

Washington and a number of others had already begun coalescing real estate investment corporations. Washington himself would participate in a second-generation Ohio Company, two companies on the coastal Virginia-Carolina border—the Adventurers for Draining the Great Dismal Swamp and the Dismal Swamp Land Company in the Carolinas—and in the Mississippi Land Company, all poised to acquire parcels of land the moment the war was over. So hungry were British Americans for land that in early 1763, Washington actually traveled to his swamp to supervise its dredging. Dozens of ordinary men, claiming preemptory rights, hauled chain, compass, and tomahawk south toward marshland and west to the Ohio Valley. They anticipated approval, not pushback, from Great Britain after seven years of war.

The Treaty of Paris, concluded amongst European nations in February 1763, disregarded the Native American claims to the Ohio Valley and the Mississippi River. The Native tribes of the Ohio Valley[2] were vehemently opposed to British expansion and launched a series of attacks to fend off British westward settlement. Averse to more prolonged and expensive wars, King George III issued a royal proclamation on October 7, 1763, that forbade his

British colonists from settling west of the Appalachian Mountains and from directly acquiring land from the Native tribes. Philip Schuyler's plan for a settlement at Detroit collapsed, and, also as a result of this proclamation, only two of George Washington's land projects could proceed publicly and legally, both of them on the Virginia-Carolina border: the Adventurers for Draining the Great Dismal Swamp and the Dismal Swamp Land Company. Unfortunately for Washington, both of his southern endeavors turned into relentless fiscal sinkholes, only useful for their timber. The king's interference in George Washington's ambitions turned the Virginian against London nabobs entirely.

The young King George III may have placated the Natives, but by contradicting the property rights of his own colonists, he set in motion a revolution. Echoing the early thirteenth-century uprising when twenty-five barons forced King John to respect their property rights, British Americans remonstrated with King George III. The very first fissure between British Americans and their monarch was about North American land. Over the next five years, whilst colonists combatted the Native Americans, British Americans also did battle with their king.

King George III not only decreed that North Americans would be deprived of land they had fought to win; he also sought to collect revenue by imposing a series of punitive taxes. Americans demonstrably objected to the Stamp Act, the already existing Navigation Acts, the Quartering Act, and the Townshend Acts. After supporting the British king for years, they were furious about increasingly restrictive trade and progressively fewer rights. On October 7, 1765, the first British North American intercolonial assembly gathered in New York City to protest the actions of an English king. On October 25, the group submitted a joint rebuke. Only four colonies, all embroiled in border disputes—New Hampshire, North Carolina, Virginia, and Georgia—did not participate.

George Washington understood that publicly and legally his Mississippi Land and Ohio Valley prospects were on hold; however, privately, he was well-poised to swoop once the king reversed his position, which Washington believed likely. For a Virginian to dream of a maritime link via the Potomac River to the interior, the more complicated problem of intercolonial cooperation was imperative. Washington already had Maryland allies in the project of making the Potomac navigable. What he needed was Ohio Valley land. In addition to King George III's 1763 dictum that prohibited the sale of much of its western territory, Pennsylvania had quantitative restrictions on the sale of real property along the desirable Monongahela River valley. Washington, however, was fixed on purchasing there. In September 1767, Washington wrote William Crawford, a surveyor friend living in southwestern Pennsylvania, with explicit instructions to purchase, on Washington's behalf, a large tract of "rich" western Pennsylvania land. Advising Crawford how to skirt both the king's and Pennsylvania law, Washington himself acknowledged that his directive was surreptitious and less than ethical:

> It is possible . . . that Pennsylvania Customs will not admit so large a quantity of Land as I require, to be entered together if so this may possibly be evaded by making several Entrys to the same amount . . . notwithstanding the Proclamation that restrains it at present . . . for I can never look upon that Proclamation in any other light (but this I say between ourselves) than as a temporary expedient to quiet the Minds of the Indians . . . any person therefore who neglects the present opportunity [sic] of hunting out good Lands & in some measure Marking & distinguishing them for their own (in order to keep others from settling them) will never regain it . . . For my own part I should have no objection to a Grant of Land upon the Ohio a good way below Pittsburg [sic] but would willingly secure some good Tracts nearer hand first. I would recommend it to you to keep this whole matter a profound Secret . . . I might be censured for the opinion I have given in respect to the Kings [sic] Proclamation & then if the Scheme I am now proposing to you was known it might give alarm to others & by putting them upon a Plan of the same nature (before we coud [sic] lay a proper foundation for success ourselves).

Philip Schuyler and the newly arrived royal governor of New York, Sir Henry Moore, evidently felt the same as Washington. In the summer of 1766, Sir Henry and Philip Schuyler traveled toward the source of the Mohawk River, where they purchased adjacent land directly from the tribal chiefs for themselves and a friend, Lord Henry Holland, a prominent Whig politician (and father of Charles James Fox, one of the British parliament's most outspoken critics of George III). The three men together also bought title to property near Fort Stanwix on the Oneida Carry, an ancient portage used by the Native tribes that linked the Mohawk River with Wood Creek. That body of water flowed into tributaries of the Great Lakes. As Schuyler's riverside land expanded, from New York Harbor up the Hudson toward Lake Champlain, and westward along the Mohawk, his acquisitions were instructional, providing a very clearly drawn blueprint for a man whose intention, like his Dutch forbears, was to gain control over and untold riches from a canal system. Lord Moore wrote of their trip to the Earl of Hillsborough, the British secretary of state for North America. In his letter, Moore described his journey with Schuyler to the Canajoharie Falls on the Mohawk River:

> At this fall is the only obstruction to the navigation between Fort Stanwix and Schenectady, my intention was to project a canal on the side of the falls, with sluices on the same plan as those built on the grand canal in Languedoc, and I stayed a whole day there, which was employed in measuring the falls and examining the ground for that purpose. Upon the meeting of the Legislative bodies I propose to lay what I have done and engage them, if I possibly can, to carry into execution a project which will be attended with such benefit to the public.

Governor Moore enjoyed his time with the Schuyler family so much that he returned to Albany again in October. Insistent on reciprocating Schuyler's hospitality, Moore welcomed the entire Philip Schuyler clan, children in tow, for a visit at the royal governor's mansion in Lower Manhattan that December. Sir Henry thought so highly of Philip Schuyler and his visionary plans for New York that he asked his real estate partner to organize and train a military regiment, commissioning Schuyler as colonel.

Philip Schuyler was a man who believed in law and order. When riots broke out against the Stamp Act and the Townshend taxes, he disapproved of the disorder but believed in conciliation. He was not a member of the Sons of Liberty but celebrated with them at a feast at Howard's Tavern in Lower Manhattan when the act was repealed. In 1766, New Yorkers who protested still toasted the king at that fete. As a member of the great Dutch New York clans, Schuyler wielded influence; as a member of the New York General Assembly he would have the political authority required to join the fight for his land and legislate an intracolonial canal system. Like his great-uncle Pieter Schuyler, who had served twice as royal governor of New York, Philip Schuyler decided to enter politics. On March 3, 1768, Schuyler was elected to the New York General Assembly.

The New York General Assembly records show Philip Schuyler's name appearing in the roll call for the first time on October 27, 1768. At thirty-four years old, Schuyler, who entered politics on a mission, immediately introduced bills to clear roads and to create new counties in both the western Mohawk River communities and in the northeast disputed lands. He also introduced legislation to make navigable creeks and streams in the vicinity of Lake Champlain. Earlier in the year, Schuyler and Governor Moore had purchased together another 4,000 acres at Fish Creek along the Mohawk River. Now, with Schuyler serving in the assembly, Moore knew he had an ally. On December 16, 1768, New York Royal Governor Moore sent a letter to the provincial assembly reiterating what he had written Lord Hillsborough the previous year. For the public record, Moore stated how much he had enjoyed his trip up the Mohawk with Philip Schuyler and parroted Schuyler's call for New York canals along the Mohawk River to the Great Lakes:

> The great inconvenience and delay, together with the expense attending the transport of goods . . . have considerably diminished the profits of the trader, and called for the aid of the legislature, which if not timely exerted in their behalf, the commerce with the interior parts of the country may be diverted into such channels, as to deprive this colony of every advantage . . . The obstruction of the navigation of the Mohawk river, between Schenectady and Fort Stanwix, occasioned by the falls of Canajoharie . . . is easily to be removed by sluices . . . [like] those in the great canal of Languedoc,

in which was made to open a communication between the Atlantic
and the Mediterranean . . . [I am now] encouraged to recommend
to the house of assembly the improvement of our inland navigation
as a matter of the greatest importance to the province, and worthy
of their consideration.

About a year after Philip Schuyler and his investment group had purchased
their parcel of land near Fort Stanwix, the British government finalized its treaty
there with the Six Nations (Mohawk, Onondaga, Oneida, Cayuga, Seneca, and
Tuscarora). The November 5, 1768, Treaty of Fort Stanwix gave King George
a measure of ease. Satisfied that he would no longer have to wage costly wars
with the Natives, His Majesty finally agreed to permit his colonists to move
westward. Open wrangling for the Ohio Valley and territory to the east of the
Mississippi River resumed and intensified. In December, George Washington
submitted a second version of the "Mississippi Land Company's Petition to
the King," in which he asked George III to grant the corporation "2,500,000
Acres of Land . . . to be located or laid off between the thirty eighth [sic] and
forty second [sic] Degrees of North Latitude, the Alligany [sic] Mountains on
the Eastward, and thence Westward to the dividing line." Washington's first
petition had been refused by Lord Hillsborough, who pointed to the parameters of the October 14, 1768, Treaty of Hard Labor with the Cherokee tribe.
Washington and his group recast their borders in their December application
but unbeknownst to him there was an insurmountable obstacle to his proposal:
another company, spearheaded by Thomas Walpole, nephew of British Prime
Minister Sir Robert Walpole, was the favored contender for many millions of
acres of land that subsumed Washington's request. Washington was not naïve
about the advantages of political families' connections. He and his partners
dissolved the Mississippi Land Company. Washington also attempted to purchase 10,000 acres of land for himself in British western Florida but was again
precluded from doing so by Lord Hillsborough.

Furious that his dreams were dashed by those in power an ocean away,
his loss was another personal reckoning: Washington would wade in the
waters closer to home where his local political positions were meaningful.

A few years earlier, he had bought the mortgage on a farm belonging to a Mount Vernon neighbor named Captain John Posey, who, deeper and deeper in debt, could never meet his obligations. In 1769, authorities foreclosed on Posey's land, and proceeds of the sale repaid Washington in full. On May 4, 1769, Washington filed a petition with the Virginia General Court, charging that his wife had not received her entire widow's dowry. With alidade in hand, George Washington had personally measured the "Tract of Land containing about 1000 acres situate near the City of Williamsburg on which are two Plantations" that had belonged to Martha's late husband, Daniel Custis. Part of the land claimed by George Washington on his wife's behalf had been inhabited by Daniel's late father, John Custis. The court agreed that Martha had been shortchanged. A compromise of some land and rental income for the widow and heir, which would be controlled by Washington, was so ordered.[3]

On Tuesday, December 5, 1769, George Washington introduced a bill to the House of Burgesses in Williamsburg, "for the clearing and making navigable the River Potowmack [sic] from the Great Falls of said River, up to Fort Cumberland."[4] Working alongside Richard Henry Lee, the bill went through committee procedural process on December 8 and 13. On December 14, 1769, the House of Burgesses "Ordered, That the Bill, with the Amendments be ingrossed"—meaning considered. There was no further action on the bill during the Christmas season; however, Washington persisted with the rest of his agenda. Insisting that there was urgency in his next matter "to prevent Emigrants from unwittingly possessing the same" lands, on December 15, 1769, he once again submitted his request on behalf of the "Soldiers who first Imbarkd [sic] in the Service of this Colony . . . That the 200,000 Acres of Land which was given to them by the Honble Govr Dinwiddies [sic] Proclamation bearing date the 19th of Feby [sic]" be honored. The council in Williamsburg, agreeing that there was no longer any legal impediment, issued the declaration, "that the Petitioners were justly entitled to the said Two Hundred Thousand Acres . . . they have leave to take up the said quantity in one or more Surveys, not exceeding twenty, on the great Canhawa [sic] and the other places particularized in their Petition." Those entitled to participate—the petitioners—included only those soldiers who had fought alongside George Washington

at the July 1754 Battle of Fort Necessity. The Council's decree authorized
Washington to apply to the College of William and Mary, whose 1693 royal
charter endowed it with the mandate to license and appoint Virginia county
surveyors, and proceed with the charting and distribution of the promised
lands. Washington, as chair of the veterans' petition committee, was now in
control of one of the largest real estate handouts in North America, and he
arranged for his friend and property scout, William Crawford, to get the job.

It had been twenty years since teenage George Washington had purchased
his first parcel of Shenandoah Valley land and sixteen since he had been promised the Ohio Valley property he had yet to own. In his capacity as the soldiers'
advocate in the House of Burgesses, Washington had kept a list of the men
who had fought with him at Great Meadows as well as each man's rank. Both
criteria were necessary to determine eligibility for Governor Dinwiddie's February 19, 1754, Proclamation of 1754 Ohio Valley land award. The information
also came in handy for Washington the real estate speculator. As he was always
concerned about appearing self-interested but had already proved willing to
circumvent the rules, Washington positioned others to shill for him. In January
1770, Washington's cousin Lund bought the rights to 2,000 acres of the soldiers' bounty from the Reverend Charles Mynn Thruston, a former lieutenant.
Lund then endorsed the document to his cousin George, who recorded the
transaction in his January 1770 cash account. On January 31, Washington
wrote his brother Charles, who was living in western Virginia (today's Charles-
town, West Virginia), about Lund's successfully concluded deal. George asked
Charles to serve him as well, not as an agent—whose purpose and client would
be known—but as a straw man, a secret henchman, surreptitiously in pursuit
of land on behalf of George Washington. Washington gave Charles the
names of a few people to approach and directed Charles to:

> purchase 12 or 15,000 Acres upon the same terms . . . Such a quantity
> of Land as this, added to what I may expect in my own Right, would
> form a Tract of so great dignity as to render it worth my while to
> send out a Person for the discovery of Land clear if possible of these
> numerous grants . . . it would be worth my while thus situated, to

buy of some . . . I shoud [sic] be glad if you woud [sic] (in a joking way, rather than in earnest at first) see what value they seem to set upon their Lands, and if you can buy any of the rights of those who continued in the Service till after the Cherokee Expedition . . . I am of opinion . . . some of those who may be in want of a little ready money, would gladly sell . . . If you shoud [sic] make any purchases, let it be done in your own name . . . In the whole of your transactions . . . do not let it be known that I have any concern therein. I have Inclosd [sic] you a copy of the Bond I drew from Thruston to Lund Washington, which will serve you for a Precedent in case you shoud [sic] make any purchase—I have put your name in the place of Lund Washington's as I would have the title given to you, & not to me . . . I shall take care to furnish you with money as you may find occasion . . . Show no part of this Letter, so that you can be drawn into no trouble or difficulty in the Affair.

George's warning to Charles that some of the claims to land were mired in overlapping grants meant that those properties would cost more to obtain. Negotiations and clear title would require several parties, be more complicated, and require extra guile. There was, however, particular interest in a parcel of 10,000 acres claimed by "a certain Ambrose Powell . . . lying above the Mouth of the great Kanhaway [sic]" that might be complicated to purchase but it was a strategic part of George's plan to own riverside property. This land claimed by Powell was not only "compended [sic] within our Grant of 200,000 Acres," but,

also fixed at a place where two or three other Grants are laid & I believe some of them older . . . yet, as it lyes [sic] in the way of a scheme I have in view; and woud [sic], in some small degree promote my Plan if I had it, I shoud [sic] be obliged to you if you woud [sic] enquire in a round about way who this Powell is, where he lives, &ca; & tell me who you think the most likely person for me to employ to purchase his right to the Grant . . . You need not let your reasons for enquiring after Powell be known . . . lest it may give him or others cause to imagine his grant is more valuable than it really is . . . inasmuch as it is totally swallowed up in other Grants . . . several of this sort may in some measure give me a prior claim to have my share of the 200,000 Acres laid of above the Mouth of the Great Kanhaway [sic] where I am told the land is very fine.

"Fine" arable land was always attractive; however, to George Washington this particular parcel at the mouth of the Kanawha was an essential component of his larger plan, as he hinted to his brother. In addition to taking charge of the Ohio Valley land apportionment and distribution, George Washington was also spearheading efforts in the Virginia legislature to make navigable the Potomac River. The Kanawha River was a tributary of the Ohio River, whose source lay just ten miles from the headwater of the north branch of the Potomac River. A Potomac-Kanawha-Ohio River conduit would provide considerable benefit for trade and growth in North America and colossal fortunes to those whose properties adjoined a canal system. Almost simultaneous with Lund's purchase of the Thruston property, Washington received a letter from Maryland ironworks owner John Semple, who wrote on January 8: "I am greatly pleased to find you are so likely to Carry the point of Improveing [sic] Potowmack [sic] River." Semple communicated to Washington his own opinions regarding Washington's bill. Washington's bill had called for private funding but Semple believed that any development project, which, Semple acknowledged, could bring enormous returns for investors, was so massive that it would really require public funding. Over the course of the next few years, Washington's thoughts would increasingly evolve to align more with Semple's.

A significant exchange of letters on the Potomac matter began with a June 18, 1770, note from Thomas Johnson, a future governor of the state of Maryland, to George Washington. This first note from Johnson to Washington would begin a lifelong friendship and partnership in public service. From Annapolis, Johnson apprized Washington that since, "others have assured me of your Friendship to the Inland Navigation on Potowmack . . . [I] inclose [sic] [to] you a Subscription Paper which is intended to be put about at our Frederick Court next Week." Johnson and Washington were contemporaries, and both were legislators. Johnson, a lawyer, was the more sophisticated policy-maker of the two and, while he advised his Virginia counterpart that it was best not to "entertain Expectations that both Legislatures will soon concur circumstantially in the same Scheme for clearing Potowmack [sic]," Johnson was, like Washington, determined. Johnson included some practical ammunition for Washington to impart in Virginia with calculations of the savings that water transport versus land carriage would bring. Johnson presented his examples in a way that he knew would be of personal value to Washington. He knew that Washington had interests in the Shenandoah Valley and in the Alexandria area. By the end of the 1760s, the Shenandoah Valley lands were favoring wheat as a crop over tobacco, and Alexandria was now becoming Virginia's premier port for the conveyance of this preferred Shenandoah crop. Johnson carefully traced the price "per Ton or 38 Bushels of wheat" from various points in western Virginia, Maryland, and Pennsylvania to the port of Alexandria.

Washington replied on July 20. First, he assured Johnson that "no person . . . wishes to see an undertaking of the sort go forward with more facility and ardour [sic] than I do." Second, Washington offered his opinion on who would invest in the scheme: "It appears to me that there will be found but two kinds of People who will Subscribe . . . Those who are actuated by motives of Publick [sic] Spirit; and those again who from their proximity to the Navigation will reap the salutary effects of clearing the River." Washington was both a patriotic Virginian and, as a waterside landowner, driven by profit. Any project concerning the Potomac River necessitated cooperation from both Virginia and Maryland landowners and legislatures. Johnson would be his Maryland ally and counterpart. Washington reminded Johnson that other colonies like Pennsylvania and New York were in a race to reach the Ohio River and the Great Lakes respectively.

Written four months after the Boston Massacre, Washington's missive did not express any notion that the British North American colonies would divorce from their mother country. It actually appears otherwise in the marketing plan he suggested to Johnson. People will be motivated, wrote Washington, if you entice them with the image of the Potomac River as corridor to Alexandria and Alexandria as the gateway to England. Washington urged Johnson to allow potential investors to dream big. His commentary was shrewd and visionary, practical and prescient. He wrote of North America as an ascending empire, though in 1770 no official break with England was yet on the horizon:

> there is the strongest speculative Proof in the World of the immense advantages which Virginia & Maryland might derive (and at a very small comparative Expence) by making the Potomack the Channel of Commerce between Great Britain and that immense Tract of Country which is unfolding to our view the advantages of which are too great, & too obvious I shoud [sic] think to become the Subject of serious debate but which thro. Illimited Parsimony & supiness [sic] may be wrested from us & conducted thro. [sic] other Channels such as the Susquehanna . . . the Lakes &c . . . if it was recommended to Publick Notice upon a more enlarged Plan, and as a means of becoming the Channel of conveyance of the extensive & valuable Trade of a rising Empire . . . I think many woud [sic] be envited [sic] to contribute their mite, that otherwise will not.

Although Washington's Potomac bill languished in the House of Burgesses, he was far from idle. On August 1, he "Met the Officers of the first Virga. Troops at Captn Weedens where we dined & did not finish till abt. Sun set" in Fredericksburg. There, the group voted approvingly to fund a trip for Washington, surveyor William Crawford, and Dr. James Craik to travel to the Ohio Valley. Despite his obligations at Mount Vernon, Washington was intent on going. As he had written his brother Charles in January, the reality of obtaining choice land in the Ohio Valley meant physically claiming it. One had to be strong and aggressive with chain, compass, and tomahawk or the property "woud [sic] soon be forfeited." Washington believed that "half the Officers in this Colony" would have neither the gumption nor the extra cash it would take to make the journey. That would mean a buying opportunity for Washington, who left home on October 5 to scout, survey, select, and demark the choicest properties.

Traveling up the Braddock Road he knew so well, Washington arrived at William Crawford's cabin along the Youghiogheny River in southwestern Pennsylvania on a Saturday afternoon, October 13. On Sunday, they visited an actively burning coal mine. On Monday morning, October 15, the men set out for Fort Pitt and their Ohio River adventure. First, to Washington's delight, they stopped to see the lush 1,600 acres purchased by Crawford on Washington's behalf per his 1767 instructions. Situated on his property was his old Fort Necessity. Under the terms of King George III's 1763 Proclamation, Washington was legally entitled to receive another 2,813 acres in the area from the new royal governor, Lord Dunmore. The group traveled on to Fort Pitt and reached the Ohio River on October 18, the same day as the signing of the Treaty of Lochaber, which opened up the lands we know as West Virginia and Kentucky to the British colonists.

As always, Washington kept track of the colorful figures with whom their paths crossed, the taverns, the local stories of Indian massacres, the fish, fowl, and wildlife, and the topography. Sailing the Ohio River in his canoe, Washington described the scenery with names like "Round Bottom," "Fish Run," and "Mingo Town." Those quaint designations have disappeared in time but in their stead remain treasured American towns like Pittsburgh, Steubenville, Marietta, Charleston, and Wheeling. The most productive part of the journey for George Washington was the discovery of a "boot-shaped peninsula ten miles wide and bordered on three sides by the Ohio"[5] where that mighty river met the Kanawha. It was there where "Washington set up his mark."[6]

Washington returned to Mount Vernon in December. On March 5, 1771, only six representatives of the approximately three hundred qualified members of the 1754 Virginia Regiment assembled at Winchester. Without having seen the land, the group accepted Washington's selection. Those in attendance also voted for Crawford to proceed with the twenty surveys approved by the House of Burgesses. Washington suggested that each soldier contribute the funds according to the size of his land award. That meant, of course, that most of the burden fell to Washington himself. On April 30, George Washington compiled the official roll call of the regiment, based on payroll and discharge date. Washington knew which of the men had died, leaving heirs to inherit, and which of the men were destitute. He contacted Crawford, his brother, and agents in London to approach those candidates likely to sell on his behalf and insisted on remaining anonymous with each and every purchase.

William Crawford set about his task and set aside the land for Washington that Washington had selected for himself. Despite a 1712 Virginia land ordinance that forbade the purchase of land tracts that were more than three times wider than they were deep, Crawford and Washington again knowingly disobeyed the law. Washington's riverfront land hugged some fifteen miles of the Great Kanawha.[7] A few members of the 1754 Virginia Regiment traveled to see Crawford's progress and tour their own parcels. When they learned what Washington had grabbed, they were furious. It was then when people began to refer to Washington's real estate acquisitiveness as "avaricious." Despite his later heroism in the American Revolutionary War, Washington would never shake his reputation among Virginians as a ruthless and rapacious real estate developer.

To avoid formal complaints, Crawford juggled some borders and, explaining his situation, apologized to an irritated Washington. Washington would gain the choicest riverfront land anyway. He collected parcels belonging to other soldiers, additional acreage from Dunmore—to whom he appealed for a colonel's share despite attaining that rank post-1754 battle—and from the House of Burgesses, arguing that his costs for the nine-week western trip, for which he was reimbursed, and Crawford's surveyance were oversized. Washington received a number of hostile letters accusing him of greed and self-interest to which he responded with shockingly insulting diatribes.

In furtherance of establishing his real estate empire, Washington crafted and published an advertisement for tenants before he even legally owned most of the Ohio Valley land. His ad appeared in the inaugural edition of the *Maryland Journal and Baltimore Advertiser* on August 20, 1773, with the false representation that he was already the landlord. It does reveal his entrepreneurial ambitions:

The subscriber having obtained patents for upwards of twenty thousand acres of land on the Ohio and Great Kanawha (ten thousand of which are situated on the banks of the first-mentioned river, between the mouths of the two Kanawhas, and the remainder of the Great Kanawha, or New River, from the mouth or near it, upwards, in one continued survey) proposes to divide the same into any sized tenements that may be desired, and lease them upon moderate terms, allowing a reasonable number of years rent free, provided, within the space of two years from next October, three acres for every fifty contained in each lot, and proportionably for a lesser quantity, shall be cleared, fenced, and tilled; and that, by or before the time limited or the commencement of the first rent, five acres of every hundred, and proportionably, as above, shall be enclosed and laid down in good grass for meadow; and moreover, that at least fifty fruit trees for every like quantity of land shall be planted on the Premises. Any persons inclinable to settle on these lands may be more fully informed of the terms by applying to the subscriber, near Alexandria, or in his absence to Mr. Lund Washington; and would do well in communicating their intentions before the 1st of October next, in order that a sufficient number of lots may be laid off to answer the demand. As these lands are among the first which have been surveyed in the part of the country they lie in, it is almost needless to premise that none can exceed them in luxuriance of soil, or convenience of situation, all of them lying upon the banks either of the Ohio or Kanawha, and abounding with fine fish and wild fowl of various kinds, as also in most excellent meadows, many of which (by the bountiful hand of nature) are, in their present state, almost fit for the scythe.

The advertisement also bared two more obsessions of Washington: it boasted of the vicinity of his properties to water, to be even more improved soon (canals); it also divulged his hope for a capital city on the Potomac River away from the powerful who resided near and ruled from Williamsburg:

From every part of these lands water carriage is now . . . easy communication . . . from Fort Pitt, up the Monongahela, to Redstone, vessels of convenient burthen, may and do pass continually; from whence by means of Cheat River, and other navigable branches of the Monongahela, it is thought the portage to Potowmack [sic] may, and will, be reduced within the compass of a few miles, to the great ease and convenience of the settlers in transporting the produce of their lands to market. To which may be added, that as patents have now actually passed the seals for the several tracts here offered to be leased, settlers . . . may cultivate and enjoy the lands in peace and safety . . . these must be among the most valuable lands . . . not only on account of the goodness of soil, and the other advantages above enumerated, but from their contiguity to the seat of government, which more than probable will be fixed at the mouth of the Great Kanawha. George Washington.

There have been varying accounts of the total amount of acreage that George Washington would finally receive for his 1754 military services. According to the appropriate designation for the rank of major, he should have been granted about 5,000. By his own account, he admits to owning some 32,373 acres purchased or appropriated from those either willing to sell, desperate to sell, or who did not meet their obligations. Legal documents from families with names like Thruston, Roots, Stobo, Vanbraam, and others suggest that Washington owned an additional 37,400 acres, making his ownership more than 70,000 acres of western Virginia land along the Great and Little Kanawha rivers. In addition to the Kanawha properties, Washington would own over 12,000 acres in the lower Potomac basin and nearly 5,000 acres in the Monongahela area—1,600 secured for him by William Crawford, 2,813 from Royal Governor Dinmore, and another three thousand from the perennially strapped farmer Captain John Posey, who had subsequently purchased cheaper western lands on Washington's suggestion. Washington would also own land in Kentucky[8] and about 1,000 acres of an approximately 7,000-acre parcel of land in New York's Mohawk River valley. At the end of his life, Washington tallied his western and Potomac properties. Excluding his Alexandria, Georgetown, and waterside "Federal City" parcels, townhouses and commercial buildings,

Washington estimated that he had clear title to about 55,000 acres of land along the Potomac and Ohio Valley tributaries. Though he tried to collate a meticulous list, it did not reflect the many thousands of acres he had sold over his lifetime.[9] Until the election of Donald J. Trump in 2016, George Washington was considered by historians to be the wealthiest president of the United States of America.[10] Washington's real estate empire, however, paled in comparison with that of Philip Schuyler's son-in-law, Stephen van Rensselaer III, whose name is a perennial on economists' lists that compute the ten richest Americans of all time.

It did not take long for English home rule to once again discomfit and thwart Washington's plans. British North American Secretary of State Lord Hillsborough was receiving mixed messages. Hillsborough's cousin was married to the newest royal governor of New York—its thirty-ninth—William Tryon. In keeping with the ritual of many newly arrived royal governors before him, Tryon made a pilgrimage to Albany for a visit with Philip Schuyler. Tryon enjoyed some time at the Schuyler family home, The Pastures—referred to by the locals as "the Mansion"—bid farewell to his wife, and journeyed northward to investigate tribal unrest. Despite having signed treaties, the Natives were demanding return of land. After listening to their grumblings, Tryon, satisfied that the treaties had met British legal standards, conveyed positive sentiments in person to cousin Hillsborough during a trip to England. At the very moment when friction over New York land had cooled down with the tribes, it heated up with New England colonists over the New Hampshire Grants, the land west of the Connecticut River. The New York General Assembly appointed Philip Schuyler chairman of the committee to assert New York's position contra New England: Schuyler consulted dozens of land grants and laws and issued a stern condemnation to the governors of Massachusetts and Connecticut. The New York Assembly ordered the colony's officers of the law to arrest squatters in the northeast territories and put them on trial. Schuyler's name became anathema in the New England colonies.

The governors of New Hampshire, Massachusetts, and Connecticut together attempted to reverse the king's Connecticut River border decree. They waged surreptitious campaigns—today known as "lobbying"—with British politicians.

The New York Assembly accused the New England governors of not only being devious and disingenuous but also being misguided in believing they had two pillars of support in the Earl of Shelburne, who merely wanted a friendly end to the dispute, and with "the lords of trade when they made their report in May, 1757, [who] were not fully informed of the true course of that part of Hudson's river." American geography remained conveniently mysterious to those embroiled in the quarrel. If the New England colonies gained jurisdiction of lands west of the Connecticut River and Lake Champlain, that would deprive Philip Schuyler of his inherited land and his dream to link New York Harbor, the Hudson River, Lake Champlain, the St. Lawrence River, the Great Lakes, and the Atlantic Ocean. Schuyler countered New England by nominating Edmund Burke as New York's agent in London. Schuyler drafted a land report on the New Hampshire Grants for Burke, to be presented at the British court. He also appeared the figure of conciliation when, on February 5, 1773, he mediated the border dispute with New Jersey.

Although Lord Hillsborough chose to dismiss the squabble between New York and New England as a matter that had been settled by King George, instead of driving investments there, he fixated on the still tumultuous Ohio Valley where, despite the Fort Stanwix Treaty of 1768, ongoing Native butchery against British colonists persisted. Men like George Washington—land speculators, traders, farmers, and merchants—who had already or had hoped to establish farms, mills, stills, and taverns, took considerable risk when they hazarded the western adventure. With no consideration for the hardships of or promises made to those who had settled in the Ohio Valley, Lord Hillsborough issued a policy statement that revived the ban on the defrayal of Ohio Valley land, declaring that Dinwiddie's February 19, 1754, proclamation was meant to exclude American-born fighters. Hillsborough's British allies found no such impediment. Virginia's royal governor, Lord Dunmore, a self-interested investor, announced that he was revoking William Crawford's surveys. Claiming that Crawford was unlicensed, Dunmore rescinded the Virginia council's 1769 order for the division of the 200,000 Ohio Valley acres. George Washington expressed outrage in a February 20, 1774, letter to James Wood: "Lord Hillsboroughs [sic] Sentiments of the Proclamation of 1763, I can view in no other light than as one, among many other proofs, of his Lordships malignant disposition towards us poor Americans; founded equally in Malice, absurdity, & error." Thomas Jefferson agreed. In his 1774 *A Summary View of the Rights of British America*, Jefferson wrote:

> It is time for us to lay this matter before his majesty, and to declare that he has no right to grant lands of himself. From the nature and purpose of civil institutions, all the lands within the limits which any particular society has circumscribed around itself are assumed by that society, and subject to their allotment only. This may be done by themselves assembled collectively, or by their legislature, to whom they have delegated sovereign authority; and if they are allotted in either of these ways, each individual may appropriate to himself such lands as he finds vacant, and occupancy will give him a title.

To Jefferson, like Washington, in North America, a chain, a compass, and a tomahawk superseded the property yens of the English king.

Washington, Thomas Johnson, and other investors from Maryland and Virginia formed the Frederick Company with the purpose of making the Potomac River navigable. The equity partners, Thomas Jefferson included, studied a proposal submitted by John Ballendine, who wished to serve as general contractor of the venture. Washington had his own copy of Ballendine's pitch pamphlet. Ballendine left for England for presumably a tour of the Bridgewater Canal and financial assistance. On September 8, 1774, the *Maryland Gazette* featured an advertisement by Ballendine, just returned

> from great Britain with a number of engineers and artificers in order to remove the obstructions to the navigation of the Potowmack [sic] River . . . others interested in this necessary work . . . [should meet him] at George Town in Maryland . . . Monday, 26th day of September . . . At which time and place he will . . . be ready to lay before them an accurate plan and estimates of the expence [sic] . . . an Act of the Virginia Assembly, and likewise a subscription from some of

the principal proprietors . . . of the Province of Vandalia now residing
in England.

Ballendine's newest investors were the same politically connected London
aristocrats who had deprived Washington of his Mississippi land scheme.
They were now trying to elbow out Johnson, Washington, and their Amer-
ican investors. Washington turned his resentment into a proactive blockade.
From September 5 to October 26, while he represented the colony of Virginia
at the First Continental Congress, Washington instigated a chorus of dissent.
The January 14, 1775, *Virginia Gazette* published an article on Ballendine's
Potomac project that reflected a significant revision:

> At a meeting of the Trustees for opening the navigation of Potow-
> mack River held at George Town Dec. 1, 1774 Thos. Johnson, Jr.,
> Attorney-at-law, [et al. from Maryland] . . . ordered and directed
> that the subscriber should on the credit and at the risk of the
> above named Trustees hire fifty slaves to labor in cutting the canals
> around the several Falls of said River; and at another meeting of
> Trustees for the purpose aforesaid held at Alexandria 19th inst.,
> present George Washington, [et al.] Gentlemen of Virginia together
> with many of the Trustees at the former meeting . . . recognized
> and approved of the order . . .

Five years after he had submitted his bill to the Virginia General Assembly
for the development of the Potomac River, George Washington, along with
likeminded Thomas Johnson of Maryland, now boldly yanked control from
Ballendine's impeccably connected London investors via the intercolonial enterprise they had earlier envisaged. Washington's Potomac River canal system
was underway.

In competition with the Washington-led consortium was a group in New
York fronted by Philip Schuyler. New York's royal governor, William Tryon,
who had accompanied Philip Schuyler on upstate journeys to the Lake Champlain area and along the Mohawk, resubmitted the proposed canal project

touted by his predecessor to the New York Assembly with amplifications. Tryon now advised the New York Assembly to construct two canal systems: one along the Oneida Carry to connect the Mohawk River with the tributaries of the Great Lakes, and another on the upper Hudson River to link it with Lake Champlain. It was no secret to anyone that Philip Schuyler would reap tremendous benefits from both projects. Royal Governor Tryon, who served as His Majesty's representative, did not put forward the suggestion to profit Schuyler. By 1775, their friendship was under a cloud shadow.

An array of British actions found unacceptable by North American colonists had provoked a series of demonstrations like the Boston Tea Party and other boycotts. For some, the call to action was taxation without representations; for others, unfair trade policies or the forced quartering of British soldiers. Philip Schuyler believed that freehold and freedom were inextricable. Known for his thoughtful deliberation and his distaste for the kinds of explosive insurrections favored by Bostonians, Schuyler was reelected to the New York Assembly by an enormous majority. Standing firm for the transfer of power into the hands of Americans, Schuyler became the unofficial champion and anonymous spokesperson for the minority of anti-royalists in the New York Assembly. Among his series of valiant and eloquent resolves on behalf of the people of the colony of New York was his response to the king's decree to prohibit communication, letters of "sedition," among the colonies after a protest document had been circulated by Massachusetts.

Like Philip Schuyler, George Washington also viewed land ownership as indivisible from a man's identity. The most egregious wrongdoings on the part of the king, the parliament, and their favorites, to Washington, was their aggregate imperious interference in his property rights. He was tired of their whims, their contradictory proclamations that propped his hopes and then dashed them. When news of the June 22, 1774, Quebec Act, ceding much of what is now Indiana, Michigan, Ohio, Minnesota, and Wisconsin to the Province of Quebec and not to Virginians or New Yorkers, reached the thirteen colonies, for many British Americans like George Washington, it was the final straw.

On Saturday, June 17, 1775, the Virginia Assembly voted on and passed "An Act for raising a Capital sum of forty thousand Pounds Sterling, by subscription, and establishing a company for the opening and extending the navigation of the River Potowmack." George Washington missed the vote. In May, he had departed Mount Vernon to attend the Second Continental Congress in Philadelphia. On June 14, 1775, the Continental Congress selected George Washington and Philip Schuyler to configure and draft rules for an American army. Four days later, George Washington, appointed as the new commander in chief of this embryonic American Continental Army, and Philip Schuyler, chosen as Washington's second of four major generals, departed Philadelphia riding side by side to protect and preserve the land and the rivers they loved. Chains, compasses, and dreams of canal systems would all prove essential to them in the fight to come.

CHAPTER 5

Currents

AN ANGRY KING GEORGE III issued his first public response to the American rebellion in a speech he gave before the British Parliament on October 27, 1775. The king vowed to quash the rising tide of independence across the ocean: "They have raised troops, and are collecting a naval force; they have seized the public revenue, and assumed to themselves legislative, executive, and judicial powers," he indignantly declared. The king then publicly hurled his wrath at "the authors and promoters of this desperate conspiracy"—America's Founding Fathers—and charged them with colluding and plotting unrest "for the purpose of establishing an independent empire."

The same powerful currents that could transport people and goods across the Atlantic and up and down the Hudson and Potomac Rivers toward the interior of the continent could also facilitate the flow of soldiers. No one understood this better than Commander in Chief George Washington and Major General Philip Schuyler. After the yearlong and ultimately victorious Siege of Boston, George Washington repositioned his troops in Lower Manhattan to defend the vital New York Harbor. Britain's overriding strategy to gain supremacy in North America was now to divide New England, where it had suffered defeat, from New York and from the rest of the colonies. On

July 17, 1776, Major General Philip Schuyler informed the commander in chief that intelligence reports brought news that British General John Burgoyne and his troops were poised to enter New York from British Canada near Lake Champlain. A month later, Washington and his army lost control of New York Harbor and Lower Manhattan in a brutal defeat at the hands of General William Howe's 32,000 troops. After a stinging setback in Harlem Heights, Washington retreated to White Plains. Further humiliation forced Washington to cross the Hudson River to New Jersey and then traverse the Delaware River to Pennsylvania, leaving Major General Philip Schuyler in complete command over the Northern Department.

To keep the enemy at bay, Schuyler used his financial acumen, his friendship with the Native Americans, and his knowledge of New York geography and waterways. In addition to his organizational skills to train men and procure equipment and foodstuffs, Schuyler drafted a multi-pronged plan that proved Washington correct in believing that Schuyler would be an invaluable asset to the Continental Army: First, Schuyler conferred with tribal chiefs at Fort Stanwix to ensure their neutrality so that British armies descending from Canada via the St. Lawrence River and Great Lakes would find no assistance. Schuyler's success with the tribes resulted in the Congress renaming the fort "Fort Schuyler," and, with tribal consent, Schuyler readied a lock at Wood Creek to connect it with the Mohawk River so that his own speedily constructed bateaux could traverse the western waters.[1]

Next, in order to confront Burgoyne's army at the northeast border, Schuyler proceeded with his longtime plan to link Lake Champlain with the Hudson River. He received the authority to measure, clear, and level waters near Fort Edward. Schuyler discussed the design and expense of the Fort Edward canal project with many influential visitors. Chaperoned by Schuyler, Morgan Lewis, a future governor of New York State who had married a Livingston, and Gouverneur Morris, a signatory of the Articles of Confederation, visited the fort and learned of Schuyler's aspirations for a New York canal system. According to Lewis, Morris was enraptured, predicting that, "[A]t no very distant day, the waters of the great western seas [will] by the aid of man, break through their barriers, and mingle with those of the Hudson."[2]

TOP: The Schuyler House, Albany, New York, built by family patriarch, Philip Pieterse Schuyler, around 1659. The house stood at the southeast corner of State Street and South Pearl Street. CENTER: Philip Hooker, *Philip Schuyler Mansion, Albany, New York*, 1818. Headpiece on manuscript description and appraisal of the property. Watercolor and brown ink on paper. Gift of Nannette Bryan, New-York Historical Society, 1961.13. The house, known as "The Pastures," broke with modest Dutch-style tradition in its more splendid Georgian-designed architecture. BOTTOM: Schuyler House Saratoga, New York. Photograph Courtesy of Saratoga National Historical Park.

Anonymous [The Schuyler Painter], *Colonel Philip Schuyler (1695–1745)*, ca.1720, oil on canvas. Gift of Henry C. Van Schaack, New-York Historical Society, 1847.1. It was from Colonel Philip Schuyler that his nephew, General Philip Schuyler, inherited an enormous parcel of land at Saratoga, New York.

Thomas McIlworth, *Mrs. Philip John Schuyler (Catherine van Rensselaer Schuyler) (1734–1803)*, 1762–1767, oil on canvas. Bequest of Philip Schuyler, New-York Historical Society, 1915.11.

Portrait of Lawrence Washington. Courtesy of Mount Vernon Ladies' Association. George Washington's elder half-brother, mentor, and the man from whom he would unexpectedly inherit Mount Vernon.

ABOVE: *East Front of Mount Vernon* by Edward Savage. Courtesy of Mount Vernon Ladies' Association. It was this Potomac River view that inspired George Washington's vision of a coastal route to the interior of North America and a capital city at Alexandria, Virginia. BELOW: *View of Fort George with the City of New York from the Southwest.* Engraved by John Carwitham possibly after William Burgis. C. 1764, hand-colored engraving on paper. Albany Institute of History & Art, gift of the estate of Marjorie Doyle Rockwell, 1995.30.8. It was New York City's natural deep-water harbor, with connectivity to both the Atlantic Ocean as well as multiple rivers, that made her a multi-ethnic colonial trading hub.

Hamilton's First Meeting with George Washington. Painted in 1856 by Alonzo Chappel (1828-1887). Scottish Rite Masonic Museum & Library, Gift of Mr. and Mrs. Richard Manney, 79.78.1. Photography by John M. Miller.

ABOVE: The Master Bedchamber at The Pastures, the Philip Schuyler home in Albany. George Washington slept here—as did Benjamin Franklin, the Marquis de Lafayette, and British General John Burgoyne. Renowned for his hospitality, Philip Schuyler placed his most important guests—friend or enemy—in his own private bedroom and decamped to less convenient quarters. Photograph courtesy of New York State Office of Parks, Recreation, and Historic Preservation; Schuyler Mansion State Historic Site. BELOW: Schuyler House Dining Room, Saratoga, New York. George Washington, Alexander Hamilton, the Marquis de Chastellux, and other luminaries dined in this very room. Photograph Courtesy of Saratoga National Historical Park.

Unidentified artist, *Entry of Washington into New York*, ca. 1857-1866, oil on canvas. Promised Gift of Elie and Sarah Hirschfeld Collection, Scenes of New York City. New-York Historical Society. Evacuation Day, Tuesday, November 25, 1783.

The two most breathtakingly beautiful, yet most challenging, locations along each of their respective waterways for those who dreamed of canal systems. ABOVE: *A View of Cohoes Falls on the Mohawk River.* Paul Sandby, painter; William Elliott, engraver, 1761. The United States Library of Congress digital collection. BELOW: *Great Falls of the Potomac.* Courtesy of Mount Vernon Ladies' Association.

The Washington Family by Edward Savage. The painting, begun in 1789, depicts the Washington family seated around a map that prominently features the Potomac River. Courtesy of the National Gallery of Art, Washington, D.C., Andrew W. Mellon Collection.

Joseph Wright, *John Jay*, 1786, oil on linen. Gift of John Pintard, New-York Historical Society, 1817.5. It was Treaty of Paris signatory and later first Chief Justice of the United States Supreme Court and Governor of New York State, John Jay, who persuaded the Congress of the Confederation in December 1784 to remove to New York City.

Robert E. Pine, *James Duane*, ca.1784, oil on canvas. Purchase, New-York Historical Society, 1948.54.

First cousins, these four women were the social, philanthropic, and cultural leaders of the first Federal City of the United States of America.

TOP LEFT: *Sarah Livingston Jay*. Print courtesy of the New York Public Library, the Miriam and Ira D. Wallach Division of Art, Prints and Photographs. TOP RIGHT: Ralph Earl, *Portrait of Elizabeth Schuyler Hamilton* (Mrs. Alexander Hamilton), (1751–1801). Museum of the City of New York, 71.31.2. BOTTOM LEFT: Ralph Earl, *Mrs. James Duane (Mary Livingston), (1738–1821)*, 1787, oil on canvas. Purchase, New-York Historical Society, 1948.55. BOTTOM RIGHT: *Portrait of Lady Catherine Alexander Duer* by Charles Wilson Peale. Courtesy of Heritage Auctions, HA.com.

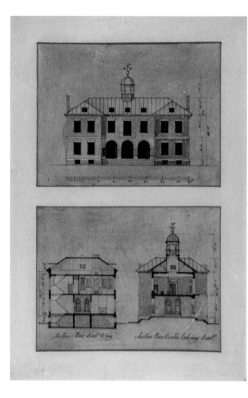

Old Federal Hall 1735. (Established as City Hall in 1699). Courtesy of the National Park Service—Federal Hall National Memorial.

Federal Hall. (As it appeared after the New York clans spearheaded its refurbishment for the inauguration of President George Washington). Courtesy of the National Park Service—Federal Hall National Memorial.

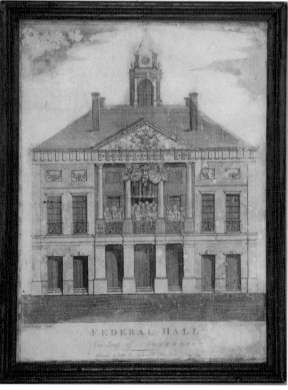

ABOVE: *Washington's Inauguration* by Ramon de Elorriaga. Courtesy of the National Park Service—Federal Hall National Memorial.

RIGHT: Unidentified artist, *Richard Varick* (1753–1831), early 19th century, oil on linen. Purchase, New-York Historical Society, 1982.15. Varick was secretary to both General Philip Schuyler and Commander-in-Chief, General George Washington, and became Mayor of New York City when it was the first federal capital of the United States under the Constitution of the United States of America. Varick was married to Maria Roosevelt, a daughter of Isaac Roosevelt, the paternal great-great-grandfather of President Franklin Delano Roosevelt.

The Republican Court (Lady Washington's Reception Day), 1861. Daniel Huntington (American 1816-1906). Oil on canvas, 66 x 109 1/16 in. (167.6 x 277 cm). Brooklyn Museum, Gift of the Crescent-Hamilton Athletic Cub, 39.536.1. First Lady Martha Washington (most prominent figure on platform left side); Betsey Hamilton (second row, second from left); John Jay (first row, first on left); Alexander Hamilton (first row; third on left); Peggy Schuyler van Rensselaer (center of female cluster behind Martha Washington); Sarah Livingston Jay (center of painting visible as the first figure among the ladies cluster to the front right depicted with her arm across her sternum); Lady Kitty Duer (fourth figure back in diagonal of ladies on the right).

Y.Z., sculp. *"What Think Ye of Congress Now? View of Congress on the road to Philadelphia,"* ca.1790, etching. New-York Historical Society Library, 44865. After the passage of the Residence Act in July 1790, which, at the time, was known to have been the outcome of behind-the-scenes maneuvering on the part of President George Washington, he and Congress were criticized by many and were severely lampooned by the press.

Unidentified artist, *Alexander Hamilton*, n.d., oil on wood panel. Gift of Ethel McCullough Scott, John G. McCullough, and Edith McCullough Heaphy, New-York Historical Society, 1971.120. Despite Thomas Jefferson's attempt to sully Hamilton's reputation for posterity, Alexander Hamilton did not "sell New York down the river."

Two other guests fascinated by Schuyler's proposed canal systems were elder statesman, Benjamin Franklin and Charles Carroll of Maryland, who journeyed north together to visit Schuyler and his blueprints. Franklin, lately returned from England, had, like Schuyler, acquainted himself with the Bridgewater Canal and had also studied the canal system in the Netherlands. On May 10, 1768, Franklin had written Sir John Pringle:

> You may remember that when we were travelling together in Holland, you remarked that the trackschuyt [sic][3] . . . was slower than usual, and enquired of the boatman, what might be the reason; who answered, that . . . the water in the canal was low . . . After our return to England, as often as I happened to be on the Thames, I enquired of our waterman whether they were sensible of any difference in rowing over shallow or deep water.

In this letter to Pringle, Franklin, a natural scientist, explained in detail that he had conducted experiments to understand the workings of canals, water depth, and displacement: "I provided a trough of plained [sic] boards fourteen feet long, six inches wide, and six inches deep, in the clear, filled with water within half an inch of the edge, to represent a canal . . . I repeated the experiment a number of times at each depth of water." Franklin then produced a table of measurements. His conclusion was that

> large canals and boats and depths of water . . . bear the same proportions . . . four men or horses would draw a boat in deep water four leagues in four hours, it would require five to draw the same boat in the same time as far in shallow water, or four would require five hours. Whether this difference is of consequence enough to justify a greater expence [sic] in deepening canals, is a matter of calculation, which our ingenious engineers in that way will readily determine.

Franklin's traveling companion, Charles Carroll of Maryland, a very rich man, had invested in Washington's Potomac River canal project twice the amount that

Washington had expended. Owner of one of the grandest and most expansive estates along the Potomac, Carroll would remain a lifelong investor in a series of projects to develop a canal system on it. Carroll's travel journal notes that he and Franklin did indeed discuss the cost of canals with Philip Schuyler:

> General Schuyler informed me that an uninterrupted water carriage between N. York and Quebec might be perfected at £50,000 Sterling expense by means of locks and a small canal cut from a branch that runs into Wood creek, and the head of a branch that runs into the Hudson River. The distance is not more than 3 miles. The River Richelieu . . . is navigable for bateaux from the Lake Champlain into the St. Lawrence.[4]

Carroll described Schuyler's lands at Saratoga as

> very good, particularly the bottom lands. Hudson's river runs within a quarter of a mile of the house, and you have a pleasing view of it for two or three miles above and below. A stream called Fishkills, which rises out of Lake Saratoga, about six miles from the general's house, runs close by it, and turns several mills; one, a grist mill, two saw mills, (one of them carrying fourteen saws,) and a hemp and flax mill . . . I requested the general to get a model made for me by the person who built it.[5]

Schuyler also shared sound property management methodology with Carroll.

> I was informed by the general that it is customary for the great proprietaries of lands to lease them out for three lives, sometimes on fee-farm-rents, reserving, by the way of rent, a fourth, or, more commonly a tenth of all the produce; but the proprietaries content themselves with a tenth of the wheat. On every transmutation of property from one tenant to another, a quarter part of what the land sells for is sometimes paid to the original proprietary or lord

of the manor. The general observed to me that this was much the most advantageous way of leasing lands;—that in the course of a few years, from the frequent transmutations of tenants, the alienation fines would exceed the purchase of the fee-simple, though sold at a high valuation. General Schuyler is a man of a good understanding improved by reflection and study . . . Saratoga [is] a most beautiful and most valuable estate. He saws up a great quantities of plank at his mills, which, before this war, was disposed of in the neighborhood, but the greater part of it sent to Albany.[6]

Benjamin Franklin departed for France on October 26, 1776, and did not have the opportunity to revisit Schuyler and observe the further development of Schuyler's wartime canal projects. Other fascinating people—friends and foes alike—would flow in and out of Schuyler's Albany mansion, The Pastures, to discuss the canals, borrow law books, request tours of rivers and forts, ask for guidance on procuring materiel for the army, or simply to meet the great man. The Pastures became an essential destination for American military leaders en route to the Canadian border. Philip Schuyler proved as gracious to his treasured guests like General George Washington, who returned on several occasions, and Washington's young aide-de-camp, Alexander Hamilton, who became family, as he was to men like Horatio Gates and Aaron Burr, who would become family nemeses.[7]

The Pastures not only provided a retreat from the north; it was also an oasis apart from constant British attack in the south. The British, in possession of Manhattan, inevitably would embark north on the Hudson River. Schuyler knew he had to prevent the British from successfully sailing upriver from the deepwater New York Harbor. He engineered an ingenious artificial obstruction that combined floating logs and chains—a medieval cheval-de-frise and two seemingly impenetrable booms—that were extended across the Hudson River at the base of the Highlands near the West Point promontory. Any sailing vessel that attempted to cross it would be cut to shreds.

For most of 1776, the ebb and flow of conquest and defeat on both sides provided no clear advantage to either the British or the Americans. It was at last at the Battle of Trenton, a small but pivotal engagement that took place at the end of December, when the Continental Army could point to significant success. The iconic portrait of George Washington crossing the stormy Delaware River on Christmas Day illustrates the rough currents through which he sailed to victory.

After Trenton, there was another kind of current—a political eddy—that would similarly impact both Washington and Schuyler. The next significant triumph for the Continental Army would take place in Schuyler territory— Saratoga, New York—in the fall of 1777. As Schuyler had predicted and for which he well prepared, Burgoyne's armies voyaged via Lake Champlain to northern New York and from the Great Lakes across the Mohawk to face the vastly outnumbered Continental Army of the Northern Department. Winding along the Hudson River for two meandering miles, the Saratoga estate of General Philip Schuyler became premier target for Burgoyne. Before his ultimate defeat in Saratoga, Burgoyne ordered his soldiers to burn down the Schuyler country seat. General Schuyler's wife, Catherine, readied her coach and hastened for The Pastures in Albany. Before leaving, Catherine van Rensselaer Schuyler, insisting that the redcoats could "eat the furniture," burned her own fields. At great speed to town accompanied by only one sentinel, Mrs. Schuyler approached the forest that separated her from her Albany mansion. Her driver hesitated, cautioning Mrs. Schuyler that, as the British were specifically targeting the general's homes, they ought to head elsewhere. Catherine van Rensselaer Schuyler refused, declaring: "The general's wife must not be afraid!" Burgoyne's army also targeted the Livingstons, setting fire to the Clermont estate and firing cannon shots through Livingston Manor, the home of Declaration of Independence signer Philip Livingston, that was located near Poughkeepsie.

Although it was Schuyler's blueprint and strategy that ultimately defeated the British, it was British-born immigrant Major General Horatio Gates who took full credit for the victory. A mistral of malevolence that stirred political crosscurrents for both Schuyler and George Washington, Horatio Gates felt he was better qualified than both Washington and Schuyler to lead the patriot army. At the beginning of 1777, Gates preyed on the representatives from New

England to the Continental Congress, urging them to dismiss the man they already abhorred. Accusing Schuyler of treason, Gates and his allies beseeched George Washington to remove Philip Schuyler from his post. Washington knew the charges were phony and refused to do so. To appease the faction within its own house, the Congress removed Schuyler with the excuse that it needed to investigate. Schuyler resigned in disgust, demanding that his name be cleared. On September 12, the eve of the battle at Saratoga, which Schuyler should have led, his second cousin, political luminary John Jay, wrote Schuyler of his disappointment and sadness at the course of events: "Washington and Congress were assured that unless another general presided in the Northern Department the militia of New England would not be brought into the fold. The congress, under this apprehension, exchanged their general [Schuyler] for the militia—a bargain which can receive no justification from the supposed necessity of the times."

Denied the chance to lead the troops at Saratoga, Philip Schuyler nonetheless gained transatlantic fame following the two game-changing skirmishes. After the British defeat, Schuyler famously offered hospitality to Burgoyne, German Baron Riedesel, commander of the Hessian mercenaries, and his baroness, Frederika Charlotte. Baroness Riedesel kept a journal of her experiences as a military wife in North America in which she wrote of her astonishment at Schuyler's civility. Owing to his cordiality to the enemy, Riedesel declared the American major general to be a true Christian in his forgiveness.[8]

Important French allies like the Chevalier de La Luzerne, appointed by King Louis XVI as Minister from France to the United States, General Rochambeau, the Marquis de Chastellux, and the Marquis de Lafayette all visited Philip Schuyler at The Pastures in Albany. Noblemen accustomed to the luxuries of Paris and grand countryside chateaux, they all commended Schuyler for his aristocratic "open house" largesse, his gentility, and the quality and sophistication of his table. In his *Travels in North-America*, Chastellux depicted Schuyler as a man who "does what he says he will do" and described Schuyler as the architect of a beautiful home and patriarch of a very attractive and spirited family. Visitors congregated in a lovely salon, enjoyed a good fire, and partook of a most satisfying dinner that was accompanied by an excellent Madeira. Quite a few people had encouraged Chastellux to visit the Schuyler family, "particularly General Washington." Chastellux felt it important for his European audience to learn specific details about the Schuyler family. He painted a verbal portrait of General Schuyler and his family: Schuyler's military service during both the Seven Years' War and the current one, Schuyler's loving marriage to the unimaginably rich Kitty van Rensselaer, Schuyler's frequent bouts with gout, and the gorgeous and lively Schuyler children.[9]

Of particular interest to Chastellux was, as he impressed on his reader, the absolute confidence and devotion between General George Washington and Philip Schuyler. Though Schuyler was no longer embroiled in battle, Washington continued to rely on his New York major general for thoughtful guidance on invasion and defense. Schuyler suggested that the Americans recapture Fort Ticonderoga. Washington replied with three carefully thought-out options, all of which incontestably revealed that George Washington was as familiar with the connectivity of the New York waterways as he was with the Potomac River and its tributaries. Chastellux, overjoyed when Philip Schuyler invited him on a journey along the Mohawk River, was awestruck by Schuyler's natural leadership skills, befitting someone well-born, and Schuyler's vision for taming and developing the seemingly infinite American wilderness. To Schuyler and Washington that goal was virtuous: patriotism and profit were not mutually exclusive.

Chasetllux, Lafayette, and the other French blue bloods who arrived to enjoy Schuyler's kindness were so grateful to Schuyler and so impressed with his generosity that some twenty years later, when the guillotine menaced the French aristocracy, complete strangers would appear at Schuyler's doorstep with letters of introduction.

The Continental Congress demonstrated that it really had no interest in pursuing trumped-up charges against Schuyler and stalled its inquiry. Schuyler, intent on clearing his name, pressed Washington for a court martial. To no one's surprise, Schuyler was completely vindicated. Swollen with the glory of Saratoga, Gates next went after Washington's job. Attaching himself to a small group of malcontented officers later called the Conway Cabal, Gates and his group attempted but failed at mutiny. Schuyler and

Washington now had one more similar experience and one more bond that created the empathy of deep friendship between them. Schuyler became so widely known as Washington's most trusted ally that another scoundrel named Benedict Arnold used Schuyler as an intermediary with Washington to obtain his post at West Point. It was on Philip Schuyler's recommendation that Washington appointed the future traitor to his position.[10]

A stream of disappointing, petty men did nothing to distract Schuyler and Washington from their patriotic mission. Schuyler resumed his role as a New York representative to the Second Continental Congress. It had taken multiple drafts and two years for the Second Continental Congress to approve the final submission of the Articles of Confederation and Perpetual Union on November 15, 1777. Hidden in plain sight in thirteen short and simply worded articles and a conclusion was the undercurrent of deep rivalry among the colonies, which is why it would take almost four years for all of the thirteen colonies to ratify the groundbreaking document. The articles bestowed the confederation with limited powers but it abrogated the rights of individual states to declare war and to negotiate with foreign governments. It was each state's responsibility, however, to raise its own army. While the Articles of Confederation endowed the Continental Congress with the ability to issue its own currency, each state could still print its own. The federal government was ordained with the power to obtain funds from foreign lenders but its only domestic source of revenue, as detailed in Article VIII, was for each state to value its own real estate, collect taxes from it, and proffer a portion of it to the confederation. Articles V and VI expressly addressed public servants and profiteering. Representatives to the Continental Congress were limited to a term of three years, "in any term of six years . . . nor shall . . . a delegate . . . be capable of holding any office under the united states, for which he, or another for his benefit receives any salary, fees or emolument of any kind." The point was reiterated: "nor shall any person holding any office . . . accept of any present, emolument, office or title of any kind whatever from any king, prince or foreign state."

The biggest sticking point for many of the states, and the reason it would take Maryland four years to officially join the union, was Article IX, which addressed border disputes, land treaties with the Native tribes, and the location of the seat of government. Article IX granted the new United States of America Congress of the Confederation the final word in determining borders:

> on appeal in all disputes and differences now subsisting or that here-
> after may arise between two or more states concerning boundary . . .
> All controversies concerning the private right of soil claimed under
> different grants of two or more states, whose jurisdiction as they
> may respect such lands . . . shall on the petition of either party to
> the congress of the united states, be finally determined . . . respecting
> territorial jurisdiction between different states.

Article IX also decreed that the, "Congress of the United States shall have power to adjourn to any time within the year, and to any place within the united states." If Article IX had not been deliberately vague about the coveted location for the seat of the new government, there would have been no union. The congress was, for the most part, meeting in Philadelphia as a geographic compromise; however, the two most powerful and richest states, Virginia and New York, rejected that locale as a long-term solution. Virginia had passed its constitution on June 29, 1776, and had moved its capital to Richmond. The New York State Assembly had ratified its own constitution on April 20, 1777, in exile as the state's commercial and legislative capital in Lower Manhattan remained occupied by the British. Both states had formed governments with executive, judicial, and legislative branches. Both states required men to be property owners to vote. For the Articles of Confederation to pass it had to placate colonies and landowning colonists at war for America's capital city.

There was no executive branch outlined in the Articles of Confederation, and the only court established in the document of "perpetual union" was an admiralty court meant to address piracy and maritime trespass. The Articles of Confederation configured the government of the United States of America as a unicameral legislative body. Each state had one vote. Representatives to the Second Continental Congress had the enormous burden of course-plotting a new nation ad hoc, building a war chest without a unified financial organi-zation, and navigating the new nation through the turbulent and changing tides of international relations. The fledgling legislature of the United States of America did not function as a technocracy but very quickly specific talents were identified amongst its leaders. Philip Schuyler was singled out for unequaled expertise, becoming the ranking financial member of the Second Continental Congress, Chairman of the Committee on Military Reform, and one of three chiefs on the committee to deal with the Native tribes; hence, he had a great deal of influence. After Maryland became the last of the states to ratify the Articles of Confederation in 1781, transforming the Continental Congress nominally into the Congress of the Confederation, another attempt was made, this time by the Congress of the Confederation of the United States of America, to finally settle the New Hampshire Grants dispute. Offered statehood as "Vermont," the people, many of whom were squatters on land belonging to the New York clans, were unhappy with the designated boundaries and rejected the opportunity to join the union. The thirteen states would continue to squabble over land and their conflicting charters for another twenty years.[11]

When the Treaty of Alliance with France was signed on February 6, 1778, the Marquis de Lafayette formally became authorized to assist the Americans with money and men. With the Marquis de Lafayette at his side, Philip Schuyler negotiated with tribal chiefs for four days in March (March 7–10, 1778) for two hundred braves to fight alongside American patriots. Seven days after they concluded their agreement, Great Britain declared war on France.

Schuyler was no longer a soldier but he remained George Washington's de facto military partner. It was Schuyler, not Arnold nor Gates, to whom Washington turned for essential intelligence and topographical data. On December 27, 1778, Schuyler wrote Washington that he was still frantically searching for a "Copy of the Account given me In 1758 by the persons employed to Explore a rout Into the St. Laurence" as he had promised but enclosed instead "a number of papers containing some Information of the western Country In 1764, and An Account of Colo: Bradstreets [sic] expedition to Frontenac . . . I should be glad to have them returned as I have no Copies." The precious documents Schuyler transmitted to Washington included a detailed description and accounting of bateaux used to travel the upstate waters during the Seven Years' War as well as a survey of landmarks and channels in northern and western

New York. This measurement table of distances and depths was similar to the ones Washington had famously produced of the Ohio Country. Schuyler also dispatched urgent communications to Washington of the imminent invasion by British Major Guy Carleton along the Canadian border and of the treachery of the Green Mountain Boys.

Washington corresponded regularly and confidentially to Schuyler about his worries that the armed forces were in dire financial straits. The paper money issued by the Continental Congress had depreciated so quickly that it had become worthless. Schuyler repeatedly used his own creditworthiness to assuage his friend's anxiety by personally funding various needs of the patriot army. As chairman of a congressional three-man committee tasked to prod each of the colonies to pay their share of the burden, Schuyler became growingly irritated by what he perceived was as an apparent ignorance of financial mechanisms on the part of his colleagues in the congress. On November 29, 1779, he wrote New York Governor George Clinton that, "[o]ur Finances are deranged to a most alarming degree, heavy demands constantly made on the Treasury which is empty."

Schuyler began to form a financial rescue plan. His pamphlet *Causes of Depreciation of the Continental Currency* explained how a package of stabilizing measures could reduce debt, provide liquidity, and fund a prolonged war. With some minor variation, the congress would implement Schuyler's program in early 1780. When financier Robert Morris was named superintendent of finance, Philip Schuyler assisted Morris in not only structuring the Bank of North America but also by becoming a rather large investor in it. Driven by patriotism and profit, Philip Schuyler, Robert Morris, and George Washington all believed that America would fail without a strong and unified continental financial system of cooperation. They would find their economic disciple in Washington's brilliant young aide-de-camp, Alexander Hamilton.

It was in 1773 when the illegitimate, impoverished teenage Alexander Hamilton sailed from the leeward island of Nevis, where he was born in ignominy, to attend the Elizabethtown Academy in New Jersey. After completing his studies there, he applied for university. Rejected from the College of New Jersey (now Princeton University), Hamilton enrolled at King's College (now Columbia

University) instead. Hamilton's plan was to study anatomy. At King's College in New York, he discovered the political and philosophical writings of Locke, Montesquieu, Hobbes, and Hume, and the legal arguments of Blackstone and Grotius. With his roommate, Robert Troup, Hamilton founded the first debating and argumentative writing society at the college. By 1774, it was clear that nineteen-year-old Alexander Hamilton's métier would not be medicine.

In November 1774, Hamilton penned a thirty-five-page essay entitled "A Full Vindication of the Measures of the Congress" meant to rebut Anglican clergyman Samuel Seabury's "Westchester Farmer" contention that the Continental Congress was acting illegally. So convinced was Hamilton in the merits of his own argument, he placed an advertisement in the December 15, 1774, *New-York Gazetteer* to gain an audience. His readers included a very critical Seabury. Although still a college student and a teenager, Hamilton responded to Seabury's countercharge with a second and even more heated challenge. Dated February 23, 1775, Hamilton's article, "The Farmer Refuted," stated, "It is the unalienable birth-right of every Englishman . . . to participate in framing the laws which are to bind him, either as to his life or property." Hamilton spelled out each and every charter that created each and every colony and posited that while Americans were indeed subjects of His Majesty the King, they were not subject to the whims of the English Parliament, which had no jurisdiction over colonial Britain. Hamilton further claimed that North America could be a self-sustaining nation of its own because North American topography was so vast and varied that anything could be farmed, fished, grown, or be produced: "Nature has disseminated her blessings variously throughout this continent." The most stunning element in twenty-year-old Hamilton's thesis was his sophisticated explanation for the abrasion with Great Britain, which we today commonly refer to as "Thucydides Trap."[12] Hamilton assessed the future of both nations, mother and colonial offspring, parent and child, as waning and rising empires, destined to rupture and compete:

> If we look forward to a period not far distant, we shall perceive, that
> the productions of our country will infinitely exceed the demands,

which Great-Britain and her connections can possibly have for them; and, as we shall then be greatly advanced in population, our wants will be proportionably increased . . . If we take futurity into the account, as we no doubt ought to do, we shall find, that, in fifty or sixty years, America will be in no need of protection from Great-Britain. She will then be able to protect herself, both at home and abroad. She will have a plenty of men and a plenty of materials to provide and equip a formidable navy . . . the special benefits we receive from the British nation are of a temporary and transient nature; while, on the other hand, those it may reap from us . . . will be permanent and durable.

After the Battles at Lexington and Concord in the spring of 1775, Alexander Hamilton spent a good deal of his time drilling with a New York regiment. On June 25, when George Washington and Philip Schuyler rode together down Broadway in Lower Manhattan, Hamilton was in the crowd cheering, unaware of his future connection to both men. Within the next year, Hamilton would fight in the artillery, assemble his own squadron, and obtain his first invitation to speak with Washington in his Harlem Heights military tent. In late October 1776, Hamilton fought among Washington's brigade at White Plains, and again was among the general's forces at Trenton and Princeton. On January 20, 1777, Washington asked Hamilton to be his aide-de-camp. They became so close that jealous underlings spread rumors that Hamilton was the general's illegitimate son, a boy he had fathered during his 1751 trip to Barbados. Like any father and son, there was sometimes friction between the two: Hamilton longed for action; unable to bear the loss should Hamilton fall in battle, Washington would deny Hamilton's serial requests.

While in his position as Washington's assistant, Hamilton fearlessly continued to publish essays against Goliaths. Affronted by Maryland representative Samuel Chase, who, with secret information about the army's wants, formed a conglomerate to monopolize the sourcing of flour, Hamilton brandished his pen as his slingshot. In the fall of 1778, using the nom de plume "Publius," Hamilton wrote a series of three excoriating letters that denounced public servants who abuse their positions for profit. His first essay, dated October 16, states:

> when a man, appointed to be the guardian of the State, and the depositary of the happiness and morals of the people . . . descends to the dishonest artifices of a mercantile projector, and sacrifices his conscience and his trust to pecuniary motives . . . no strain of abhorrence . . . nor punishment, the vengeance of the people can inflict, which may not be applied to him, with justice. If it should have happened that a Member of C[ongre]ss . . . has been known to turn the knowledge of secrets, to which his office gave him access, to the purposes of private profit . . . he ought to feel the utmost rigor of public resentment, and be detested as a traitor of the worst and most dangerous kind.

Hamilton's final letter in the series, dated November 16, was instructional and, like his 1775 treatise "The Farmer Refuted," disclosed a prescient and farseeing view of America: "The station of a member of C[ongre]ss, is the most illustrious and important of any I am able to conceive. He is to be regarded not only as a legislator, but as the founder of an empire." To Hamilton, if Columbia, as the North American British colonies had been known since the 1730s, was an embryonic empire to be defined by the humane credo that every citizen had the inalienable rights to liberty, property, and the pursuit of happiness, her imperial ethos had to be inseparable from abiding integrity.

Sometime between December 1779 and March 1780, Alexander Hamilton pseudonymously penned his own ideas for a financial rescue plan and addressed it to "a member of that body [the Continental Congress] in whose power alone it is by well digested system to extricate us from our embarrassments. I have pitched upon you from a personal knowledge of your abilities and zeal." The essay was assuredly in response to Philip Schuyler's *Causes of Depreciation of the Continental Currency* and, although there has been nonsensical speculation, it unquestionably was written to Schuyler, the legislator charged with attacking the nation's financial woes. Hamilton reaffirmed Schuyler's position that, "the object of principal concern is the state of our currency." In his self-styled "dis-quisition," Hamilton laid out the relationship between patriotism and profit, the delicate balance that would drive the future of the United States of America to greatness:

> no plan could succeed which did not unite the interest and credit of rich individuals with those of the state . . . this scheme stands on the firm footing of public and private faith, that it links the interests of the state in an intimate connexion [sic] with those of the rich individuals belonging to it, that it turns the wealth and influence of both into a commercial channel for mutual benefit.

Hamilton explained that he had reasons for requesting anonymity but would reveal himself to the letter's recipient should there be a request for him to do so:

> If the outlines are thought worthy of attention and any difficulties occur, which demand explanation or if the plan be approved, and the further thoughts of the writer are desired, a letter directed to James Montague Esqr. Lodged in the Post Office at Morris Town will be a safe channel of any communications you may think proper to make and an immediate answer will be given. Though the Writer has rea-sons which make him unwilling to be known, if a personal conference with him should be thought material, he will endeavour to comply.

It was neither reticence nor modesty that motivated Hamilton to veil himself as the author of a financial prescription; however, in comparison with someone like Schuyler, a property owner of means who conducted transatlantic business, Hamilton's economic panorama was somewhat rudimentary at that point in time. Hamilton's portfolio of commercial knowledge had to mature. Philip Schuyler would be his instructor.

When Hamilton began constructing this epistle, around Christmastime in 1779, Philip Schuyler was at home with his family in Albany. Washington had hoped to join the Schuyler family but could not get away from his Morristown encampment. The army continued to struggle with a severe want of resources. On January 16, 1780, Schuyler wrote Washington:

> Whilst I regret with Anxious Concern the Causes which deprive me and mine of the satisfaction and happiness we promised ourselves from an Interview with You and Your lady at this place I lament with all the feelings which Affection can Inspire the pain and distress you are exposed to from the Miserably deranged State of our public Affairs, the fatal Influence pervades Into every quarter, and is Sensibly felt here, the public officers are without money and without Credit.

Schuyler had been waiting in Albany to show Washington designs for army "Makisson[s]" and snowshoes. Since Washington was unable to make the journey, Schuyler formed an alternative plan: "I shall transmit a pair as a Sample by my daughter who takes the Advantage of a visit Mrs Renselaer [sic] is going to pay In Jersey to make her respects to Your Lady." Schuyler's second-born daughter, Elizabeth ("Betsey"), was traveling to Morristown to visit her paternal aunt, Gertrude Schuyler Cochran. Mrs. Cochran was married to Dr. John Cochran, surgeon general to the army and personal wartime physician to Commander in Chief Washington.

Betsey Schuyler arrived in Morristown, New Jersey, with her chaperone and a military escort. Washington wrote Schuyler on January 30, 1780: "Your fair daughter, for whose visit Mrs Washington & myself are greatly obliged, did me the honr [sic] to present your favor of the Instt [Schuyler's January 16 letter] . . . you have my hearty thanks." In the note, Washington exchanged strategy with Schuyler about "securing the enemys [sic] Vessels on lake Champlain . . . onondago [sic] River . . . & border of the lake ontario [sic]" and confided that his "Army [was] put to the severest trial—Sometimes it has been 5 or Six days together without bread. At other times as many days without meat."

In a personal vein, Washington reassured his friend that he had, "furnished Mr Van Ranselaer [sic] with a flag to convey a Letter to New York . . . a necessary compliance with the rules of the enemy" and had assumed an avuncular role toward his daughter: "I have the pleasure to inform you that Miss Schuyler is well as you will probably learn from her own pen as she has promised to give me a letter to put under my cover to you. Mrs Washington & the Gentn [sic] of my family join in best respects & good wishes . . . sincere regard and affect Dr Sir Yr Most Obedt & obliged Sert [sic]."

The "Gentn [sic] of [Washington's] family" included many gallant officers delighted to dine and dance with Betsey Schuyler and her Livingston female cousins. The wartime currents of people who drifted and swirled in and out of Washington's orbit, and the swelling tide of republicanism caused a tsunami in the social order. Prerevolutionary status quo would have preordained a marriage between Elizabeth Schuyler and a member of the clans. By the time Philip Schuyler returned to the congress on March 7, Elizabeth Schuyler had become enthralled with and had promised to marry—subject to her parents' approval—Alexander Hamilton. A letter dated March 17 from Hamilton to "My dearest girl" reveals that there was ardent affection between them. On a short trip to Amboy, Hamilton expressed his fear that she would leave Morristown to visit her father in Philadelphia: "[I]t will be a tax upon my love to part with you." This letter was also an acknowledgement and response to one she had written him, which was filled with, "the sweet effusions of tenderness . . . My Betseys [sic] soul speaks in every line and bids me be the happiest of mortals . . . You give me too many proofs of your love to allow me to doubt it . . . I possess every thing [sic] the world can give."

To many people's surprise, especially those who thought Philip Schuyler was an autocratic snob, Schuyler was delighted with the match. He had only one condition, which he conveyed to Hamilton in a letter dated April 8, 1780: "Mrs. Schuyler did not see her Eldest daughter married. That also gave me pain, and we wish not to Experience It a Second time."[13] Schuyler advised his future son-in-law that he would "probably be at Camp In a few days, when we will adjust all matters." With some degree of pride, Schuyler added: "You have been mentioned in private Conversation to go as Secretary to the Embassy at the Court of Versailles."[14] As a surrogate son to the commander in chief of the armed forces, Hamilton was an object of curiosity. As the future son-in-law of grandee Philip Schuyler, Hamilton became conspicuous. Schuyler cautioned Hamilton that he was now thrust into a spotlight that inspired envy: "Beware of

Communications to this quarter which you would not wish the world to know. This hint will prevent you from writing but by a safe hand." Despite his own warning that there would be spies and enemies everywhere, Schuyler, in his note to Hamilton, actually passed on very delicate information to Hamilton, which he hoped and suspected would be forwarded to General Washington.

On March 9, only two days after Schuyler had arrived in Philadelphia, the Continental Congress approved his financial rescue package. Schuyler soon disheartened when he learned of a cyclone of criticism intensifying against Washington. A congressional cabal had formed to displace the commander in chief and replace him with an oversight committee. Schuyler thought the entire plan counterproductive, and, to ensure fairness for his friend, Schuyler demanded, as a former major general, to be chairman of the so-called committee on military reform.

As he had signaled to Hamilton, Schuyler set out for Washington's headquarters. Schuyler arrived in Morristown in mid-April purportedly to dissect systemic problems in the Continental Army. Washington had every confidence in Schuyler that the report to the Continental Congress would be sympathetic. Schuyler submitted his report to the congress in May. To conciliate Washington's opponents, Schuyler proposed the formation of a congressional committee to coordinate the French and American officers. Washington, who thoroughly understood the nuanced situation, made his preferences public: "There is no man who can be more useful as a member of the Committee than General Schuyler. His perfect knowledge of the resources of the Country, the activities of his temper, His fruitfulness of expedients and his sound Military sense make me wish above all things [that] he may be appointed."[15] The following year, after all thirteen states would at last ratify the Articles of the Confederation—Maryland being the final one, on January 30, 1781—the newly minted Congress of the Confederation would begin the organization of executive departments. Washington, a steadfast champion of Philip Schuyler, wrote his friend of his, "infinite pleasure . . . that you are generally spoken of for the department of War. At the same time I learn with pain . . . from Colo. Hamilton that your acceptance of it is doubtful if the Choice should fall on you. I am perfectly aware of all your objections . . . but they ought not to prevail."[16]

In the company of Washington during the spring of 1780, Philip Schuyler had the opportunity to observe firsthand the interaction between the general and his future son-in-law. He was heartened by Hamilton's dedication to his new country and to the commander in chief and by Washington's unapologetic respect for Hamilton's abilities. Hamilton, however, was often embarrassed by Washington's paternal attention.

Mrs. Schuyler joined her husband in Morristown. She had been the recipient of a florid and flattering letter from her daughter's fiancé, in which Hamilton expressed profuse gratitude for consenting to give her daughter's hand in marriage. Catherine and Philip Schuyler together presented their own proposal to Betsey's fiancé in person: there would be a wedding later in the year at the family home in Albany.

Hamilton and Schuyler grew comfortable with each other during a steady round of late evening androcentric chats. They were of one mind on many subjects, and Schuyler was especially encouraged that Hamilton—aka "James Montague"—was in passionate agreement about the urgency for one cohesive monetary system for all of the United States of America. Evaluating Hamilton as loyal and of fine character, Schuyler would refer to him in letters to his daughter as, "my beloved Hamilton." The young man from Nevis, a tropical storm of lightning intellect, demonstrated his devotion to his adopted America. He persisted with ardor to petition sympathetic members of the congress to wake up to their patriotic responsibilities.

Though Schuyler's bill had helped reduce the nation's debt, the financial picture was far from rosy. At Washington's side every day, Hamilton was horrified by the dearth of basic necessities for the fighting men. The army continued to go hungry, barefoot, and unpaid. In the summer and autumn of 1780, Alexander Hamilton crafted a series of letters meant to outline and cure the defects of the current state of affairs. Notably, in a September 3, 1780, letter to New York representative James Duane (married to Mary Livingston, a cousin of Betsey Schuyler), Hamilton called for a new constitution, suggested a national bank, and proposed a stronger central government with individual heads of departments—Philip Schuyler, secretary of war, for example—with authority to regulate trade and collect taxes.

In addition to his duties as a representative to the Continental Congress, Philip Schuyler was elected one of twenty-four state senators to the New York State Assembly. British occupation forced the legislative body to move circuitously from Kingston to Poughkeepsie to Fishkill and to Albany throughout the war. In early December, the Schuyler family was in Albany awaiting the arrival of Alexander Hamilton, who traveled from Washington's latest encampment in New Windsor, New York. On December 14, 1780, the feisty upstart from a remote Caribbean island married heiress Elizabeth Schuyler at her father's eighty-acre Albany estate. The bride's mother, Catherine van Rensselaer Schuyler, was visibly pregnant with her fifteenth child. Hamilton, who had spent his life escaping his disreputable fatherless origins, was instantaneously brought into the fold of a respectable, large, and loving family. The propitious alliance for Hamilton, who wore diamond buckles on his shoes to the wedding that were a gift from Lafayette, intensified jealousy amongst Hamilton's detractors but delighted Washington, who had similarly "married up."

Relations between the Schuylers and the Washingtons were happily familial. Elated when asked to be godfather of Philip and Catherine's fifteenth child, Catherine van Rensselaer Schuyler, born on February 20, 1781, Washington, who could not be present at the March 4 christening, dispatched his wife, Martha, who traveled from New Windsor to Albany as her husband's baptismal proxy.

Two weeks before the cozy event that linked the Washington and Schuyler families even closer, Alexander Hamilton came perilously close to destroying the bond. Despite his fluency in French, Hamilton did not get the post to France. Neither was he permitted to further test his mettle on the battlefield. He was aching to escape his desk job, so, on February 16, in New Windsor with the general, Hamilton manufactured an offense so that Washington would send him into exile (the trenches). As he wrote his new father-in-law, Philip Schuyler, on February 18, 1781, "I am no longer a member of the General's family." Hamilton recounted the story of how, after being summoned to meet with Washington, he ascended the stairs to the general's office and was briefly intercepted by the Marquis de Lafayette. Explaining to the Frenchman that he was hurrying to meet with the commander in chief, Hamilton arrived slightly delayed at the top of the stairs. He reported his exchange with Washington to Schuyler: "Col Hamilton (said he), you have kept me waiting at the head of the stairs these ten minutes. I must tell you Sir you treat me with disrespect." Hamilton explained to Schuyler that he replied, "without petulancy, but with decision 'I am not conscious of it Sir, but since you have thought it necessary to tell me so we part.'"

Hamilton stormed off. In "less than an hour after, [Tench] Tilghman [another of Washington's assistants] came to me in the Generals name assuring me of his great confidence in my abilities, integrity usefulness &c [sic] and of his desire in a candid conversation to heal a difference which could not have happened but in a moment of passion." Hamilton told Tilghman that he would not under any circumstances appear for an interview and dispatched Tilghman with his decline and little explanation. Hamilton opened his heart to Schuyler as a son:

> I always disliked the office of an Aide de Camp as having in it a kind of personal dependence. I refused to serve in this capacity with two Major General's at an early period of the war. Infected however with the enthusiasm of the times, an idea of the Generals character which experience soon taught me to be unfounded, overcame my scruples and induced me to *accept his invitation* to enter his family. I believe you know the place I held in The Generals confidence and councils of which will make it the more extraordinary to you to learn that for three years past I have felt no friendship for him and have professed none. The truth is our own dispositions are the opposites of each other & the pride of my temper would not suffer me to profess what I did not feel . . . At the end of the war I may say many things to you concerning which I shall impose upon myself 'till than an inviolable silence. The General is a very honest man . . . His popularity has often been essential to the safety of America, and is still of great importance to it. These considerations have influenced my past conduct respecting him, and will influence my future. I think it is necessary he should be supported . . . I have said to make no other

impression than to satisfy you I have not been in the wrong. It is also said in confidence, for as a public I [sic] of the breach would in many ways have an ill effect . . . but my resolution is unalterable. As I cannot think of quitting the army during the war, I have a project of re-entering into the artillery, by taking Lieutenant-Colonel For- rest's place . . . If a handsome command for the campaign in the light infantry should offer itself, I shall balance between this and the artillery . . . A command for the campaign would leave me the winter to prosecute studies relative to my future career in life. With respect to the former, I have been materially worse for going into his family. I have written to you on this subject with all the freedom and confidence to which you have a right and with an assurance of the interest in all that concerns me. Very sincerely & Affectionately.

To his friend James McHenry, whom he called "Mac," Hamilton wrote, "The Great man and I have come to an open rupture . . . he charged me in the most affrontive manner with treating him with disrespect . . . Except to a very few friends our difference will be a secret."

On the twenty-fifth, Schuyler replied to Hamilton that he had received a letter from Washington with no mention of the spat. Schuyler advised Hamilton with all paternal kindness that Hamilton was too virtuous and too vital to the cause to allow one moment between two exhausted warriors to interfere with his duty to the general and to the nation. Schuyler also cautioned Hamilton that he was so invaluable as an aide to Washington that his resignation could cause an international incident. At the end of the note, Schuyler, a concerned father and patriot, gently advocated to Hamilton to desist his notion that he was more useful on the battlefield:

Last night your favor of the 18 Inst: was delivered to me. I confess that the contents surpized [sic] and afflicted me, not that I discover any impropriety in your conduct . . . you are incapable, but as it may be attended with consequences prejudicial to my country which I love, which I affectionately love . . . Long before I had the least

Intimation that you intended that connection with my family, which is so very pleasing to me, and which affords me such entire satisfaction I had studied Your Character, and that of the other Gentlemen who composed the Genrals [sic] family . . . in you only I found those qualifications so essentially necessary to the man who is to aid and council a commanding General, environed with difficulties of every kind, and these perhaps more, and of greater magnitude, than any other ever has had to encounter . . . The public voice has confirmed the Idea I had formed of You . . . men of genius Observation and Judgement think as I do . . . Your quitting your station must therefore be productive of very material Injuries to the public, and this consideration . . . impels me to wish that the unhappy breach should be closed, and a mutual Confidence restored. You may both of you Imagine when you separate, that the cause will remain a secret, but I will venture to speak decidedly istinct, [sic] and say It is impossible, and I fear the Effect, especially with the French Officers, with the French [sic] Minister, and even with the french istin [sic] Court; these already Observe so many divisions between us; they know and acknowledge your Abilities and how necessary you are to the General. Indeed how will the loss be replaced? . . . It is evident my Dear Sir that the General conceived himself the Agressor, [sic] and that he quickly repented of the Insult . . . It falls to the lott [sic] of few men to pass thro [sic] life without one of those unguarded moments which wound the feelings of a friend . . . The necessity now exists in the distresses of Your country. Make the sacrifice, the greater it is, the more glorious to you, your services are wanted, they are wanted in that particular station which You have already filled so beneficially to the public, and with such extensive reputation . . . I say not a word about your project [to join a battalion] as I hope there will be no Occasion to attempt it.

Hamilton heeded his father-in-law's advice and accompanied Washington to Newport as interpreter for Washington, who was meeting with French

General Jean-Baptiste-Donatien de Vimeur, le comte de Rochambeau. After concluding their rendezvous, Washington returned to his New Windsor, New York, headquarters but Hamilton moved to the Schuyler family mansion in Albany. All three men—Washington, Hamilton, and Schuyler—tried to pretend that nothing had happened. Philip Schuyler wrote his friend offering information that Washington needed with his usual gentility and intimacy. On April 3, 1781, in response to Washington's letter dated March 23, Schuyler mentioned Martha Washington's happy visit with the Schuyler family, during which time he had escorted her to view the New York State Assembly in action. Schuyler also reacted with empathy to Washington's distaste for the scandal brewing around General Gates. Washington had made it known that he wanted Philip Schuyler to head the Department of War. Schuyler's New England nemeses had, as expected, preferred General Gates, who was, at the time, under investigation for misconduct. Schuyler confidentially agreed with Washington, stating in this letter that a Gates "nomination" put forth by his allies, "would be too glaring an abuse of power" unless he "exculpated himself."

Schuyler, Hamilton, and Washington were self-consciously aware, and more so than most, that they were actually founding and creating a New World empire. It is evident in their actions, their choices of words, and their tireless debates about the future of their country. In the April 3 communiqué, Schuyler commiserated with Washington that he "lamented" those who were "charged with the Affairs of an Empire," but who had limited comprehension of the importance of the undertaking. Instead, they were bungling the opportunity, consumed with "narrow minded prejudices and local politics." Schuyler, Hamilton, and Washington wanted the factions and pettiness to stop. The confederation of thirteen states had to band together as one.

For Schuyler, it was time to settle old squabbles for the good of the whole nation. Appointed surveyor general of the state of New York, Schuyler set out to stop the private sales of western New York land between Americans and Native Americans pending the state's final assessment of its borders. He was also adamantly determined to settle the state's eastern border with the people who lived in western New England. Schuyler wrote Washington on

May 4, 1781, about his ongoing frustration with the endless New Hampshire Grants border disputes; he had even offered to forfeit some of his own lands but his generosity was rebuffed:

> The conduct of the Vermontese is mysterious and if the reports which generally prevail are well founded their measures will certainly be attended with dangerous consequences to this and the other united States . . . I was anxious for ceding [sic] the Jurisdiction beyond a twenty mile line from the Hudsons [sic] river, that their I [sic] might be immediately acknowledged and they made useful to the Common cause but the Governor put a stop to the business.

Schuyler, Washington, and Hamilton concurred that the rebellions of the men in Vermont were not only treasonous to the war efforts but also counter-productive to the reality of empire-building. Vermonters rejected both New York's proposal and statehood.

Schuyler turned his attention to productive matters: In addition to his own dual legislative duties, he continued to gather intelligence from the north and share it with the commander in chief and supervised the construction of 127 river-going bateaux so that Rochambeau and his men could invade Manhattan via the lower Hudson River. The contruction fo the bateaux, which were being fabricated with local—a good deal of it Schuyler—timber, was proceeding apace, Schuyler wrote Washington, despite, "the inability of the public to make good any further engagements in specie payments."[17]

The meeting between Rochambeau and Washington in Newport resulted in a plan to attack Manhattan. In the summer of 1781, Washington inched his headquarters menacingly closer to the island, at one point residing at van Cortlandt Manor, which belonged to the family of Philip Schuyler's mother. Alexander Hamilton and his bride leased a house downriver from Albany, across the Hudson from the frequently repositioning commander in chief so that Hamilton could ready for a military post: he sailed regularly to Washington's encampment and wrote frequent notes imploring his former boss to send him into combat. The general remained silent.

It was impossible for Hamilton to remain idle. While he waited for an affirmative signal from Washington, Hamilton composed a series of fiery, ambitious, and exhaustively researched articles meant to sway legislators and the public to the exigency of fiscal uniformity. Hamilton's plan was progressive, and he had to tread carefully. In *The Continentalist* number 1, published on July 12, 1781, in the *New-York Packet, and the American Advertiser*, Hamilton began inductively and non-threateningly with well-known historic references. After lulling his audience with the familiar, Hamilton, the provocateur, charted an exercise in comparative empires between legendary ancient realms and the newborn United States of America. That sophisticated assessment, in the minds of men like Hamilton, Schuyler, Washington, Benjamin Franklin, and a few others, was not in the vocabulary of the ordinary American citizen, who thought of himself as a "Yorker" or "Virginian." Hamilton cautioned that it was provincialism that had decimated dominions of yore and that Americans owed it to the magnificently crafted structure of the United States of America to avoid the "narrow coloneal [sic]" tribalism of the past. Athens and Sparta disintegrated because they were, "distracted [by] . . . the want of a solid fœderal [sic] union to restrain the ambition and rivalship [sic] of the different cities." He avowed that if American legislature could overcome "local interests" and truly conduct itself in concert as one "FOEDERAL GOVERNMENT," the United States of America would endure.

In *The Continentalist* number 2, published on July 19, 1781, Hamilton again addressed analogies between the antique world and the nascent United States of America. The renowned kingdoms of the past were inferior, maintained Hamilton, because they retained "controul over the persons and property of the subjects." America's citizens would enjoy freedoms and the right to own property but, cautioned Hamilton, America's superiority could dwindle if Americans rejected standardization that benefited its majority. Sparta and Athens, Hamilton explained, were, "at perpetual varience [sic] among themselves. Sparta and Athens contended twenty-seven years for . . . dominion of Greece." It was far more productive and beneficial to the success of an empire to follow the example of the "United Provinces" of the Netherlands, whose citizens valued "frugality, industry and commerce; peace, both at home and abroad." Hamilton argued that seven provinces had coalesced with one, "predominant . . . policy" "both at home and abroad." Hamilton had now written two *Continentalist* essays with a mirror to the past to forewarn that fractures between states never remained confined. They would exacerbate and cause destructive, irreparable, empire-wide ruptures.

On July 31, Hamilton at long last received his long-awaited commission to lead a battalion. Shortly afterward, two more of the *Continentalist* series appeared that forcefully bore into the nub of his theory that "political societies, in close neighbourhood [sic], must . . . be strongly united under one government."[18] He pinpointed land and border disputes as "pretexts for war" among the states. He admitted that the increase in fighting men, money, and materials available to combat the British had improved owing to foreign aid but warned that, whilst Americans could, for the moment, rely on assistance from the Netherlands and France, Americans could be sidelined if any two of the European powers struck their own treaty. Hamilton pleaded for independence through financial solvency: "the successive shocks in our currency" were America's most formidable enemies. In bold capital letters, Hamilton urged, "ENLARGE THE POWERS OF CONGRESS . . . preserve us from being a CONQUERED PEOPLE now . . . make us a HAPPY PEOPLE hereafter."

Hamilton's meatiest and most specific essay to date, *The Continentalist* number 4, was published on August 30. In it, Hamilton presented the Americans with a complete and dimensional program for the fiscal health of the United States of America. He believed that these measures needed to be appended to the Articles of Confederation. This addendum, according to Hamilton, should bestow the federal government with the "power of regulating trade," "a moderate land-tax," "a moderate capitation tax," "the disposal of all unlocated land, for the benefit of the United States," and "[a] certain proportion of the product of all mines, discovered, or to be discovered." In Hamilton's view,

> the great defect of the confederation is, that it gives the United States
> no property . . . no revenue, nor the means of acquiring it . . . power
> without revenue in political society is a name. While Congress con-
> tinue altogether dependent on the occasional grants of the several

States, for the means of defraying the expences [sic] of the FOED-
ERAL [sic] GOVERNMENT, it can neither have dignity vigour
[sic] nor *credit*. CREDIT supposes specific and permanent funds for
the punctual payment of interest, with a moral certainty of a final
redemption of the principal.

In *The Continentalist* number 4, Alexander Hamilton, the future mastermind
of Federalism and the uniform treasury system of the United States of America,
is revealed. Offering a prescient and powerful lesson in finance, Hamilton
awakened his audience to the realities of their day:

> The most wealthy and best established nations are obliged to pledge
> their funds to obtain credit; and it would be the height of absurdity in
> us, in the midst of a revolution, to expect to have it on better terms. This
> credit being to be procured through Congress, the funds ought to be
> provided, declared, and vested in them. It is a fact, that besides the want
> of specific funds, a circumstance which operates powerfully against our
> obtaining credit abroad, is, not a distrust of our becoming independent,
> but of our continuing united . . . There are some among us ignorant
> enough to imagine, that the war may be carried on without credit.

He further explained to his audience the difference between Americans and
their European counterparts: while rich people in the Netherlands had cash, "there
are few men of large fortunes in this country, and these for the most part in land."

Although Hamilton had vied for the position of superintendent of finances,
that position went to financier Robert Morris. Morris regularly consulted Philip
Schuyler and depended on the New Yorker for advice and investment into the
newly formed Bank of North America. Hamilton wholeheartedly applauded
the course of action but displayed a bit of jealousy vis-à-vis Morris:

> Congress have wisely appointed a Superintendant [sic] of their
> Finances; a man of acknowledged abilities and integrity, as well as
> of great personal credit and pecuniary influence . . . He has very

judiciously proposed a national bank, which, by uniting the influence
and interest of the monied men with the resources of government, can
alone give it that durable and extensive credit of which it stands in need.

One of those "monied" men was Hamilton's father-in-law, Philip Schuyler,
whose prominence had recently nearly cost him and his family their lives.

From the early spring of 1781, Philip Schuyler had been warned that
he and his family were enemy targets. On August 8, 1781, Schuyler wrote
George Washington that it was on Saturday, July 29, when he had learned
that a serious approaching conspiracy was looming. Schuyler, who was widely
known to both sides of the combat as one of the commander in chief's most
reliable sources of intelligence, an effective disseminator of counterespionage,
and a fountain of sound advice for Washington's other subordinate major
generals, assured the general that he had been taking "every precaution
for my security . . . [and had been] clos[ing] my back doors at sunset."
The Pastures brimmed with Schuyler children. Both Angelica and Betsey
had arrived for a visit. With Angelica were her three-year-old son, Philip
Schuyler Church, and her one-year-old daughter, Catherine. Angelica and
Betsey were both pregnant. Schuyler explained the scene to Washington.
On August 7—the night before he wrote Washington:

> The Enemy finding It Impossible to surprize [sic] me out of my
> house, attempted last night about 9 oClock to take me in it, forced
> the Gate of a Close court Yard and entered thro [sic] the Kitchen,
> four white men whom I had in the house having flown to their
> arms very gallantly disputed the passage into my hall, where I was at
> supper, and gave me time to gain my bedchamber, where my arms
> were deposited, the Enemy's members prevail'd [sic], they secured
> two of my men, wounded a third and obliged the other to fly out
> of the house for safety, some then entered, whilst others surrounded
> the house, those in the quarter exposed to my fire retired on the
> first discharge, those that had got in the Saloon, leading to my bed
> room, retreated with Great precipitation, on hearing me call "come

on my lads surround the house, And Secure the Villains who are plundering," I believe this little incident saved me, for although the townsmen run with all possible celerity to my assistance assoon [sic] as they heard the firing, yet they came too late to overtake the enemy, who Carried off the two men, and part of my plate . . . the party . . . Consisted of about twenty.

Out of respect for Schuyler, some friendly Oneida and Tuscarora braves combed the Mohawk River trails for the scoundrels, but the invaders intentionally scattered and could not be found. Years later, some of the stolen Schuyler family silver was mysteriously found, but its bearer remained mum as to how it had come into his hands.

The plans to invade Manhattan were put on hold when Washington got word that French Admiral François Joseph Paul de Grasse was sailing a sizeable flotilla from the Caribbean to the Chesapeake Bay. Rochambeau and his men changed their plans to reconnoiter with Washington in Virginia. On September 9, 1781, after an absence of six-and-a-half years, George Washington returned home to the terra rossa of Virginia.

Washington remained at Mount Vernon for only three days. He, Rochambeau, and their amalgamated armies, among them Alexander Hamilton, to whom Washington begrudgingly put in charge of a brigade, sailed and marched southeast along the tidewater estates that had inspired envy, motivation, and the lust for land in young and grown-up George Washington. For three weeks, 17,000 men led by George Washington embroiled in a relay of bloody battles until the British surrender at Yorktown on October 19, 1781.

From Saratoga on November 2, Philip Schuyler wrote Washington:

Yesterday a letter from Colo: Hamilton announced the glorious success which has resulted from your operations in Virginia accept my Dear Sir such congratulations as flow from a heart replete with every sentiment of affection, esteem and gratitude and permit me to super add a wish that you may, not only live, to compleat [sic] the business, which Your perseverance through the vast variety of

difficulties which have intervened, has brought thus far towards a
happy conclusion, but also long to enjoy the well earned [sic] fruits
of your arduous labours [sic].

Schuyler also informed the victorious American general that all was not
quiet in the north. There were continued enemy insurrections upstate New
York at Fort Ticonderoga and in Tryon County. The "Vermonters" continued
to stage uprisings against their New York neighbors.

There was no doubt that, despite the victory at Yorktown, Washington had
to return with his army to protect the northeastern states from British Canadian
cross-border invasions. He did go home for a well-earned interlude, but what
was supposed to be a happy respite turned into an unhappy weeklong stay from
November 13–20. Two days after his arrival, his stepson, Jacky, who had served
at Yorktown, died from camp fever. Washington also rode to Fredericksburg to
pay his respects to his mother, but she was not (after writing him to visit her
anytime) at home. He did, however, manage to find the time to purchase another
parcel of land adjacent to Mount Vernon. Six weary years in battle did nothing
to dim George Washington's acquisitiveness for land. In fact, his march along
the tidewater plantations reinvigorated his purpose. On November 17, whilst
at Mount Vernon, Washington wrote his neighbor, Benjamin Tasker Dulany:

> I learn from Mr Lund Washington that the Land formerly belonging
> to Mr Manley, is again about to be offered for sale, & that you & I
> are like to be the only competition in the purchase of it—That I often
> treated with Mr Manely in his life time, & since his death with his
> Executor for that Tract; is a fact which cannot be unknown to you:
> Equally true is it, that if the Land is exposed to public sale, I shall bid
> for it . . .the intention of this Letter is to make you a proposition, &
> explain my motives for it . . . It is to purchase the reversion of your
> Land in this neck, at the same time I make that of Mr. Manleys . . .
> It may be asked, why . . . I would choose to be the purchaser . . .
> The answer is plain . . . although it shou'd not fall into my hands
> immediately, to have in expectation . . . all the Lands in this neck.

Washington concluded his sometimes sad and frustrating week at home determined to head north to quell the pockets of ongoing turmoil. A short detour to Philadelphia turned into four months. From November 1781 to March 1782, Washington divided his time with members of the congress on official business—it was the first time that he and fellow Virginian James Madison would meet—which was to remind the legislators that the war was not over. Despite Washington's serious purpose, grateful Americans were intent on feting him. Philadelphia was alight with tableaux and festive soirees to honor their commander in chief. To lift the spirits of his grieving wife, Washington brought Martha to every celebration. On January 2, 1782, the couple attended a performance of a Beaumarchais comedy. They also attended another play, *The Lying Valet*, by British dramatist David Garrick, during which the actors pointedly addressed its prologue and voiced a plea for "a new Athens rising in the west" to audience member George Washington.

On January 22, 1782, Elizabeth Schuyler Hamilton gave birth to a baby boy. The couple named the infant Philip Schuyler Hamilton. The young Alexander Hamilton family remained at The Pastures in Albany while the family patriarch dived into his work as surveyor general of the state of New York. In February, Schuyler voluntarily swore an oath to the people of New York that he had no conflict of interest in performing his duty because he had not "directly or indirectly purchased any lands . . . from any commissioner . . . authorized or appointed to sell any of the lands confiscated to this State . . . since the present war with Great Britain." Schuyler had to sort through dozens of faded and conflicting centuries-old land grants, nebulous contracts that had been allegedly signed with Native chiefs, mediate arguments between neighbors, and immerse himself in feudal clan documents. He also had to supervise the definitive distribution of western New York State land that had been promised to patriot soldiers. In a similar role to Colonel George Washington at the end of the Seven Years' War, Philip Schuyler ascertained eligibility and registered applications. Dissimilarly, however, Schuyler had not preselected choice parcels of land for himself; he had sworn previously that he would not. In fact, he was so scrupulous that he turned over all forms pertaining to his sister and her husband, Washington's physician, Dr. Cochran, to New York representative to the Congress of the Confederation and future mayor of New York City James Duane. Duane, was, of course, married to Schuyler cousin Mary Livingston but it was nearly impossible to avoid a clan member amongst the decision-making political circles of New York. Duane was able, without Schuyler's participation, to guarantee 2,000 acres for the Cochrans in western New York State. Some of those western lands were confiscated and appropriated from the Native tribes who had not cooperated with the Continental Army. A chain, a compass, and a tomahawk would no longer suffice as the legal final word in New York State.

Alexander Hamilton was setting out on his own path in the legal community. In the spring of 1782, he became a citizen of New York State and began preparing to sit for the New York State bar exam.[19] He also resumed writing his *Continentalist* essays. His fifth in the series, published on April 18, 1782, argued that the federal government needed to get more aggressive in collecting revenue in order to pay its creditors. A percentage of all import duties belonged to the federal government, he maintained. Hamilton further reasoned that, "[t]o preserve the ballance [sic] of trade in favour [sic] of a nation ought to be a leading aim of its policy," and then summarized his version of the history of modern trade:

> Trade may be said to have taken its rise in England under the auspices of Elizabeth . . . France was much later in commercial improvements . . . The Dutch, who may justly be allowed a pre-eminence in the knowledge of trade, have ever made it an essential object of state. Their commercial regulations are more rigid and numerous, than those of any other country; and it is by a judicious and unremitted vigilance of government, that they have been able to extend their traffic to a degree so much beyond their natural and comparitive advantages . . . No mode can be so convenient as a source of revenue to the United States. It is agreed that imposts on trade, when not immoderate, or improperly laid, is one of the most eligible species of taxation.

The United States of America, even after the victory at Yorktown, remained a loosely connected confederation of former colonies with divergent interests and unequal capabilities. In this April 1782 essay, Hamilton acknowledged that while America had an entire coastline available for seagoing trade, not every port or maritime city had developed into a transoceanic center of commerce. He pointed to Connecticut, New Jersey, and Pennsylvania as states with Atlantic Ocean borders and robust river systems whose citizens relied on imports, mostly from New York. Hamilton's suggestion: that these states develop their ports at places like Amboy and New London to increase import tariffs for the good of the federal government. Hamilton's interest in federal revenue collection was noticed. The superintendent of finance, Robert Morris, asked Hamilton to perform the unpopular job of collecting taxes owed by New York State to the federal government. Morris offered Hamilton remuneration—a small percentage of whatever Hamilton could collect. Hamilton turned him down: He was studying for the bar exam and he knew that there would be very little reward. Most of lower New York State was still occupied by the British, and its legislature, like most of the other states, viewed its financial obligation to the federal government as voluntary. Morris then increased the offer, and Hamilton accepted half-heartedly but with a plan. He would get his father-in-law to assist him with state officials.

In the spring of 1782, General George Washington departed Philadelphia to assess his army's situation in New York. The Battle of Yorktown by no means meant an end to local skirmishes between British and American soldiers. Washington reestablished himself at the Newburgh, New York, encampment, where he would reside for a good part of the following year.

In late June, Washington ferried across the Hudson River to be with his friend Philip Schuyler and the Schuyler family for a weeklong visit. From June 26 to July 1, Washington enjoyed the legendary Schuyler hospitality at both Schuyler homes, in Albany and at Saratoga. That summer, the Philip Schuyler households became the vortex of Federalist currents. The general and his right-hand major general, two political and philosophical allies, engaged in many intermittent conversations on issues that would have alarmed provincialists. Guest and host both thought it imperative for the Congress of the Confederation—and not each individual state—to secure forts and borders, to provide funding for a national military, and to proceed with a unified, not haphazard, itinerary for negotiations with the Native Americans. They also discussed other common interests like canals, crops, and husbandry.

Having resided in close quarters for over a week with two of the most ardent proponents of Federalism and two of the largest and most strategic landowners in America, Alexander Hamilton published his *Continentalist* number 6, which, unsurprisingly, specifically addressed the role of property in the United States of America. It was appropriately published on July 4, 1782.

To date, the Congress of the Confederation had been empowered with collecting revenue from each state via only one source: the assessment of land. To Washington, Schuyler, and Hamilton, the lack of cooperation on the part of the states was a crowbar effort that resulted in insufficient and unreliable proceeds for federal government. There was, according to all three men, an exigent need for immediate reform. By the summer of 1782, Hamilton, Schuyler, and Washington were all calling for the Congress of the Continental Confederation to endow itself with the ability to access greater and more consistent resources. In *The Continentalist* number 6, Hamilton predicted an ominous future for the new republic if it did not: "Let us see what will be the consequences of not authorising [sic] the Fœderal [sic] Government" to enact a nationwide economic agenda.

America had to find a multipronged way to collect revenue. Relying on the states to impose suffocating taxes on private property as the federal government's sole source of income would cause negative reprisals. Hamilton was not naïve: "[T]he avarice of many of the landholders will be opposed to a perpetual tax upon land" but, he noted, their objections actually had merit. Elevated taxes on private property would result in a wider adverse chain of reaction that would impact everyone; they would "render landed property fluctuating and less valuable," wreak havoc with the price of crops, and hurl farmers into poverty.

There was another way to ensure income for the new federal government from its very own territory. In *Continentalist* 6, Hamilton laid out his vision that America would be "hereafter less exposed to wars by land, than most other countries." This magnificent, somewhat isolated continent on which the United States of America was housed offered the new nation "an immediate" "source of revenue" via its "unlocated lands." There would no longer be capricious kings who doled out charters willy-nilly or unpredictable and temporary royal governors who promised land and reneged on awards. Hard-won American land that was not already in private hands belonged to the Confederation, which had the right, the duty, to build a fiscally sound United States. It was incumbent on the federal government to receive its support from, "the whole society," not just from the gentry class. To Hamilton, the United States of America presented a clean slate of creative opportunity that ought to function in unison as

> something noble and magnificent in the perspective of a great Fœderal [sic] Republic, closely linked in the pursuit of a common interest, tranquil and prosperous at home . . . but there is something proportionably diminutive and contemptible in the prospect of a number of petty states, with the appearance only of union, jarring, jealous and perverse, without any determined direction . . . weak and insignificant by their dissentions . . . Happy America! If those, to whom thou hast intrusted [sic] the guardianship of thy infancy, know how to provide for thy future repose; but miserable and undone, if their negligence or ignorance permits the spirit of discord to erect her banners on the ruins of thy tranquility!

Within days of the publication of *Continentalist* 6, Alexander Hamilton himself became one of those to whom "guardianship of thy infancy" was passed. At twenty-seven years of age, he was appointed a representative from the state of New York to the November 1782 session of the Congress of the Confederation. While Hamilton had been composing his *Continentalist* 6, his father-in-law, Philip Schuyler, was drafting a bill for the New York State legislature with his son-in-law's responsibilities and theories in mind. Philip Schuyler introduced a bill to the New York State Assembly requesting that that legislative body reaffirm its obligation to pay its share of taxes owed to the federal government. Schuyler's bill, which passed in the New York State Assembly on July 21, 1782, also called for the groundbreaking step of the "assembling of a general convention of the United States, specifically authorized to revise and amend the Confederation."

Philip Schuyler and many of his neighbors were holders of continental securities. He and Hamilton convened a meeting of their neighbors at the Albany City Hall so that they could bring concerns to both the state and federal legislatures. New Yorkers were also uneasy because British soldiers were nipping along the entire perimeter of the state. With no treaty in sight, restless and resentful redcoats intermittently invaded to intimidate. New York needed more protection, especially in the north, which required more money. Schuyler continued to serve General Washington as a quartermaster and provided the soldiers stationed in New York with nourishment and equipment. Hamilton passed the New York State bar, and soon thereafter he departed for Philadelphia. Although Betsey and their baby stayed behind, his father-in-law, mother-in-law, and their baby daughter, Catherine, shortly followed Hamilton to Philadelphia with seventeen-year-old John Schuyler on horseback next to their coach. Installing Alexander Hamilton at the Congress of the Confederation was going to be a Schuyler family affair. Schuyler knew that his presence in Philadelphia would be of great value to his son-in-law, who would benefit from the powerful legislator's introductions. Traveling south along the east bank of the Hudson River, Schuyler stopped to inspect the portion of the Claverack property that he had inherited from his mother; his wife, Catherine, was also heiress to this New York property, whose boundaries were in dispute with the state of Massachusetts. The Schuyler family arrived in Philadelphia some eight days after having left Albany and could not wait to return to New York. On December 2, 1782, Philip Schuyler wrote George Washington:

> My children are so exceedingly anxious to return to Albany and so prepossessed with an Idea that they cannot recover their health whilst they remain here, that I propose to move them as soon as they shall be deemed capable of the Journey—It is at present my in tention [sic] to apply for Sir Guy Carltons leave to pass the Harbour [sic] of New York in a Shallop from Elizabeth town. If it is not improper I have to Intreat Your Excellency that directions may be given to the

officers commanding at the posts in the river to permit the vessel which may convey may be to pass—If such an order should Interfer [sic] with any arrangements you may have made, I beg to be advised of It in which case I will attempt to procure a vessel within our lines and embark there for Fish Kill, or further up If the state of the river will permit. I have the Honor to be with Great Esteem, and affection Your Excellency's Most Obedient Servant.

The Schuylers did leave Philadelphia fairly quickly, leaving Hamilton behind in Philadelphia to settle into his role as a member of the Congress of the Confederation. Cognizant of the dual possibilities that his tenure could be short—the term for each representative was one year with a maximum possibility of three years in office over the course of a six-year period—and that the expected cessation of hostilities could prompt state legislatures to shed fealty to the union, Hamilton felt pressed to achieve his goals. When this tidal wave from Nevis with his incandescent intelligence met a likeminded legislator from Virginia, the pair determined to awaken the congress from its inertia. Although Alexander Hamilton and James Madison were temperamental opposites—Hamilton was brash, egotistical, and outspoken; Madison was shy, reflective, bookish, and sickly—both were intent on strengthening the central government. First and foremost, they wanted to weave together an economically solvent republic.

In addition to Madison and his father-in-law, Philip Schuyler, Hamilton's other great champion and steadfast ally remained George Washington. Although, like any father and son, they had argued intermittently, as Hamilton's torrent of energy was sometimes too demanding of the commander in chief, they always seemed to find a way toward understanding and forgiveness. It was during the opening days of 1781, approximately two years before Hamilton was engaged in his Federalist efforts in Philadelphia, when newlywed Alexander Hamilton had resigned in a huff from service to Washington and had written his new father-in-law and Washington supporter, Philip Schuyler, that he was disgusted with the nation's commander in chief. Although he never lost his filial rank with Washington, Hamilton, at the beginning of 1783, now a federal legislator and father himself, made every effort to reingratiate himself with the general in a steady stream of letters. After having not written his commander in chief for more than a year, on February 13, 1783, Alexander Hamilton picked up his pen to write George Washington. Hamilton's icebreaking note transmitted a tone of perceptible humility: "Flattering myself that your knowledge of me will induce you to receive the observations I make as dictated by a regard to the public good, I take the liberty to suggest to you my ideas on some matters of delicacy and importance." Restating information that no one knew better and grieved over more than General George Washington, Hamilton wrote: "The state of our finances . . . [are] never more critical." Hamilton conveyed his awareness that a "torrent" of dissatisfaction was swelling amongst Washington's army owing to nonpayment. For Hamilton, "[t]he great *desideratum* at present is the establishment of general funds, which alone can do justice to the Creditors of the United States . . . restore public credit and supply the future wants of the government."

Using Hamilton's *Continentalist* essays as a paradigm, Hamilton and Madison, like rolling thunder, barraged their colleagues for a resolution that would force the states to take their financial responsibilities to the confederation seriously. On February 17, 1783, only two months after Hamilton arrived in Philadelphia, the Congress of the Confederation entered into record:

> Whereas by the eighth article of the confederation and perpetual union, it is agreed and declared, that all charges of war . . . shall be defrayed out of a common treasury . . . Resolved, that the legislature of each state be, and they are hereby required, to take such measures as shall appear to them most effectual for obtaining a just and accurate account of the quantity of land in such state.

Washington was pleased that Hamilton was once again communicating with him and admitted so to his former aide de camp; he wanted to be Hamilton's sounding board. Though Washington repeatedly stated in public and in writing that he would not comment on politics, in his letters to Hamilton in the spring of 1783 he was so honest and forthright about his real political leanings it was clear that the pair had an unshakeable bond of trust. On March 4, Washington wrote Hamilton from his headquarters in Newburgh, New York, that he had "often thought . . . that the public interest might be benefitted, if the Commander in Chief of the Army was let more into the political & pecuniary state of our affairs than he is." Washington further commented that "as Citizen & Soldier . . . the sufferings of a complaining army on one hand, and the inability of Congress and tardiness of the States on the other, are the forebodings of evil." He warned Hamilton that "the blood we have spilt in the course of an Eight years [sic] war, will avail us of nothing" if "the great defects of their Constitution" were not corrected to empower the central government with solvency.

On March 12, the same day that the congress received the provisional peace treaty, Washington again wrote Hamilton. Washington rarely displayed his temper in public; in this letter to Hamilton, however, he unleashed his fury, not directed at Hamilton, but toward the ongoing intrigues of his enemies and their allies in the congress. An emissary from the Congress of the Confederation had arrived at the general's headquarters with news that the army was going to be dissolved. Not only was that news to Washington but also the appearance of this messenger, who caused a "storm" of emotion amongst the soldiers, created a bigger problem for Washington amongst his officers. Washington replied to the envoy that his army, "would not disband untill [sic] they had obtained" payment; neither would he dismiss his men prematurely as there were still random skirmishes with redcoats in sensitive border areas. A revolt, headed by Philip Schuyler's nemesis, Horatio Gates, was brewing. Fearing a mutiny, Washington summoned some of his principal officers to a meeting on March 15 to air their grievances. He well knew that their issues were about money. Nonpayment was a powder keg waiting to explode. It was a deft move on Washington's part to listen and to agree.

Philip Schuyler was not surprised that Horatio Gates was up to his old tricks and determined to be by Washington's side in Newburgh that Saturday. Schuyler, however, was torn. The New York State Assembly's Friday, March 14, session was going to address two matters close to Schuyler's heart: his July 21, 1782, act (that furnished the federal government with New York State tariff revenues) was about to become law, and the New York State Assembly was planning to approve an offer that had been in committee negotiations since January 29. On Friday, March 14, 1783, the New York State Assembly did indeed agree to grant the Congress of the Confederation a considerable amount of money and land to design and build a permanent postwar seat of government—the new capital city of the United States of America—at Kingston, New York.

Schuyler breathlessly arrived at Newburgh and witnessed Washington's masterful leadership in the face of disgruntled subordinates. Two days after the quelled mutiny, Schuyler, back at his state assembly seat in Kingston on Monday, March 17, described the entire scene to his soon-to-be son-in-law, Stephen van Rensselaer III: "Never through all the war" had Washington realized "a greater victory than on this occasion." That same day, March 17, Alexander Hamilton, joining his father-in-law in a chorus of compliments, wrote Washington to extol the general's conduct: "Your Excellency has in my opinion acted wisely. The best way is ever not to attempt to stem a torrent but to divert it." Like the prodigal son, Hamilton had returned. A floodgate of feelings poured out. Hamilton confided that he was dismayed by those in Philadelphia with "a fatal opposition to Continental views." He could not abide the men telling him to be patient when he found an urgent and immediate need for a uniform federal financial plan.

On March 18, Washington wrote Elias Boudinot, then president of the Congress of the Confederation, his own account of the March 15 standoff. He also pleaded with the congress to get federal funding to his men. Hamilton, Madison, and three other representatives had formed a funding committee, which presented a comprehensive refunding program to the congress. For more than a month, Robert Morris had been haranguing the members of the congress to establish permanent revenues to satisfy, at the very least, interest on the national debt. In James Madison's "Notes on Debates," he chronicled the varying pressures placed on members of the legislative body to force them to come to a compromise on soldiers' pay. From the seventeenth to the twenty-second of March, the topic of the federal government assuming all states' debts with regard to the war was addressed in heated debate; for that to occur, it was necessary for the Congress of the Confederation to alter Article VII. To demonstrate the urgency of the situation, Washington's letter to Boudinot was read aloud on the floor of the congress on March 24, 1783. Along with it, a letter from the Marquis de Lafayette was also orated, informing the legislative body that the early draft of a peace treaty between Great Britain, France, and Spain had been signed in January. Hamilton immediately and dutifully dashed off a note to Washington:

> Your Excellency will before this reaches you have received a letter from the Marquis De la Fayette informing you that the preliminaries of peace between all the belligerent powers have been concluded. I congratulate your Excellency on this happy conclusion of your labors. It now only remains to make solid establishments within to perpetuate our union to prevent our being a ball in the hands of European powers bandied against each other at their pleasure.

A congressional committee was appointed to respond to Washington's March 18 letter to Boudinot. The group determined that Alexander Hamilton should be the one to write the commander in chief on its behalf: if there was any bad news to convey to General Washington, it was tacitly and unanimously agreed that the blow would be softened if Washington received it from Hamilton.

The following day, March 25, Hamilton wrote Washington, admitting that he had been requested to explain to Washington the circular dilemma that was plaguing the members of the congress. While Washington spent every day squelching a tempest, the congress had been dithering with hypothetical debates: To continue to keep an army in peacetime terrified the new American congress; to pay the soldiers, when very few states were adhering to the payments suggested by the Articles of Confederation, presented an insurmountable barrier. Supposing that money did become available for disbursement, the determination as to what to pay each soldier, who might have accepted certificates or land for service, posed entangled conversations that stalled solutions. Hamilton wrote Washington

> to communicate our embarrassements [sic] to you in confidence and to ask your private opinion. The army by their resolutions

express an expectation that Congress will not disband them previous to a settlement of accounts and the establishment of funds.
Congress may resolve upon the first; but the general opinion is that
they cannot constitutionally declare the second. They have no right
by the Confederation to *demand* funds, they can only recommend;
and to determine that the army shall be continued in service 'till the
states grant them, would be to determine that the whole present
army, shall be a standing army during peace unless the states comply
with the requisitions for funds. This it is supposed would excite the
alarms and jealousies of the states and increase rather than lessen
the opposition to the funding scheme. It is also observed that the
longer the army is kept together, the more the payment of past dues
is procrastinated . . . It is further suggested that there is danger in
keeping the army together, in a state of inactivity . . . Congress are
doing, and will continue to do, everything in their power towards
procuring satisfactory securities for what shall be found due on such
settlement . . . On one side the army expect they will not be disbanded
'till accounts are settled & funds established, on the other hand, they
have no constitutional power of doing any thing [sic] more than
to recommend funds, and are persuaded that these will meet with
mountains of prejudice in some of the states.

Hamilton was eminently aware that the official message, which reflected
congressional indecisiveness, would upset Washington, so he enclosed with
that communication a second, more personal note to express his private
commiseration:

The inclosed [sic] I write more in a public than in a private capacity.
Here I wrote as a citizen zealous for the true happiness of this country,
as a soldier who feels what is due to an army which has suffered
everything and done much for the safety of America . . . I cannot as
an honest man conceal from you . . . Republican jealousy has in it a
principle of hostility to an army whatever be their merits, whatever

be their claims to the gratitude of the community. It acknowledges
their services with unwillingness and rewards them with reluctance.

In his reply, dated March 31, Washington once again expressed his unmiti-
gated faith in Hamilton's discretion. As Washington had broadcast repeatedly,
a soldier was meant to be apolitical. Washington had held his tongue except
to a privileged few: Philip Schuyler was one of them; Alexander Hamilton,
another. Like a father to his son, Washington consistently and without cen-
sorship confessed his innermost ruminations, and he implored Hamilton in
this letter to be likewise reciprocal when they reunited:

> My wish to see the Union of these States established upon liberal &
> permanent principles, & inclination to contribute my mite [sic] in
> pointing out the defects of the present Constitution, are equally great.
> All my private letters have teemed with these Sentiments . . . I shall
> be obliged to you however for the thoughts which you have promised
> me on this subject, and as soon as you can make it convenient. No
> man in the United states is, or can be more deeply impressed with
> the necessity of a reform in our present Confederation than myself.
> No man perhaps has felt the bad effects of it more sensibly; for to
> the defects thereof, & want of Powers in Congress may justly be
> ascribed the prolongation of the War, & consequently the Expences
> [sic] occasioned by it.

On April 4, Washington wrote Hamilton again:

> I read your private letter of the 25th with pain . . . I hope no resolu-
> tion will be come [sic] to for disbanding or separating the Lines till
> the Accts. are liquidated. You may rely upon it, Sir, that unhappy
> consequences would follow the attempt . . . I will now, in strict
> confidence, mention a matter which may be useful for you to be
> informed of. It is that some men (& leading ones too) in this Army,
> are beginning to entertain suspicions that Congress, or some members

of it, regardless of the past sufferings & present distress, maugre the justice which is due to them, & the returns which a grateful people should make to men who certainly have contributed more than any other class to the establishment of Independency, are to be made use of as mere Puppits [sic] to establish Continental funds . . . the Army . . . is a dangerous instrument to play with . . . Upon the whole, disband the Army, as soon as possible but consult the wishes of it; which really are moderate . . . compatible with the honor, dignity, and justice which is due from the Country to it.

On April 8, Hamilton responded with agreement that the, "idea of not attempting to separate the army before the settlement of accounts corresponds with my proposition . . . to let them have some pay had also appeared to me indispensable . . . To morrow [sic] we confer with the Superintendant [sic] of Finance on the subject of money." Hamilton, in a prescient commentary on what would become the two divergent political factions in the entire history of the United States, wryly wrote that he would himself not be surprised

to hear that I have been pointed out as one of the persons concerned in playing the game . . . There are two classes of men Sir in Congress of very Different views—one attached to state, the other to Continental politics . . . The advocates for Continental funds have blended the interests of the army with other Creditors from a conviction, that no funds for partial purposes will go through those states to whose citizens the United states are largely indebted.

The success of the union, according to Hamilton, was based on the restoration of public credit. Insolvent America had lost face with her European financiers: "Taxation in this Country, it was found, could not supply a sixth part of the public necessities . . . to obtain further loans in Europe it was necessary we should have a fund sufficient to pay the interest of what had been borrowed & what was to be borrowed." Hamilton relayed to Washington his own frustration with the members of the Congress whom he felt were intransigent in what he believed to be a shortsighted and selfish position: they wanted each state to pay its own soldiers. Some of the states had smaller armies than others; some of the states had suffered little damage from the war. Some of these representatives were using the army as a pawn

> against the funding system . . . The matter with respect to the army which has occasioned most altercation in Congress and most dissatisfaction in the army has been the half pay . . . The inequality which would have arisen in the different states when the officers came to compare . . . would have been a new source of discontent . . . such a reference was a continuance of the old wretched state system, by which the ties between the Congress and the army have been nearly dissolved—by which the resources of the states have been diverted from the common treasury & wasted; a system which Your Excellency has often justly reprobated.

Hamilton closed the note with a postscript. Like a son in need of approval from a proud father, his alleged afterthought read: "I am Chairman of a Committee for peace arrangements."

In another letter to Washington, another formal one on behalf of the congress, which was dated the following day, April 9, Hamilton conveyed the news with official pomp: "Congress having appointed a committee consisting of Messrs. Madison, Osgood, Wilson, Elseworth [Oliver Ellsworth] and myself to consider what arrangements it will be proper to adopt in the different departments with reference to a peace; I am directed by the Committee to address your Excellency on the subject of the military department." He signed off, "Alx Hamilton Chairman."

At twenty-eight years old, Alexander Hamilton had been appointed chairman of the committee, which, according to the *Notes of Debates in the Continental Congress*, was tasked to

> report the proper arrangements to be taken in consequence of peace.
> The object was to provide a system for foreign affairs, for Indian

affairs, for military and naval peace establishments; and also to carry
into execution the regulations of weights & measures & other articles
of the Confederation not attended to during the war. To the same
Come. [sic] was referred a resolution of the Executive Council of Pa.,
requesting the Delegates of that State to urge Congs. To establish a
general peace with the Indians.

Washington responded formally to the committee's request through Hamilton on April 16 and requested "Time to collect & concenter my Ideas on this Subject." Washington assured the committee, through Hamilton, that he understood that these were matters were of "very great importance," and that he would communicate his judgements, "in the best Manner I am able & at the earliest period in my power." Washington submitted his plan for peace through Hamilton to the committee on May 2, 1783. Along with that formal response, Washington, per their established pattern, enclosed a second more private note.

Before his deliberations were complete, George Washington exchanged several letters with Hamilton. On April 16, he wrote:

My last letter to you [April 4] was written in a hurry, when I was
fatigued by the more public—yet confidential letter which . . .
accompanied it; possibly, I did not on that occasion express myself
(in what I intended as a hint) with so much perspicuity as I
ought . . . I do not, at this time, recollect the force of my
expression . . . My meaning, however, was only to inform that there
were different sentiments in the Army as well as in Congress,
respecting Continental & State Funds; some wishing to be thrown
upon their respective states rather than the Continent at large, for
payment & that, if an idea should prevail generally that Congress,
or part of its members or Ministers, bent upon the latter, should
delay doing them justice, or *hazard* it in pursuit of their favourite
[sic] object; it might create such divisions in the Army as would
weaken, rather than strengthen the hands of those who were

disposed to support Continental measures—and might *tend* to defeat the end they themselves had in view by endeavouring [sic] to involve the Army. For these reasons I said, or meant to say, the Army was a dangerous Engine to work with . . . no Man can be more opposed to State funds & local prejudices than myself, the whole tenor of my conduct has been one of continual evidence . . . I should do injustice to report & what I believe to be the opinion of the Army were I not to inform you, that they consider you a friend, Zealous to serve them, and one who has espoused their interests in Congress upon every proper occasion . . . At this moment, being without any instructions from Congress, I am under great embarrassment [sic] with respect to the Soldiers for the War & shall be obliged more than probably from the necessity of the case, to exercise my own judgment without waiting for orders, as to the discharge of them.

There is no doubt from this exchange of letters between Washington and Hamilton that the two men enjoyed a mutual reliance that gave the reticent Washington the freedom to express his true political beliefs. There is also no doubt from this exchange of letters that both Washington and Hamilton, along with Philip Schuyler, were in the vanguard along with a small handful of American leaders who urged a uniform federal fiscal program. Schuyler had pleaded for it in his days as a representative to the congress; Hamilton had published articles on the topic and then fought in conjunction with James Madison to pressure the congress to speed up adherence to and reform of the Articles of Confederation; George Washington stated and reiterated his preferences plainly, once again, in this April 16, 1783, letter to Hamilton, that, "no one can be more opposed to State funds & local prejudices than myself." On April 18, the Congress of the Confederation approved the funding committee's proposals for military pensions and a new impost, but the tax would not only have an expiration date; it would also continue to be assessed by individual states.

The final version of the peace treaty had not arrived, and would not for another seven months, but preparations for peace stimulated a return to personal concerns for many Americans. In April 1783, Philip Schuyler went home to his Albany mansion, resumed daily stewardship of family landholdings, signed a new rental agreement with a tenant farmer in Saratoga, reoccupied himself as a diligent trustee of his late father-in-law's properties, and, at the request of the heirs of his late friend John Bradstreet, sifted through real estate partnership agreements for legal title.

Statesman and war hero Major General Philip Schuyler, like George Washington, remained in the public sphere. In addition to his name appearing in the Congress of the Confederation as a leading candidate for the position of secretary of foreign affairs, Schuyler announced his candidacy for governor of the state of New York. The moment Schuyler stepped forward as a gubernatorial contender, like a sudden gust of wind, a rumor suspiciously billowed accusing Schuyler of impropriety during his tenure in the New York State Assembly. The previous year, in July 1782, the assembly had passed a property law. Now that Schuyler had chosen to run for office against incumbent Governor George Clinton, Schuyler was speciously denounced for profiting from the 1773 surrender of some van Rensselaer lands. Schuyler was charged with receiving additional Claverack acreage in exchange for his participation in the enactment of the bill. Schuyler vehemently denied the charges, challenging anyone to "prove it," but lost the race to Clinton nonetheless. The election also cleaved the famed New York clans into two political factions: those who desired a strong federal government versus those who wanted to retain local power. Clinton's running mate as lieutenant governor was a van Cortlandt; some also standing quietly behind the victors, who might well have breathed life into the hateful allegations against Schuyler, were Livingstons. After a 643 to 3,584 loss, Schuyler reoccupied himself with his duties as surveyor, processing application after application for soldiers who sought payment for their service. Schuyler also poised and readied himself for the seemingly unlimited real estate opportunities that peace would bring.

George Washington, also engrossed in preparations for peace, wrote Alexander Hamilton on April 22, 1783, that he "had a meeting with the Secretary at War for the purpose of making arrangements for the release of our Prisoners." Washington's own soldiers were aching for home. "I believe it is not in the power of Congress or their officers, to hold them much, if any, longer, for we are obliged at this moment to increase our Guards to prevent rioting." His men, close to explosion, still had not been paid: "And here, my Colo. Hamilton, let me assure you, that it would not be more difficult to still the raging Billows in a tempestuous Gale, then to convince the Officers of this Army of the justice or policy of paying men in Civil Offices full wages, when *they* cannot obtain a Sixtieth part of their dues."

Washington's weariness and yearnings for home mirrored those of his battle-fatigued warriors. Their fate, like his, awaited both instruction and reward from the congress. In this April 22 letter to Hamilton, George Washington, for the first time, staged the case for his own remuneration to a sympathetic but targeted audience. Alexander Hamilton was not only a surrogate son but also a now powerful member of the congress. Washington confessed his apprehension to Hamilton: "My anxiety to get home increases with the prospect of it, but when is it to happen?" He also shared his reveries: "I write to you unreservedly [about] my anxious desire of enjoying some repose" at Mount Vernon. Washington painted the scene of this happy homecoming punctured by the "necessity of my paying a little attention to my private concerns, which have suffered considerably in Eight years absence."

Many American patriots had sacrificed in countless ways. Washington, here, was strictly pointing to his financial losses: the commander in chief had abandoned his farms, deserted his real estate, and ignored his businesses. A conspicuously disseminated report, that George Washington had refused the five-hundred-dollar-a-month salary offered to him as commander in chief, was not entirely the whole truth. Uncirculated was the fact that Washington did insist on being reimbursed for his expenses for the duration of the war, and he spent lavishly for parties, equipage, and finery as befitting the aristocratic Virginia gentleman he aspired to be but could not afford to be. From the time when he arrived in Boston in 1775 and rejected the home of the president of Harvard as too modest a residence, Washington set a tone of entitlement and immoderation. His personal entourage included two chefs, a personal staff of ten men, and a number of slaves, who all traveled with him. His wife, Martha, had made six journeys to her husband's roving headquarters during the war. Washington submitted all of these costs as his due. His April 22 note to Hamilton was a forewarning to an active member of the congress that, as his service protracted without the final treaty, "expences [sic] accumulated."

The commander in chief may have taken no salary but he billed the United States government for his unrestrained cost of living.

In 1775, the Continental Army had assembled with no money, but a pledge was made to its patriot fighters. They would receive pay and, if victorious, land. George Washington had received a similar guarantee from a royal governor, but that vow was reneged. In his April 22, 1783, letter to Hamilton, Washington stood his ground on his own behalf and on behalf of his subordinates: "I have not heard that the Congress have yet had under the consideration the Lands . . . [that] have been promised to the Army," he advised. As the highest-ranking member of the triumphant patriot army, Washington expected some of that American bounty. By 1783, fifty-one-year-old George Washington had been investing in land for thirty-three years. For twelve-and-a-half years of his life, he had fought in two wars rewarded in part by the right to own private property, and he wanted more of it.

In early June, the Congress of the Confederation was embroiled in the seemingly endless debate over Virginia's terms for cession of western lands. The complexities of apportioning lands gained through the new treaty, lands previously awarded to companies like Washington's competitor, the politically powerful Vandalia group, Native American claims, and the ongoing border issues amongst the states would not likely resolve quickly. On June 17, George Washington wrote President Elias Boudinot a note "for the consideration of Congress" that contained

> a Petition from a large number of Officers of the Army in behalf of them selves, [sic] and such other Officers and Soldiers of the Continental Army as are entitled to rewards in lands, and may choose to avail them selves [sic] of any Previledges [sic] and Grants which shall be obtained in consequence of the present solicitation.

The matter of fighting and dying for land was so important to Washington that in this note he publicly, purposefully, and uncharacteristically offered his own position on a political matter:

Altho' I pretend not myself to determine, how far the district of unsettled Country which is described in the Petition is free from the claim of every State, or how far this disposal of it may interfere with the views of Congress—Yet it appears to me this is the Tract which from its local position and peculiar advantages ought to be first settled in preference to any other whatever . . . by the disbanded Officers and Soldiers of the Army—to whom the faith of Government hath long since been pledged, that lands should be granted at the expiration of the War, in certain proportions, agreeably to their respective grades.

I am induced to give my sentiments thus freely on the advantages to be expected from this plan of Colonization—because it would connect our Government with the frontiers—extend our Settlements progressively—and plant a brave . . . hardy . . . People . . . who would be always ready & willing to combat, to secure the borders and defeat any enemies of the United States.

Washington continued by reminding the congress that not only had they promised American soldiers land, for which they had risked their lives but that after everything these men had sacrificed, they deserved no less than a, "pleasant retreat in old age—and the fairest prospects for their Children."

Washington's eyes were on the future, and in what he called his "last official communication," he wrote a formal letter "To the States" that circulated in the congress and in the newspapers. From his headquarters at Newburgh, Washington gave his "final blessing to that Country, in whose service I have spent the prime of my life." With great sagacity, he cautioned his fellow citizens not to squander their victory. Americans were now

the sole Lords and proprietors of a vast tract of Continent, comprehending all the various Soils and Climates of the World . . . Heaven has crowned all its other blessings by giving a fairer opportunity for political happiness, than any other Nation has ever been favored with . . . the foundation of our Empire was not laid in the gloomy Age of ignorance and superstition, but at an Epocha when the rights

of Mankind were better understood and more clearly defined, than
at any former period . . . we have a disposition to seize the occasion
and make it our own . . . there is an option still left to the United
States of America; that it is in their choice and depends upon their
conduct, whether they will be respectable and prosperous or con-
temptible and Miserable as a Nation. This is the time of their political
probation . . . This is the moment to establish or ruin their National
Character for ever [sic]—This is the favorable moment to give such
a tone to our foederal [sic] Government . . . or this may be the ill
fated [sic] moment for relaxing the powers of the Union, annihilating
the cement of the Confederation and exposing us to become the
sport of European Politicks, [sic] which may play one State against
another . . . to serve their own interested purposes . . . silence in me
would be a crime.

Washington proceeded to list four "things, which I humbly conceive are
essential to the well being [sic], I may even venture to say to the existence, of
the United States as an independent Power." His prescription included: "An
indissoluble Union of the States under one federal Head"; "A sacred regard to
the public Justice"; "The adoption of a proper Peace Establishment"; and the
shedding of local "prejudices . . . to make those concessions which are requisite
to the general prosperity . . . in some instances, to sacrifice their individual
advantages to the interest of the community." Washington rejected political
and financial sectionalism, stating that

It is only in our United Character, as an Empire, that our Independence is acknowledged, that our power can be regarded or our Credit
supported among foreign Nations . . . the United States are . . . to
render compleat [sic] justice to all the public Creditors, which so
much dignity and energy . . . it shall not be carried into . . . a National
bankruptcy, with all its deplorable consequences . . . so pressing are
the present circumstances . . . let us then as a Nation . . . fulfill the
public Contracts which Congress had undoubtedly a right to make

for the purpose of carrying on the War, with the same good faith we suppose ourselves bound to perform our private engagements . . . Rewards . . . to the Soldiers . . . as compensation for their Services . . . the donation of Lands, the payment of Arrearages . . . the gratuity of one years [sic] full pay which is promised to all . . . exemption from Taxes for a limited time . . . or any other adequate compensation or immunity, granted to the brave defenders of their Countrys cause . . . I cannot omit to mention the obligations this Country is under to that meritorious class of veteran . . . who have been discharged for inability . . . an annual pension for life; their peculiar sufferings . . . the Militia of this Country must be considered as the Palladium of our security.

This June 1783 farewell from the nation's victorious commander in chief revealed to a public audience his mindset that to steer the right course, to steady and buoy the ship of state, it was essential to implement a uniform system of credit and funding, to eschew the British pound sterling in favor of American money, and to unshackle American commerce from the suffocating British mercantilist policies. In this moving adieu, George Washington declared his early support for an unambiguously Federalist fiscal program.

PART II

A TALE OF
TWO CITIES

CHAPTER 6

Wandering in Exile

THE FIRST AND SECOND CONTINENTAL Congresses in 1774 and 1775 had convened in Philadelphia, Pennsylvania. Throughout the War of Independence, the legislative body was somewhat peripatetic. From December 20, 1776 to February 27, 1777, the Continental Congress assembled in Baltimore, Maryland. From March 4, 1777 to September 18, 1777, the congress returned to Philadelphia. For one day—September 27, 1777—the Continental Congress met in Lancaster, Pennsylvania. From September 30, 1777, to June 27, 1778, the Continental Congress held their sessions at the York, Pennsylvania, court house. It was at York, Pennsylvania, where the warring colonials adopted their first and revolutionary Articles of Confederation and signed their Treaty of Alliance with France.

From July 2, 1778, through February 1781 the legislative body, still called the Continental Congress, convened in Philadelphia. From March 1, 1783, once the newer Articles of Confederation was ratified by all thirteen states, the lawmakers continued to assemble in Philadelphia as the renamed Congress of the Confederation. While the revamped Articles of Confederation had purposefully omitted the designation of a permanent seat of government in order to foster cooperation, Philadelphians understandably claimed it as their preserve.

It was certainly no secret that many members of the United States of America Continental Congress and Congress of the Confederation detested Philadelphia and wanted to wrest the seat of government away for a variety of reasons: some perceived its financial success as amoral, some detested the fact that Quakers refused to join the war, some wanted a less cumbersome journey to legislative meetings, some dreamed of the tribute and prestige that rich men and power would bring to their own hometowns. When asked to attend the First Continental Congress in 1774, George Washington wrote Thomas Johnson on August 5 that since there had been an agreement to meet in Philadelphia, the Virginia delegation would "abide by the General Choice of Philadelphia, tho. [sic] judged an improper place." On March 7, 1777, John Adams wrote his wife, Abigail, from Philadelphia with a very harsh assessment of the town and its people. He also shockingly commented that should the British gain control of the city, it would be no great loss to America: "This City is a dull Place . . . chiefly Quakers as dull as Beetles . . . America will lost nothing, by Hows [sic] gaining this Town . . . We may possibly remove again from hence, perhaps to Lancaster or Reading." On July 6, 1782, Virginian Arthur Lee wrote Massachusetts delegate Francis Dana that the congress ought not to remain, "in this *Tory City* [that] has accumulated all the money here." "The residence of Congress in the bosom of *Toryism*" disgusted Lee.

An anonymous letter from someone calling himself "Aratus" was transmitted to Virginia representative Theodorick Bland Jr., circulated amongst the members of the congress, and subsequently published in various newspapers. Dated November 17, 1782, from Baltimore, this eighteenth-century Aratus[1] pleaded for the Congress of the Confederation "to render Annapolis the permanent metropolis of America." He offered lifestyle temptations to the legislators. They would live and eat well: Annapolis was a town replete with "elegant houses" ready for their arrival, a "market" "well supplied [sic] with "fish and oysters" and "all kinds of wild fowl." Aratus explained that, in addition to publishing his proposition, he was strategically targeting certain "acquaintances in the different parts of the continent, Pennsylvania, Jersey, New York and Delaware excepted, which states, it is natural to suppose, will be averse to the measure."

In one part of his letter, Aratus took a very serious tone, warning the members of the congress to think carefully about remaining in Philadelphia. Aratus reminded the legislators of the episodes wherein they had been insulted and assaulted by unworthy, ungrateful, and disreputable citizens. These townspeople had not even been prosecuted for their aggressive and lawless actions. The article by Aratus provoked an undercurrent of concurrent murmur.

The January 1783 discussions in the New York State Assembly that resulted in the March 14 resolute act to proffer Kingston, New York, as the new federal seat of government arrived at the Congress of the Confederation on April 1, 1783. On May 4, Philip Schuyler wrote his son-in-law Alexander Hamilton from Saratoga that, "If that body should seriously determine on a permanent residence in this state . . . I make little doubt but that the cession of Jurisdiction will be made agreeable to their wishes." Schuyler was working on another matter that his son-in-law had requested: The Congress of the Confederation was interested in portioning western New York State lands to comply with the 1776 promise to soldiers as payment for services. New Yorkers were willing to participate in a nationwide effort to reward their fighting heroes but before any formal agreement would pass in the state legislature, the local representatives required clarification on distribution size, quantity, and guidance on legal title, according to Schuyler. Schuyler also wrote Hamilton with directness that the New York State Assembly wanted something further—a tax break: "I attempted during the last meeting to make the landed provision you mention . . . If Congress in the recommendation would declare that we should have credit for the Amount on the same terms as we shall Sell to our own citizens, the request would *certainly* be complied with."

Shortly after the Congress of the Confederation received New York's offer to remove the seat of government to Kingston, New York, the state of Maryland made a similar proposal to instead house the federal government in Annapolis, sweetening the pot with the offer of a three-hundred-acre federal district and thirteen grand residences, one for each of the delegations. The Congress of the Confederation received the Maryland offer on June 2, 1783. On June 3, 1783, President of the Congress of the Confederation Elias Boudinot submitted a letter to the delegates delineating two offers that required "the consideration and assent of Nine States." There was, however, an insufficient number of representatives present, which Boudinot admonished was "extremely humiliating to us, as well as disadvantageous to the union." On June 8, Boudinot wrote New Jersey Governor William Livingston, a cousin of Philip Schuyler and member of the clans, to ask if Livingston wanted to extend an offer from their own state to house the seat of the federal government. On June 10, the Congress of the Confederation voted to address the issue of a permanent seat of government and to discuss any offers on the first Monday in October.

James Madison's "Notes on Debates" reflect that on Thursday, June 19, 1783, "Information was recd. [sic] from the Executive Council of Pennsylvania [that about 500 soldiers] were on the way from Lancaster to Philadelpa. [sic] . . . declaring that they would proceed to the seat of Congress and demand justice, and intimating designs agst. [sic] the Bank." Madison further noted that, "Mr. Izard, Mr. Mercer & others being much displeased, signified that if the City would not support Congress, it was high time to remove to some other place." "Aratus" could not have imagined how prophetic his words would be.

Owing to the report that hostile soldiers were on the march to cause mischief at the state house (Independence Hall) and at the Treasury, Alexander Hamilton requested that the congress convene for an irregular summit on Saturday, June 21, 1783, at the state house, where Pennsylvania Governor John Dickinson and the Executive Council were also to assemble to address the same issue. It was a sultry day. Tempers flared. The governor of Pennsylvania made a very bad decision, which caused the legislators to remove the seat of government from Philadelphia, and it would never return.

At about three o'clock in the afternoon, Alexander Hamilton, James Madison, Elias Boudinot, and many of our most cherished Founding Fathers were startled by a frightening racket that seemed to be coming from outside the state house. When they peered out the windows, they saw some five hundred angry Revolutionary War veterans dressed in uniform surrounding Independence Hall. The soldiers pointed their bayonets through the windows directly at the heads of the legislators demanding back pay. Many of the soldiers had been given interest-bearing certificates for their services that were now worthless; some had been promised parcels of land to farm, and others an assortment of material goods, none of which had materialized. Washington had repeatedly warned his young protégé, Alexander Hamilton, that American soldiers were at their breaking point.

It had been nearly two years since the British had surrendered at Yorktown, and, although a preliminary peace treaty had been submitted to the congress, the legislature had still not resolved how to satisfy its war reparations: foreign creditors, American creditors, and soldiers all waited for reimbursement. The soldiers had fought for one nation, but the Articles of Confederation had granted sovereignty to each individual state to collect revenue. The United States of America as one functioning entity was simply unable to seize money from these independent states and, therefore, could not honor most of its financial debts. In 1783, the perfect union had amassed debts totaling over forty-three million Continental dollars to its own citizens and to Dutch bankers and over twenty-five million dollars to France. According to the Congressional Research Service, that sum would translate into about two-and-a-half billion 2021 US dollars—roughly two-and-a-half times the cost of the Civil War. Those numbers, however, need to be adjusted to understand that in relation to the GDP of that time period, the true impact of that debt would be more than a trillion dollars in today's economy, the total cost of all post-9/11 wars in the Middle East combined.

Many of the desperate and incensed soldiers who surrounded the Pennsylvania State House, in addition to being armed, were drunk. They shouted at the statesmen that there would be no escape for such villains, too cavalier to feed hungry families. The politicians waited anxiously to be rescued but Pennsylvania Governor Dickinson refused to come to their aid for fear of being unpopular among his own constituents, many of whom were creditors of the fledgling United States of America.[2]

Fearing for their lives, our nation's heroes managed to escape the building and catch a ferry across the Delaware River to New Jersey. Forced to flee like outlaws, they would be safer in New Jersey, another state under its own jurisdiction with its own laws, a different governor, who presided over his own statewide autonomous army, and another currency. Elias Boudinot had dispatched an urgent communiqué to Washington, who received it on June 24.

In his response to Boudinot, Washington called the events of June 21 an "infamous and outrageous Mutiny" and assured the president of the Congress of the Confederation that cries for help were not belated. Washington had "instantly ordered Three compleat [sic] Regiments of Infantry and a Detachment of Artillery to be put in motion as soon as possible; This Corps . . . will consist of upwards of 1500 effectives." The commander in chief further expressed his outrage, calling the protestors "the Pennsylvania Mutineers." Washington's position was that the rebelling soldiers had insulted "the Sovereign Authority of the United States."

Within one week after the debacle in Philadelphia, the congress found itself situated in the small college town of Princeton, New Jersey, where the family of Mrs. Boudinot resided. As the United States of America had just defeated the greatest army and navy in the eighteenth-century world, a convention of its legislative body—a union of thirteen far-flung states—might have been compared reverently with the Council of Nicea. Instead, legislators faced continued humiliation. The Congress of the United States convened not in a lavishly appointed capitol building but in the second-floor library at Nassau Hall. The town itself was incommodious; many of the legislators had to share beds. James Madison wrote his father that he and another Virginia representative not only shared a bed but they were housed in "one room scarcely ten feet square."[3] Benjamin Rush wrote fellow Pennsylvania delegate John Montgomery that the members of the Congress of the United States of America were being treated shamefully. They were, "abused, laughed at & cursed in every Company."[4]

Most of the members of the congress assumed that once things settled down in Philadelphia they would return there. Some, however, accused Alexander Hamilton of engineering an exit so that New York's offer of Kingston as the permanent capital would prevail. Hamilton, who had actually displayed great courage when he attempted to negotiate with the soldiers outside Independence Hall, wrote James Madison the moment they had settled in at Princeton:

> I am informed that among other disagreeable things said about the
> removal of Congress from Philadelphia it is insinuated that it was a
> contrivance . . . I am told that this insinuation has been pointed at

me in particular . . . As you were a witness to my conduct and opinions through the whole of the transaction, I am induced to trouble
you for your testimony upon the occasion. I do not mean to make a
public use of it; but through my friends to vindicate myself from the
imputations I have mentioned. I will therefore request your answers
to the following questions: Did that part of the resolutions which
related to the removal of Congress originate with me or not? Did I
as a member of the Committee appear to press the departure; or did
I not rather manifest a strong disposition to postpone that event as
long as possible, even against the general current of opinion? I wish
you to be as particular & full in your answer as your memory will
permit. I think you will recollect that my idea was clearly this: that
the . . . removal . . . might have an ill appearance in Europe—and . . .
it was prudent to delay it.

Despite a compilation of factual evidence, Alexander Hamilton would be
accused for years as the mastermind behind the removal of the seat of government to New York City.

Pennsylvania Governor John Dickinson began an urgent campaign to convince the congress to return to Philadelphia. He promised no further violence
but delegates viewed his pleas with skepticism. Many also viewed the course
of events as a moment of destiny.

The vote to create a permanent capital city was scheduled for Monday,
October 6. Shortly after Maryland and New York presented their proposals
to the congress, Virginia extended her own offer of three hundred acres at
Williamsburg, up to £100,000 to construct delegate residences, and an autonomous federal district of approximately twenty-five square miles. Delaware
put in a bid for an area between the Christina and Brandywine rivers. New
Jersey offered Princeton and Nottingham in western New Jersey followed by
other suggestions like Newark and Boudinot's hometown of Elizabethtown.
It was clear to the Pennsylvanians that no one was interested in returning to
Philadelphia, so their delegates proposed Germantown, which was received
with no enthusiasm by the other representatives. They were still sore from the

Pennsylvania governor's lack of protection. In fact, no offer was to be considered with any degree of seriousness without the assurance of an autonomous federal district apart from citizen rule.

The Virginians then advocated something new: they extended an offer to Maryland to agree to a capital city on the Potomac River at Georgetown. Each state would cede property and both states would benefit from a permanent seat of government at that location. This suggestion, which entailed the cooperation between two states, prompted Pennsylvania once again—this time with New Jersey—to propose a site on the Delaware River like Trenton, New Jersey, that also demonstrated an interstate kind of fairness.

All of these offers were deliberated, copied, distributed, and mailed to local political officials and landowners. Still, the congress remained in uncomfortable exile. On July 12, Virginia Governor Benjamin Harrison wrote his delegates in Princeton that the removal of the congress to Princeton was received with "general Satisfaction here . . . nothing could justify your staying so long after the various insults you have received but the Advantages derived from the Bank during the war." New England delegates agreed, and so did Elias Boudinot, who wrote Pennsylvania delegate Benjamin Rush on July 25 that Philadelphians had no right "to Complain of our sudden departure & long delay from that City . . . she has been richly repaid in return." Despite "a very respectful and affectionate Address from the Citizens of Philadelphia,"[5] as Boudinot wrote prominent Philadelphian Thomas Willing, the congress was not returning to Philadelphia. On July 28, James Madison reaffirmed that sentiment in a letter he wrote Edmund Randolph: "This question if decided at all in the affirmative must be preceded by despair of some of the competitors for the permanent residence, almost all of whom now make a common cause agst. [sic] Philada. [sic]."

Madison, in his usual Socratic way, presented every argument for and against each location. He dismissed the "scanty accommodations at Princeton . . . more fully felt," the "numerous" and "generous" offers, and the fear that Virginia would lose the bidding war if, once New York were evacuated by the British, Virginia would become "less eligible . . . farther from the South . . . farther from the Center, and making a removal to a Southern position finally more difficult, than it would be from Philada. [sic]. Williamsbg [sic] seems to have a very slender chance . . . Annapolis, I apprehend wd. [sic] have a greater no. of advocates. But the best chance both for Maryland & Virga. [sic] will be . . . [their united] double jurisdiction on the Potowmack." He warned a second time that even a temporary movement by the Congress to "be carried into N. York before a final choice be made . . . it wd. be difficult to get them out of the State." Madison made it clear to Randolph, as he would to others, that he was more than happy—and viewed it as almost a duty and a mission—to do any and all bidding for Virginia's—and the nation's—greatest hero, George Washington.

Another measured discourse on the subject of the permanent seat of government appeared in a July 29 article in the *Maryland Journal and Baltimore Advertiser*. The author, who called himself "A True American," noted that profit and patriotism seemed inextricable from partisan desires to gain the capital city for one's own state. He reflectively posed the debate questions frequently on the lips of the members of the congress as well as in the thoughts of ordinary Americans: Would the decision to situate a permanent capital city rest on principles or on financial gain? On trade or on other less pragmatic considerations? Would the United States of America set its course on the righteousness (the 1630 John Winthrop sermon gleaned from Jesus's "city upon a hill") or revenue? To the eighteenth-century American, were patriotism and profit mutually exclusive or was the desire for success threaded into the American patriotic fiber?

The "True American" acknowledged that, "several of the central states now warmly contend for the honour [sic] of furnishing a place for the permanent residence of Congress . . . advantageous and brilliant offers." He was concerned that if the seat of government were placed at a city that was also the nation's commercial hub, "the undue preponderating weight and influence of any one place . . . is . . . contrary to . . . equal freedom . . . [and would grant supremacy of that] state over the rest of the union." The anonymous scribe opined that the truly fair and moral solution would be to place the seat of government in the dead center of the empire, and then presented a remarkably erudite historical survey of ancient empires, legendary rulers like Cyrus of Persia, Alexander the Great, Caesar, Constantine, and Emperor Charles V, and their designated capital cities. After a methodical explanation of how the demises of many

capital cities were predictable, the "True American" turned his attention to the
Republic of the Seven United Provinces of the Netherlands, whose financial
capital was separate from its seat of government. The "True American" begged
the congress to create an "American Hague," independent of commerce and,
thus, a symbol of equality and impartial sovereignty, at a geographically central
location. Since the American empire had not yet sprawled to the Pacific but
undoubtedly would, the "American" recommended no need for speed in the
decision. Let the congress remain a roving one.

It is not surprising that many of the author's musings echoed hypotheses
found in Adam Smith's *The Theory of Moral Sentiments*. Adam Smith's focus
on prosperity and morality would be a thread that linked him with American
concerns throughout his career, culminating with his 1775 seminal work, *An
Inquiry into the Nature and Causes of the Wealth of Nations*. Private libraries
were always a rich man's pride, but copies of *The Theory of Moral Sentiments*,
published in 1759, also could be found in roughly 20 percent of the ninety-two
libraries that existed in the pre–Revolutionary War thirteen colonies, and, by
the end of the war, in 40 percent of them. Americans before the war actually
enjoyed a higher literacy—70 to 75 percent of white men knew how to read—
than did their counterparts in European countries. Bostonian females could
boast a greater than 70 percent literacy rate. In addition, copies of books
could be purchased inexpensively for a couple of British shillings.

George Washington had bought his stepson, Jacky, a copy of *The Theory
of Moral Sentiments* in 1773 in preparation for Jacky's short-lived academic
career at King's College, and Washington himself possessed a copy of Smith's
An Inquiry into the Nature and Causes of the Wealth of Nations in his Mount
Vernon library. Robert Morris, Edmund Randolph, and Alexander Hamilton
all had read *Wealth of Nations* before Evacuation Day, and James Madison had
put the book on the list for a proposed congressional library that same year.

Other germinal books on the list that Washington ordered for Jacky in 1773
included, "Vattel's Law of Nature," "Montesquieus Spirit of Laws," "Lock on
Government," "Grotius de Jure Belli & Pacis," and "Hutchinson's Ethicks,
Law of Nature, Moral Beauty & ca,"[6] but it was the Scottish Enlightenment
authors like Adam Smith, David Hume, and Lord Kames, whose *Historical*

Law-Tracts inspired Jefferson to campaign against entail who were particularly influential in the new republic. Smith frequently focused on the relationship between money and morals. He also repeatedly directed his reader to examine the historically important strategic locations of capital cities. Smith reiterated litanies of fabled civilizations and their loci of power. Offering example after example, Smith underscored the importance of situating capital cities near water for trade and travel for both commercial and military purposes and "to that part of the empire which contributed most to the general defence [sic] and support of the whole." Smith predicted in *Theory of Moral Sentiments* that the "distance of America from the seat of government [London]" would cause political upheaval because exiled citizens created their own new polities.

Smith's lesson can be expanded. Many origin myths began with stories of exile. In the Judeo-Christian tradition, Adam and Eve were expelled from the Garden of Eden to wander. Abraham was told by God to leave his home and family. Noah, tossed on the seas, allegedly sailed the Mediterranean and portioned out Africa, Asia, and Europe to this three sons, Shem, Ham, and Japheth, who became the founding fathers of the three continents. Moses and the people of Israel wandered the desert before settling Canaan. Jesus was born when Mary and Joseph were in exile on a pilgrimage. The Sumerian epic of Gilgamesh recounts the story of the founding of Sumer, which began with a great flood. The deified hero of this story, Utnapishtim —Ziusudra—was brought to live forever in Dilmun, the equivalent of the Judeo-Christian Garden of Eden, by the gods. Ninhursag, the Earth Mother, Enki, the god of water, and Ninlil, who breathes life into the wind, preside over the paradise, whose "waterways, rivers and canals . . . flow to quench the thirst of all beings and bring abundance to all that lives." The Phoenician Queen Dido journeyed from her home in Lebanon to Carthage. Greek mythology told of Jason and the Argonauts and Odysseus. The Roman poet Virgil transformed the Hellenic figure Aeneas into a wandering exile who became an Italian founding father. The brothers Romulus and Remus, abandonded to roam, begat Rome.

Nordic figures Erik the Red and his son, Leif Erikson, were the primogenitors of explorers like Henry Hudson, the Spanish conquistadores, Jacques Cartier, and others, who voyaged to the New World to establish settlements.

Their wanderlust inspired rootless groups like the Pilgrims, who had lived in exile in the Netherlands, to brave the journey to Massachusetts. The French Huguenot Protestant ancestors of American Founding Fathers like John Jay and Elias Boudinot were also adrift after the persecutory October 22, 1685, Edict of Fontainebleau. From La Rochelle to the Netherlands to England, these maltreated migrants roamed the seas until they reached the shores of North America and established thriving communities. The 1478 Spanish Inquisition that caused a Jewish diaspora sent Sephardic Jews into exile to more tolerant European countries like the Netherlands, and ultimately to Dutch colonies like Brazil and New Amsterdam. Sephardic French-born Elias Lagarde arrived in Virginia aboard the HMS *Abigail* in 1621. Several displaced Sephardic Jewish families winded their way from many ports in Europe to Charleston, Savannah, Newport, Rhode Island, and Philadelphia by the mid-seventeenth century. In the summer of 1654, twenty-three Sephardic Jews boarded the *Valck*—"falcon" in Dutch—and sailed from the Dutch colony of Recife in Brazil. Their ship got blown off course and arrived at Cuba, where they embarked on another ship, the *Santa Catarina*. Often called the "Jewish *Mayflower*," the *Santa Catarina* arrived at New Amsterdam harbor that September and disgorged Manhattan's first community of Jewish settlers. That same year, they established the first synagogue in North America, Shearith Israel.[7]

On September 25, 1771, two young men, friends and classmates of future president of the United States James Madison, delivered a commencement address at the College of New Jersey—now Princeton University—that offered a different paradigm for an American origin myth. Instead of utilizing the exile tradition, Philip Freneau and Hugh Henry Brackenridge collaborated on a topographical poem steeped in ancient tradition and most recently that of Denham's seventeenth-century "Cooper's Hill" and Alexander Pope's "Windsor-Forest." The hero of the students' epic poem, "The Rising Glory of America," was the unparalleled physical beauty that contoured the entire continent of North America. The "roaring" "Niagara," mountains of "Apalachia [sic]," "chrystal [sic] currents" of streams and rivers, the "verdant banks," "the lands / of Carolina, Georgia and the plains / Stretch'd out" depicted a vast and vital empire of manifest destiny. Configured by God, America was, "Paradise a new," according to Freneau and Brackenridge, and her greatness would eclipse the Old World: "And thou Patowmack navigable stream, / Rolling thy waters thro' Virginia's groves, / Shall vie with Thames, the Tiber or the Rhine." America's capital city, a symbol of liberty and freedom, would be sacred: "No more of Memphis," "No more of Athens" and "No more of Rome." Instead, a "new Jerusalem . . . Shall grace our happy earth."

In 1780, Revolutionary War chaplain, diplomat, and future land speculator Joel Barlow began his own attempt at a national epic with "The Vision of Columbus." Barlow's panegyric, which would be reworked and again revised and published over a period of twenty years, offered a lengthy philosophical view of America's birth. Like George Washington and Philip Schuyler, Joel Barlow envisioned the United States as a thalassocracy of

Canals . . .
And distant streams and seas and lakes unite[d] . . .
From fair Albania [Albany, New York], tow'rd the falling sun
Back thro' the midland, lengthening channels run
Meet the far lakes, their beauteous towns that lave
And Hudson join to broad Ohio's wave.
From dim Superior, whose unfathom'd sea . . .
lead their watery pride . . .
To Mississippi's source the passes bend,
And to the broad Pacific main extend.

Three years after Barlow had begun his poem in the midst of the War of Independence, both the federal government of the United States of America and her greatest hero lingered in exile. On July 15, 1783, George Washington wrote Philip Schuyler that his own present, unanchored state provided a propitious moment for him to explore the generative terrain and bubbling waters of upstate and western New York:

The present irksome Interval, while we are awaiting for the definitive Treaty, affords an opportunity . . . to make a Tour to reconnoitre [sic]

those places where the most remarkable Posts were established, and the ground which became famous by being the theatre [sic] of Action in 1777—On our return from thense, we propose to pass across to the Mowhawk [sic] River in order to have a view of that Country which is so much celebrated.

In accordance with Washington's request, Schuyler prepared "light Boats" ahead of time in order to avoid delays during their expeditions. The commander in chief departed Newburgh on July 18 and arrived at Schuyler's Albany home on Saturday, July 19. In Albany, Washington was greeted by town officials, a thirteen-gun salute, and a reception at Mayor John Beekman's house. Among Washington's entourage was Italian Count Francesco dal Verme, who recalled in his journal that they "lodged with General Schuyler, a very rich man, whose home is as magnificent as it is well situated on a hill . . . [with] a panoramic view" of the Hudson River.[8]

On Sunday, July 20, Washington and Schuyler traveled to Saratoga, where Washington inspected Schuyler's sawmills. Dal Verme noted that Schuyler's mills had fifteen saws with the capability of cutting sixteen boards at the same time. He and Washington were greatly impressed. After a day in Saratoga, Washington and his companions went on to visit the northern forts. Washington wrote the details of his perambulatory journey to the Marquis de Chastellux:

> I have lately made a tour through the Lakes George & Champlain as far as Crown Point—then returning to Schenectady, I proceeded up the Mohawk river to Fort Schuyler, crossed over to the Wood Creek which empties into the Oneida Lake, and affords the water communication with Ontario. I then traversed the Country to the head of the Eastern branch of the Susquehanna & viewed the Lake Otsego, & the Portage between that lake & the Mohawk river at Canajohario.
>
> Prompted by these actual observations, I could not help taking a more contemplative & extensive view of the vast inland navigation of these United States, from Maps & the information of others; and

could not be but struck with the immense diffusion and importance of it; and with the goodness of that Providence which has dealt her favors to use with so profuse a hand. Would to God we may have wisdom enough to make a good use of them. I shall not rest contented 'till I have explored the Western part of This Country, & traversed those lines (or great part of them) which have given bounds to a New Empire.

During his crisscross of northern New York State, Washington had the opportunity to meet with Oneida tribesmen, who expressed their grievances with the American commander in chief. Washington wrote Chastellux that sowing this new empire would require assiduousness. Though patriotic, he resigned himself to, first and foremost, turning his "attention . . . to the deranged situation of my private concerns which are not a little injured by almost nine years absence and total disregard of them."[9]

Washington had not been merely curious about seeing the forts and meeting with the Indigenous peoples. Seven years at war had dulled nothing in his acquisitive desire for land. The nearly three-week, 750-mile meandering reaffirmed Washington's belief that New York could be the gateway to the west. His initial goal was to own property near the Saratoga "Mineral Spring," as he wrote New York State Governor Clinton, like his friend Philip Schuyler. Washington and the New York governor formed a land investment partnership. Unfortunately, the Saratoga deal did not work out. Next, Clinton and Washington attempted to purchase land near "that part of the Oriskany track on which Fort Schuyler stands." That plan also failed. Finally, Clinton successfully assembled three separate parcels of land on the north side of the Mohawk River that had been part of the earlier Coxe Patent. He was able to purchase more than 6,000 acres in what later became Oneida County for £1,062.50. Washington was extremely pleased with his partner for the "amazingly cheap"[10] transaction. Clinton outlaid the funds; Washington gave the governor an IOU, and it would take the commander in chief at least four years to reimburse the New Yorker. By 1793, about 4,000 acres of the 6,000-acre packet had been sold for over £3,400—a return of more than 300 percent of their original investment. A year after Washington's successful transaction, two other Virginians—James Madison and James Monroe—would also purchase Mohawk Valley land in a joint venture.

While Washington was on his tour of northern New York, Philip Schuyler penned an advisory letter to the Congress of the Confederation on the proper policy and treatment of Native Americans in the subsuming of western territory. Washington returned to Albany on August 3, 1783 and stayed overnight again at The Pastures. When he bid adieu to Schuyler on August 4, the friends had no idea that, despite an ongoing exchange of letters and similar professional undertakings for both private and public concerns, they would not see each other again until 1789. Still, throughout the years, the men remained likeminded and confident in each other's support—the only issue that would divide them would be the location of America's capital city.

Shortly after Washington's departure from Albany, Alexander Hamilton returned to the Schuyler mansion after an absence of nine months. In Princeton that summer, the air had been filled with a constant ebb and flow of rumors that the definitive peace treaty had arrived aboard this ship or that. Whilst the congress waited in Princeton for news, in Paris, on September 3, 1783, Benjamin Franklin, John Adams, and John Jay gathered with British emissaries on the left bank at the Hôtel d'York to sign the final version of the Treaty of Paris, which officially ended the war. The Congress of the Confederation would not receive the true document until November.

On September 10, the peace commissioners who signed the Treaty of Paris—John Adams, Benjamin Franklin, and John Jay—informed President Boudinot that "On the third Instant, Definitive Treaties were concluded." As Hamilton had warned, the June 21, 1783, Philadelphia mutiny, exacerbated by the ongoing indeterminate location for a seat of government, did indeed have wider consequences that had caused a transatlantic ripple. The trio in Paris explained to Boudinot that the British had relished the stories of cacophony in America and subsequently stalled the negotiations with the "vain Hope from the exagerated [sic] Accounts of Divisions among our People, and Want of Authority in Congress, that some Revolution might soon happen in their Favour." They cautioned that "the late & present Aspect of Affairs in America has had, and continues to have, an unfaourable [sic] influence, not only in Britain but throughout Europe." Adams, Franklin, and Jay advised Boudinot that many Europeans who had read the Articles of Confederation with admiration now wondered why Americans, who had fought so nobly, could not "be brought to act as a Nation." A transient and toothless government "lessen'd [sic] the Dignity" and "diminished" the luster of the new nation in the eyes of the world.

Over two hundred years of criticism has been levied against Alexander Hamilton as the agitator who snared the seat of government to New York City, but Hamilton was in Albany with his wife and family while the members of the Continental Congress remained in Princeton to lobby one another and form voting blocs in anticipation of the October 6, 1783, motion to locate the permanent seat of government. Whilst Hamilton was organizing his books and papers in anticipation of establishing his law office in New York City, it was the legislators in Princeton, and not Hamilton, who were fielding threats of secession from disgruntled Pennsylvanians. New Yorker Ezra L'Hommedieu wrote Governor George Clinton on August 15, 1783, that he had arrived on the sixth of August, "a few days after Colo. Hambelton [Hamilton] was gone." He then imparted the news that the Pennsylvanians were increasing the pressure for the congress to return to Philadelphia:

> Philadelphia are now exceeding anxious for the Return of Congress to that City. 'Tis no wonder: they now see that it makes an Add'n of 100,000 Dollars at least to The State p. Annum. 'Tis said if Congress do not goe [sic] back, the Union will be dissolved; the State of Pennsylvania will be so convulsed that they will not be in a Capacity of Contributing to the Necessities of the United States; they say if Congress would remove there but six weeks, to shew that there was no misunderstanding, all would be Peace & Quiet; & if they then removed, there would be no blame or uneasiness. 'Tis very doubtful to me if Congress ever return to Philadelphia and it is as doubtful where they will agree to have their Place of residence.

On August 29, the Pennsylvania General Assembly passed a resolution that offered the Congress of the Confederation "commodious and agreeable" lodging, and offered the congress its own jurisdiction if it were to make Philadelphia its permanent seat of government. On August 30, James Madison wrote his father:

> I inclose [sic] you one of the latest papers containing the address of the Presidt. [sic] to the Assembly of Pena [Pennsylvania] . . . they are . . . about to address Congs. On the event which occasioned their removal, & to provide especially for the protection of Congs. In case they sd. [sic] deem Philada. the fittest place for the transaction of business until a final residence shall be chosen. What effect this may have is uncertain.

Despite torrential efforts by the state assembly of Pennsylvania to induce the Congress of the Confederation to return to Philadelphia, members of the federal legislature declared themselves to be unamenable to any location in Pennsylvania. On September 20, 1783, James Madison wrote recently widowed Thomas Jefferson that he had remained in Princeton throughout the summer awaiting the October 6 vote:

> The first Monday in next month is fixed for a decision . . . after which it may still be necessary to choose a temporary residence untill [sic] the permanent one can be made ready. I am utterly unable to foretell . . . My plan of spending this winter in Philada . . . was not entirely abandoned untill [sic] Congress left that City and shewed [sic] an utter disinclination to returning to it.

Leading up to the October 6 vote, an outpour of offers besieged the representatives of the congress. Some came from very unexpected sources. On August 21, 1783, Secretary of the Congress Charles Thomson wrote his wife:

> The President of Congress has not provided a house for himself nor is it likely he will find one here to suit him. I find Elizabethtown has been talked of at his table as a proper place for the residence of

Congress. He has a house there which he says has twenty rooms and which he will let for the use of the President. It is true the place is infested with mosquitoes in summer and lying low and near marshes may be liable to intermittents [sic] in the spring and fall, but these are trifling when it is considered that by fixing the residence of Congress there the value of his estate will be increased and he will have an opportunity of letting his house at a good rent.

Secretary Thomson expressed his opinion that Elizabethtown, Boudinot's choice for the location of the seat of government, was more expensive than Princeton because of its proximity to New York City. Declaration of Independence signer Lewis Morris also offered to house the seat of government at his baronial 2,000-acre estate, the Manor of Morrisania. Situated at the junction of the East and Harlem Rivers in the South Bronx, it would have been a very easy commute by water or land. Morris preempted concerns about jurisdiction in his proposal that included an independent and cost-free twenty-five square miles of his property. His bid would arrive after the vote.

Even before the representatives had spent one month in Princeton, there was unilateral agreement that Princeton would be a dismal place to be in wintertime. Ezra L'Hommedieu chorused his colleagues in his August 15 letter to Governor Clinton that, the Congress of the Confederation would without doubt remove yet again to another location, "before winter, as tis thought they cannot be accommodated in that Season of the Year." Seasonal considerations prompted one of the more outlandish suggestions to only convene in fair weather in a variety of locations. The Congress of the Confederation would convene ad infinitum as a roving legislature with alternating seats of government. This idea prompted public ridicule from Pennsylvania representative Francis Hopkinson. In his article "A Summary of Some Late Proceedings in a Certain Great Assembly," Hopkinson sarcastically called the member who proposed this idea "ingenious" and farcically plotted a blueprint for such an arrangement: The Congress could build an equestrian statue large enough to fit every congressional member. This horse should then travel with the members in it—like the infamous Trojan horse—and would be designed with compartments for secret papers and air vents. This peripatetic horse provided a fantastic advantage for the American people: there would be no need to build an expensive federal city. The serious side of the Hopkinson vignette was that New England states were so opposed to a permanent capital city in Philadelphia that they had, in fact, formed a coalition with the southern states to establish two seats of government: one along the Potomac near Georgetown and another on the banks of the Delaware River near Trenton, New Jersey.

While it would seem that sectional interests would define the decision for the location of the capital city, the odd coupling of the New England states with southerners also reflected their joint antipathy toward the overriding federal fiscal power symbolized by Philadelphia as a result of the Bank of North America being housed there. The point was driven home by the Congress of the Confederation that it would never return to Philadelphia even before the October 6 vote when, on September 22, 1783, a "Motion *in Re* Jurisdiction of Congress Over Permanent Site" was entered into the congressional record stating, "That the district which may be ceded to & accepted by Congress for their permanent residence, ought to be entirely exempted from the authority of the State ceding the same; and the organization & administration of the powers of Govt. within the sd. [sic] district concerted between Congress & the inhabitants thereof."

The motion to establish a federal city opened as expected on Monday, October 6, 1783. As usual, Virginia delegate James Madison kept meticulous notes for the benefit of posterity that detailed the factions and reasonings of our Founding Fathers in their quest to fix America's capital city. Madison divided his observations of the proceedings into "Permanent seat of Congress" and "Temporary seat of Congress." Under the section "Permanent," he wrote:

North River [Hudson River]—recommended for the permanent seat of Congs. Chiefly by its security against foreign danger

Falls of Potowmac [sic]—By 1. Geographic centrality—2. Proximity to western Country already ceded—3. Inducement to—further Cessions from N. C. S. C. & Georgia—4. remoteness from the influence of any overgrown commercial city.

Falls of Delaware—By 1. Centrality with regard to number of inhabitants. 2. Centrality as to no. of States & of Delegates. 3 facility of obtaining intelligence from sea.

Beneath his column designated Temporary seat of Congress, Madison listed:

Princeton—in favor of it, 1. Its neighbourhood [sic] to the Permanent seat at,[11] 2. Inconvenience of a removal. 3. Beneficial effect of a frugal situation of Congs. On their popularity throughout the States. 4 the risque [sic] in case of removal from Princeton of returning under the commercial & corrupt influence of Philada.—against it—1. Unfitness for transacting the public business. 2 deficiency of accommodation, exposing the attending members to the danger of indignities & extortions, discouraging perhaps the fittest men from undertaking the service & amounting to a prohibition of such as had families from which they would not part.

Trenton. Argts. In favor & agst. It similar to those respecting Princeton. It was particularly remarked that when the option lay with the President & committee between Trenton & Princeton the latter was preferred as least unfit to receive Congs. On their removal from Philada.

Philada. In favor of it. 1. Its unrivalled convenience for transacting the public business & accommodating Congress. 2. its being the only place where all the public offices particularly that of Finance could be kept under the inspection & controul [sic] of & proper intercourse with Congs. 3. Its convenience for F. Ministers, to which, caeteris paribus, [sic] some regard would be expected. 4. The circumstances which produced a removal from Philada. Which rendered a return as soon as the insult had been expiated, expedient for supporting in the eyes of foreign nations the appearance of internal harmony . . . In addition to these overt reasons, it was concluded by sundry of the members who were most anxious to fix Congs. permanently at the falls of the Potowmac that a temporary residence in Philada.

Would be most likely to prepare a sufficient number of votes for
that place in preference to the Falls of Delaware and to produce a
reconsideration of the vote in favor of the latter.

The debate over a temporary return to Philadelphia went on at length. In
his October 13, 1783, letter to fellow Virginian Edmund Randolph, Madison
expanded on his notes with the actual voting record of his colleagues. It is a
fascinating study of a moment in time because the reasons and factions would
shift dramatically over the next seven years. In October 1783, New Jersey felt
that Philadelphia's supremacy would be a geographic threat; New England
opposed for moral concerns. Madison made it clear to Randolph that on the
whole, because of extreme "resentment agst. Philadelphia," the serious choice
"lay between the falls of the Potowmack [sic] and those of the Delaware."

New York City was considered. Pennsylvania, Delaware, Virginia, and North
Carolina voted in favor of New York; Massachusetts, Connecticut, Rhode
Island, and New Jersey voted no; Maryland and South Carolina divided the
vote. The two states that did split the vote were both missing representatives,
which changed the predicted outcome; however, there had been a strategy
planned to neuter any vote to remove to New York. According to Madison:
"[i]f either of the divided States had . . , [resulted] in . . . [an] affirmative it
was the purpose of N. Jersey to add a seventh vote in favor of Phil," despite the
fact that the New Jersey representatives were adamantly against Philadelphia.

The legislature polled its members on Annapolis: "The arguments in favor
of Annapolis consisted of objections agst. Philada. Those agst. It were chiefly
the same which had been urged in preference of Philada. On the question [to
place the seat of government at Annapolis] the States were Masts. Cont. R. I.
Delaware, Maryland & N. C. ay. N. Y. N. J. Pa. Virga. No. S. C. divided,"
wrote Madison to Randolph. Virginia was also missing a few delegates, whom
Madison knew would cast their vote in favor of Annapolis, as Virginia "would
be promoted by it."

Alexander Hamilton took no part in either the jockeying that led up to
the October 6 vote on the seat of government or in the vote itself. He had
resigned from the Congress of the Confederation in July, joined his wife in

Albany in August, and was in the process of launching his own law office in New York City. On October 16, 1783, James Madison finally responded to Alexander Hamilton's letter in which Hamilton asked his friend to absolve him of malicious accusations that he had actively exerted effort to remove the seat of government from Philadelphia. Madison began by apologizing that he had not received Hamilton's letter of July 6 until the evening of October 15, and Madison agreed that "even after the delay which has taken place, my recollection enables me with certainty to witness the uniform strain of your sentiments as they appeared both from particular conversations with myself, and incidental ones with others in my presence." Madison confirmed that Hamilton "was opposed to the removal of Congress except in the last necessity; that when you finally yielded to the measure it appeared to be more in compliance with the peremptory expostulations of others than with any disposition of your own mind, and that after the arrival of Congress at Princeton your conversation shewed [sic] that you received the removal with regret [rather] than with pleasure."

The October 7, 1783, resolution to place the seat of government of the United States of America on the Delaware River displeased the southerners, who wanted a capital city along the Potomac. The vote was immediately challenged: Maryland's delegates informed the congress that they wanted to change their vote to the Potomac. Other southerners threatened to approve a return to Philadelphia while the new capital city was under construction. Some threatened to refuse to fund the new seat of government. The proposal of a dual seat of government also resurged. On October 21, 1783, a dual residency act was passed, granting the seat of government "ambulatory" residence between Trenton and Annapolis.

On November 4, the congress adjourned and planned to reconvene in Annapolis on November 26. On November 10, Thomas Jefferson, who was to begin his term as a representative from Virginia to the Congress of the Confederation, wrote his brother-in-law Francis Eppes from Philadelphia that he had "arrived at this place, not hearing till I had almost reached it that Congress had determined to remove for a time to Annapolis." He had decided to forego the autumn meetings in Princeton because the congress, "would be employed

in chusing [sic] their president and other formalities of no public consequence."
Under the new presidency of General Thomas Mifflin, he explained to Eppes,
the plan for dual residence of the congress between Trenton and Annapolis was
again altered to include temporary accommodations at Georgetown, "which
is then to be substituted for Annapolis. This however is not to be considered
as an ultimate determination. Trenton alone had been fixed on. The Southern
delegates, extremely dissatisfied with this, contrived after an interval of many
days to get a vote for Georgetown in the terms you have seen."

Still in Philadelphia on November 11, Jefferson reported to Virginia Governor Benjamin Harrison with Madisonian detail on the whipsaw activities in
the congress that he had only received "from the information of others." His
Excellency "would doubtless . . . have heard" of the "determination of Congress
as to their future residence" and "soon after" "of . . . subsequent determination
on the same subject." Jefferson reaffirmed Madison's news that "Philadelphia
had no attention as a permanent seat" and summarized the situation as one
where the southern states would not agree to anything north of the Potomac
River, and the northern compromise for geographic consideration to the south
was the falls of the Delaware River. Thomas Jefferson, a Virginian and proponent of the southern seat of government, added a farsighted thought that
newly formed western states might have the opportunity to participate in the
decision to situate America's capital city: "The establishment of new states
will be friendly or adverse to Georgetown according to their situation. If a state
be first laid off on the lakes it will add a vote to the Northern scale, if on the
Ohio it will add one to the Southern."

Some citizens in Maryland had a similar idea. The Maryland state legislature passed a November 1783 Act, "for making the river Susquehanna
navigable from the line of this state to [Love Island] tidewater." William
Augustine Washington, Charles Carroll of Carrollton, and forty-three other
men formed a canal company capitalized with £18,500 and a pledge of
another £1,500. The mouth of the river was at Havre de Grace, which was
favorably located in proximity to Philadelphia and Baltimore; it was also,
importantly, situated on a main thoroughfare to the western lands. The
idea of a transcontinental empire reinvigorated the campaign to reject and

nullify the expected in favor of something new and daring. Why not place the nation's capital out west? Along the Ohio River? Or on the Mississippi River, which could serve as a wall of defense as well?

Security for the United States would be an ongoing concern. British to the north along the Canadian border, Spanish and French at the southern and western borders, and pockets of hostile Native tribes all poised for bloodshed, yet the Congress of the Confederation beckoned George Washington to Princeton to discuss disbanding the militia. Still in exile from his beloved Mount Vernon, Washington explained in a note from Princeton to the Marquis de Chastellux that he was "waiting for the ceremonials" that the conclusory declaration of peace would bring. Those documents would not arrive until October.

Washington was not at all idle, however, whilst he waited. He was, in fact, fully engaged with the members of the congress in their efforts to carve America's frontiers. The Treaty of Paris would determine North American boundaries between European nations and the United States of America, but made no mention of tribal landholdings, as if the Indigenous peoples were invisible. Washington wrote James Duane, the newly appointed chairman of a congressional committee on Indian affairs, that it was essential for the disposition of western lands to be handled correctly. There were many delicate components to consider before negotiations with Native tribal chiefs began. Washington opined that, with regard to "Indian Affairs . . . my Sentiments with respect to the proper line of Conduct to be observed towards these people coincides precisely with those delivered by Genl Schuyler…in his Letter of the 29th July to Congress."[12] Having been an active speculator in land, Washington offered shrewd advice based on his own experience. He also expressed some cynicism based on his own transactions that failed. Washington had sequentially lost American land to powerful and politically connected British investors. Washington claimed to have disdain for any system of preference, and, without any irony, deemed it corrupt:

> To suffer a wide extended Country to be overrun with Land jobbers—Speculators, and Monopolizers or even with scatter'd settlers is, in my opinion inconsistent with that wisdom & policy which our true

interest dictates, or that an enlightened People ought to adopt . . . to aggrandize a few avaricious Men to the prejudice of many and the embarrassment of Government for the People engaged in these pursuits without contributing in the smallest to the support of Government . . . [will result] more than probable in a great deal of Bloodshed . . . disposing of the Cream of the Country at the expence [sic] of many suffering Officers and Soldiers who have fought and bled to obtain it, and are now waiting the decision of Congress to point them to the promised reward of their past dangers and toils, or a renewal of Hostilities with the Indians . . . How far agents for Indian Affrs [sic] are indispensably necessary I shall not take upon me to decide; but if any should be appointed, their powers in my opinion should be circumscribed, accurately defined . . . it will be found, that self Interest was the principle by which [British] . . . Agents were actuated.[13]

James Duane, who had married a Livingston heiress, had, like Washington, a personal financial stake in the final territorial outline of his own state. The Marquis de Chastellux had called the Livingston properties an entire "district"—similar to a royal holding in France. Washington drew for Duane an astute parallel, demonstrating their similar interests, that reaffirmed Philip Schuyler's expert counsel:

it is my opinion that if the Legislature of the State of New York should insist upon expelling the Six Nations from all the Country they inhabited previous to the War, within their Territory (as general Schuyler seems to be apprehensive of) that it will end in another Indian War. I have every reason to believe from my enquiries, and the information I have received, that they will not suffer their Country . . . to be wrested from them without another struggle . . . The same observations, I am perswaded [sic], will hold good with respect to Virginia . . . the Settlement of the Western Country and making a Peace with the Indians are so analogous that there can be no definition of the one without invoking considerations of the other.[14]

Schuyler and Washington were so likeminded and compatible as friends that Philip Schuyler was one of the few people alive to whom George Washington would close his letters, "affectionately." On November 10, 1783, Philip Schuyler wrote Washington, signing off "with unfeigned affection," that, indeed, tribal enemies were circling the perimeters of New York State: "the british [sic] have constructed barracks sufficient for four hundred men opposite to Niagara in addition to those there occupied by their ranging corps during the war . . . is there not some danger, that on receipt of the definitive [sic] treaty, they may evacuate the Fort at Niagara and expose it to distruction [sic] by the Indians?" Despite the pervasive and looming danger there and in New York City, which was still occupied by British forces, the Congress of the Confederation gave Washington the orders to furlough his army. The congress did not see this decision as a foolhardy one, as it anticipated the final peace treaty and sought to avoid further financial obligation.

Washington issued his official "Farewell Orders" to the men, some of whom had fought for eight years and had still not gotten paid. His address was impassioned, personal, and, at the same time, comprehensive. He began by recapping their remarkable service as outnumbered underdogs who had surprised the world. They had prevailed with unexpected victory. They were vastly outnumbered, lacked formal training, and endured "extremes of hunger and nakedness." Washington expressed great personal pride in this "band of brothers" who had also set aside "violent local prejudices" to form "inviolable attachment and friendship" as Americans. In many cases, until the war the one thing that Washington's men had had in common, the thing that bound them, was the British pound sterling.

Washington reaffirmed that the abstract "thanks of their Country" would arrive in tangible form of "considerable assistance in recommencing their civil occupations, from the sums due to these from the Public." The soldiers were understandably worried that remuneration for their extraordinary years of service would never be forthcoming. Washington understood and verbalized their concern then stated that it was inconceivable to him "that any one of the United States [sic] will prefer a National Bankrupcy" to honoring the debit owed its warriors. He felt strongly that financial default by the United States would result in the "dissolution of the Union." The United States of America had to pay its soldiers and the rest of its debts in toto to avoid collapse. The general reiterated his

> frequently given . . . opinion . . . [but] unless the principles of the
> Federal Government [are] properly supported, and the Powers of
> the Union encreased, the honor [sic], dignity, and justice of the
> Nation . . . [will] be lost for ever . . . [I] cannot help repeating on
> this occasion, so interesting a sentiment, and leaving it as . . . [my]
> last injunction to every Officer and every Soldier.

To seize a moment that he knew his troops would remember, Washington further conveyed that his political views were indivisible from the personal advice he wanted to impart to all of them. They would now be tested as individuals and would be assessed by history as the founders of a nation. He wished those who had served under his command "enlarged prospect of happiness" and success in the "persuits of Commerce and the cultivation of the Soil." Prosperity, attained via the "virtues of economy [sic], prudence and industry," should be seen by his men as not only a private ambition but also a key patriotic goal. Washington's charge to his soldiers to reap private gain for the greater public good was a strong parallel to the philosophical "happy coincidence" and "invisible hand" symbioses proposed by economist Adam Smith.

Washington further dispatched his soldiers on a mission to "carry with them" their "strong attachments to the Union" when they returned to their "different parts of the Continent." Though they had shed their uniforms, he instructed, the battle to shape the empire was just beginning. They had to teach their neighbors the lessons they had learned in the theater of war: that victory required a unified, overarching strategy and their new political structure required a strong federal government.

Though his men were returning to their homes and farms, General George Washington was still wandering in exile. From Poughkeepsie, New York, Washington wrote Philip Schuyler on November 15, 1783:

It gives me great pleasure to inform you that Sir Guy Carleton has announced to me his intention to relinquish the Posts which he holds on York Island [Manhattan] as far as McGowens pass inclusive on the 21st Instant and Herricks and Hamstead [Hempstead, Long Island] with all to the Eastward, on Long Island on the same day and if possible to give up the city with Brooklyn on the day following—and Paulus Hook—Denyces and Staten Island as soon after as practicable. From this disposition, I have great hopes, in case no accident should happen to retard them, that I shall have the pleasure to congratulate you on the full possession of the State by its Government before the last of this Month.

Three days later, on November 18, 1783, General George Washington departed his Newburgh headquarters, turning his back on the Highlands of New York on a journey he knew by heart. Northern New York State had been formed by ancient Precambrian crystalline bedrock. Three billion years later, metamorphic and igneous rocks formed above it. Flooded by waters in the Paleozoic age, the majestic sedimentary stratified mountains of New York State formed the profile in whose shadow George Washington meandered southward for days. Tarrytown, Yonkers—where he dined with his friend General Lewis Morris—and the Bronx—to rest overnight at a home owned by the van Cortlandt family—can all boast of taverns and residences where George Washington trod, drank, and ate.

The forces of wind, melting glaciers, and erosion that had pummeled the lowlands of New York for a billion years could not compare with the devastation that Washington witnessed when he arrived at the threshold of New York City. After seven years of British occupation, the island of Manhattan had transformed from a sylvan to a scabrous landscape. British warships stationed on the East River had been used as prisons, and when patriot soldiers died, they were thrown overboard; it was not unusual for New York City residents to see dead bodies wash up on shore near their fish and food markets. New York City's population had been halved during the war, numbering about 12,000 after the 1781 British surrender at Yorktown.

It took more than two years after the formal capitulation by the British for their militia to leave New York City. Scheduled for Tuesday, November 25, 1783, Evacuation Day was a crisp, clear, and windy autumn day in New York City. At the northwest heights of Manhattan, poised atop the ground of Inwood marble, General George Washington sat with statue-like dignity, patiently astride his horse Blueskin, waiting for the thunderous boom that would prompt his advance from the citadel, now named in his honor. It was a jubilant yet bittersweet moment for the general and for his entourage. It had been there on November 16, 1776, when 3,000 patriots had been killed or captured. For Washington, it was a personally unpleasant reminder that seven years earlier he had retreated in shame past Colonel Roger Morris's home, whose *maîtresse de maison*, Mary Philipse, had rejected his proposal of marriage in favor of Colonel Morris.

The general's chestnut-colored Nelson was his favorite horse for battle, but for public dazzle, he chose the pale-gray Blueskin to set off his uniform for artists and spectators. Next to him, on a bay, was New York Governor George Clinton. Behind the two men were the members of the council for the southern district of New York. Among them was Congressman James Duane, whose Gramercy Park farm had been torched by the enemy. Exiled New Yorkers were coming home.

Some eight hundred gloveless soldiers in threadbare uniforms formed a phalanx behind their commander in chief. With a northwest wind at their backs, the cavalcade made its way slowly southward down through Harlem Heights and the Boston Post Road. Triumphant but somber, as a former British soldier and a man who had spent much of his life at war, Washington had anticipated retaliation, but to his surveyor's eye, as he elucidated in his diary, the site of pollarded trees and barren orchards, the shells of burnt little wooden Dutch farmhouses, and the dried-up wells and trenches gave him a frisson of horror. Already known as the "Father of the Country," Washington mourned with the pain of a parent the deaths of the young men, his stepson included, whom he had guided into manhood.

The British had scheduled their departure for noon but dilatory officers ran an hour late, leaving vindictive finishing touches. Fort George, located at the southern sea level tip of Manhattan, now deserted, was left with a parting gift for the Americans. Waving from the top of its flagpole was the Union Jack. Adding further insult, the British had thoroughly greased the pole to prevent the Americans from hoisting their own standard. When the American patriots discovered that no man could climb the slime, they defiantly sent for nails and ladders.

General Henry Knox had preceded the American commander in chief to secure order. He and Washington reconnoitered at the Bull's Head Tavern on the Bowery. The Westchester Light Horse brigade followed four abreast in the rear. With General Washington in the lead, they passed scorched mansions, broken windows, and looted stores. New Yorkers had waited for hours, lining the streets. Down Chatham Street to the Tea Water Pump near Pearl Street, the procession gained momentum and emotional energy from the crowds. People poured out of doorways and began to stride apace the parade. As Washington rode toward Broadway, soldiers and citizens alike began to weep and shout with joy. This jubilant march, whose final destination was to be at the corner of Thames and Broadway, struck observers as a symbolic pageant of liberation. According to Governor George Clinton's retelling of the day, which became apocryphal New York lore, George Washington turned to him and, despite having witnessed miles of despoil and desecration, predicted, "This will surely be the city of empire!"

That evening gorgeous fireworks illuminated the skies over New York City. Governor Clinton hosted a grand dinner at, ironically Fraunces Tavern, originally a home of the loyalist De Lancey family. George Washington and other dignitaries presided over thirteen exuberant toasts to the Confederation. Governor Clinton announced that the state government was now returning to its prewar seat—New York City. The next morning, the fourth Congress of the Confederation convened at Annapolis, Maryland, yet another temporary seat of government.

Continued celebrations kept George Washington in New York City until December 4, when, once again at Fraunces Tavern, Washington bid his soldiers and New York family goodbye. "With a heart full of love and gratitude, I now take leave of you," he tearfully told them.

On that same day, December 4, 1783, Virginia delegate to the Congress of the Confederation Thomas Jefferson wrote George Rogers Clark from Annapolis about western exploration and to express his exasperation with the congress, "lately agitated by questions where they should fix their residence . . . Still we consider the matter as undecided."

While America's Odysseus was finally going home, the Congress of the United States of America remained itinerant.

CHAPTER 7

Hadley's Quadrant & Parallel Dreams

ALONG WITH THE OPULENT INTERIOR decorations that Philip Schuyler brought back with him from England in 1761 were two seemingly unspectacular but remarkably serviceable instruments. One, called a theodolite, was used to gauge angles on land. The other, the only recently invented Hadley's Quadrant, measured the heavens from the horizon at sea. Pragmatic and far-seeing, these two instruments are the perfect symbols to describe the dual natures of friends Philip Schuyler and George Washington. "You are a philosopher," Schuyler wrote Washington five days before Christmas 1783. They were both philosophers, stargazing astronomers, imaginative mariners, and intuitive hydrologists as well as grounded agronomists, geologists, experts in husbandry, methodical bookkeepers, and hard-headed pre-industrialists. Two toughened military strategists, they were also sentimental men. Washington had openly shed tears before bidding farewell to his soldiers; Schuyler, in his December 20, 1783, note to Washington, expressed that he was filled with "emotions too sensible for communication" for his friend.

Washington responded to Schuyler's letter a month later. He had winded his way on a roundabout journey from New York through town after town, where Americans hailed him along his route. On December 23, Washington was decommissioned in Annapolis and finally arrived at Mount Vernon on Christmas Eve. The winter of 1783–84 was an especially harsh one in northeastern Virginia. The roads had frozen and were covered with banks of snow, preventing Washington from visiting and receiving visitors. Although, in his January 21, 1784, response to Philip Schuyler, Washington portrayed himself as a retired farmer by the "fire side," that restful scene was misleading. Washington loved to project the image of himself as Cincinnatus—the retired warrior who had lain down his arms and returned to his farm—but Schuyler knew him well and had predicted in his December epistle, "you will probably hardly be inclined to retire."

The War of Independence had elicited a federal spirit that had subsided as soldiers returned to their quotidian occupations. The theodolite and the Hadley's Quadrant in Philip Schuyler's possession could also be seen as symbols for the postwar rivalry between the two most powerful states—Virginia and New York—as the leaders of each state ferociously sought to dominate the other through their western territorial claims and their teeming water networks. Now that the British were gone, a lust for hegemony educed a jingoism between the two states.

George Washington and Philip Schuyler were called upon to lend gravitas and expertise to the factions representing their respective states in state and federal legislatures. River toll collections, the improvement of ports and trade, the development of inland seaway connectivity, the successful settlement of territorial claims with both the Native tribes and other states, and the location of the seat of government claimed the attention of state and federal leaders.

New York wanted all of the land to the Great Lakes, which was contested by both Indigenous tribes as well as the state of Massachusetts; Virginia offered to cede land north of the Ohio River if the Congress of the Confederation awarded her permanent and incontrovertible rights to the Ohio Valley. Vermonters also would not acquiesce an inch of land to the New Yorkers, whose Dutch patents had antedated their claims. Philip Schuyler had fiercely defended federal sovereignty and the Articles of Confederation, whose Article IX, Section 4 stipulated that the United States Congress had the sole right to manage, "all affairs with the Indians, not members of any of the states," and Section 1 of the same article granted full authority to the federal government to enter "into treaties and alliances," but as commissioner of Indian affairs of New York State, in January 1784, Schuyler drafted legislature that gave New York State complete sovereignty over the Six Nation territories west to Lakes Ontario and Erie. As a result of Schuyler's bold assertions, the Congress of the Confederation would remove him as northern Indian commissioner and offer to reinstate him, which Schuyler would decline in favor of representing the interests of New York State. Retaining his duties as New York State surveyor general and New York State commissioner for Indian affairs, a post he would hold for twenty-two years, Philip Schuyler was determined to settle peaceably with the Iroquois Confederacy western New York territorial disputes. New York Congressman James Duane, who had been placed in charge of the committee on Indian affairs by the Congress of the Confederation and had communicated with George Washington on treating with the Native tribes, also advised New York State Governor Clinton—in a similar vein as had Schuyler—throughout the winter and spring of 1783–84 on the interpretations and loopholes in the Articles of Confederation that could be used to New York State's advantage. It was George Washington who had counseled Duane that Duane needed to tend to his own real estate interests while his committee formulated a federal plan for dealing with the Native tribes.

Housebound but not at all the idle retiree, within days of his Mount Vernon homecoming, George Washington turned his attention to his own properties. In February, he sent a note through his brother Charles Washington to his tenants in Berkeley County, Shenandoah Valley, that "if they do not settle & pay up their arrearages of Rent very soon I shall use the most efficatious [sic] means to do myself justice." Only one tenant paid up. Washington also penned several newspaper advertisements, combed his documents and papers with ferocity, and contacted public officials because, unlike Philip Schuyler, whose land holdings were upheld by incontestable deeds, most of Washington's claims—especially those in the Ohio Valley—were never properly patented. Also, unlike Schuyler, most of whose property lay in one state, Washington claimed lands that were far-flung. By the end of the War of Independence, George Washington claimed a real-estate portfolio of interests in Virginia,

Maryland, New York, Pennsylvania, what is now West Virginia, Ohio, Tennessee, Kentucky, and Carolina-Virginia border. Throughout the war, Washington had maintained unwavering binocular focus on both the American empire and his own. In addition to the parcels of land that Washington had purchased in the New York State Mohawk Valley the previous summer, and the farms he had gobbled during his short stop at Mount Vernon in 1781, Washington obdurately persisted in securing incontrovertible rights to every inch of land that had been promised to him by the British royal governors.

On February 1, 1784, Washington wrote Botetourt County Surveyor Samuel Lewis, the son of recently deceased Brigadier General Andrew Lewis, who had been an officer under Washington's command. Apparently, the younger Lewis had succeeded his father as county surveyor general. Washington wrote:

> In my researches after papers, I find Memorandums of warrants, which had been put into the hands of the Surveyor of Bottetourt [sic] to execute; particularly one in my own right, under the Royal Proclamation of 1763 for 5000 acres, which appears to have been executed in part on the 6th of Nove [sic] 1774 by a survey for 2950 on the Great Kanhawa [sic], adjoining to (what is commonly called) the Pokitellico [sic] Survey for 21,941, acres, And in a Letter of the 15th of Feby 1779 from Genl [sic] Lewis (whose death I sincerely regret) I find a paragraph containing these words: "With regard to what you ask respecting Lands, no patents have been granted for any by the Proclamation of 63, but one which Doctr [sic] Connelly obtained by favor of Lord Dunmore."

No longer the young, insignificant soldier that men of importance trifled with, General George Washington was now the hero and father of a nation. He was going to use his clout, the political favors he claimed to detest, to extract what he felt was rightfully his. Washington solicited Lewis's support:

> I have now to beg the favor of you Sir, to give me such further information respecting the application of my warrants which have come

into your office, as it may be in your power to do; & to inform me at the same time whether the Survey of 2950, acres made for my benefit, has ever been returned to the Secretarys [sic] office: Also, whether a patent for the Tract including burning Spring has ever been obtained—for what quantity of acres—what improvements are on it, with such other particulars as maybe interesting for me to know—particularly, in what County it lies—how far it is from the Kanhawa in the nearest part—& from the mouth of the Cole river, where it forms its junction with the latter.

For Washington to secure those legal deeds, it was imperative for Virginia to get final approval from the Congress of the Confederation on her land cessions and federally recognized borders.

Virginia representative to the Congress of the Confederation Thomas Jefferson, who was busy in Annapolis advancing Virginia's interests, found it hard to get business done without a quorum. It seemed to Jefferson that his own state's assembly could achieve more for the people of Virginia than whatever he could accomplish at the federal legislature. Extremely frustrated, he wrote James Madison on February 20, 1784, from Annapolis that while the federal government dithered with Virginia's land proposals, more and more Virginians were investing in more and more interior land: "Monroe is buying land almost adjoining me. Short will do the same. What would I not give you could fall into the circle . . . Think of it . . . There is a little farm of 140 as. [sic] adjoining me." Jefferson urged Madison to get the State Assembly to spring into action in sorting out its territorial claims and its water rights. He instructed James Madison to make use of George Washington, whose interests were known to all:

Because the Ohio, and it's [sic] branches which head up against the Pawtomac [sic] affords the shortest water communication by 500 miles of any which can ever be got between the Western waters and Atlantic, and of course promises us almost a monopoly of the Western and Indian trade, I think the opening this navigation is an object on which no time is to be lost . . . Could not our assembly be induced to lay a particular tax which should bring in 5. Or 10,000£ a year to be applied till the navigation of the Ohio and Patowmac [sic] is opened, then James river and so on through the whole successively. Genl. Washington has that of the Patowmac [sic] much at heart. The superintendance [sic] of it would be a noble amusement in his retirement and leave a monument of him as long as the waters should flow. I am of opinion he would accept of the direction as long as the money should be to be employed [sic] on the Patowmac [sic], and the popularity of his name would carry it thro' [sic] the assembly.

It was urgent, he wrote, and he was especially alarmed by "a design agitating to sever the *Northern Neck* [of Virginia] and add it to this state [Maryland]." Jefferson was also dismayed that his efforts to push a location on the Potomac River as the seat of government had stalled. "Georgetown languishes. The smile is hardly covered now when the federal towns are spoken of. I fear that our chance is at this time desperate. Our object therefore must be if we fail in an effort to remove to Georgetown, to endeavor then to get some place off the waters of the Chesapeak [sic] where we may be ensured against Congress considering themselves as fixed."

On January 4, 1784, the Virginia state legislature had passed George Washington's long-term pre–Revolutionary War project, "An Act for Opening and Extending the Navigation of the Potomack [sic] River." Thomas Jefferson, who knew that Washington wanted to spearhead the development of canal systems in Virginia and that this endeavor was one of Washington's lifelong passions, also understood that Washington, who needed to appear to be the Virginia gentleman farmer, was going to pretend to resist a return to politics. Jefferson knowingly played this game by inundating Washington with a spate of entreaties throughout the month of March. On March 6, 1784, Jefferson gave Washington a teasing indication that he was going to press the former commander in chief to engage: "The present hurry forbids me to write to you on a subject I have much at heart, the approaching & opening the Navigation of the Ohio & Potowmac [sic]. I will trouble you by the next post."

Jefferson's lengthy March 15 letter fleshed out a variety of the issues shared by both men with the purpose of cajoling Washington. Jefferson began with the report that despite a Congress "crippled" by nonattendance, "the deed for the cession of Western territory by Virginia was executed & accepted on the 1st instant." Jefferson explained to Washington what course of action would most benefit Virginia in her decision to partition her western lands that mirrored Washington's own strategy when he selected property:

I hope our country will herself determine to cede still further to the meridian of the mouth of the Great Kanhaway, further she cannot govern; so far is necessary for her own well being [sic], the reasons which call for this boundary (which will retain all the waters of the Kanhaway) are 1. That within that are our lead mines. 2. This river rising in N. Carola [sic] traverses our whole latitude and offers to every part of it a channel for navigation & commerce to the Western country; but 3. It is a channel which can not [sic] be opened but at immense expense and with every facility which an absolute power over both shores will give. 4. This river & its waters forms a band of good land passing along our whole frontier, and forming on it a barrier which will be strongly seated. 5. For 180 miles beyond these waters is a mountainous barren which can never be inhabited & will of course form a safe separation between us & any other state 6. This tract of country lies more convenient to receive it's [sic] government from Virginia than from any other state. 7. It will preserve to us all the upper parts of Yohogany & Cheat rivers within which much will be to be done to open these which are the true door to the Western commerce.

Jefferson then traced a tour from Washington's interior waterside parcels of land to his tidewater interests to reel in the "reluctant" general:

the union of this navigation with that of the Patowmac [sic] is a subject on which I mentioned that I would take the liberty of writing to you. I am sure it's [sic] value and practicability are both well known to you. [sic] this is the moment however for seizing it if ever we mean to have it . . . we must . . . In our own defence [sic] endeavor to share as large a portion as we can of this modern source of wealth & power.

Jefferson further prodded Washington by reminding him that a race was on between Virginia and New York:

the Western country is under a competition between the Hudson, the Patomac & the Missisipi [sic] itself . . . there will therefore be a rival-ship [sic] between the Hudson & Patowmac [sic] for the residue of the commerce of all the country westward of L. Erie, on the waters of the lakes, of the Ohio & upper parts of the Missisipi [sic] to go to N. York that part of the trade which comes from the lakes or their waters must first be brought into L. Erie, so also much that which comes from the waters of the Missisipi [sic], and of course must cross at some portage into the waters of the lakes, when it shall have entered L. Erie, it must coast along it's [sic] Southern shore on account of the number & excellence of it's [sic] harbours [sic], the Northern, tho' [sic] shortest, having few harbours [sic], & these unsafe, having reached Cayahoga to proceed on to N. York will be 970 miles from thence & give portages, whereas it is but 430 miles to Alexandria, if it turns into the Cayahoga & passes through that, Big beaver, Ohio, Yohogany (or Monongalia & Cheat) & Patowmac [sic], & there are but two portages, for the trade of the Ohio or that which shall come into it from it's [sic] own waters or the Missisipi [sic], it is nearer to Alexandria than to New York by 730 miles, and is interrupted by one portage only. Nature then has declared in favour [sic] of the Patowmac [sic], and through that channel offers to pour into our lap the whole commerce of the Western world, but unfortunately the channel by the Hudson is already open & known in practice; ours is still to be opened, this is the moment in which the trade of the West will begin to get into motion and to take it's [sic] direction, it behoves [sic] us then to open our doors to it.

Finally, Jefferson flattered Washington—"what a monument of your retirement would it be!"—and assured Washington that Washington's involvement would be absolutely devoid of any appearances of self-dealing. After all, it was Jefferson who had already buttonholed "my friends in the General assembly . . . to have a tax laid . . . to be employed first in opening the upper waters of the Ohio & Patowmac [sic], where a little money & time will do a great deal, leaving the great falls for the past part of the work." Jefferson reasoned with Washington that "when you view me as not owning nor ever having a prospect of owning one inch of land on any water either of the Patowmac [sic] or the Ohio . . . my goal in this busines is public & pure."

Washington's long interest in waterside property and the development of the canal systems was so widely known that many others came forth to solicit his participation in canal schemes. During the war, Washington had attended the wedding of Catherine ("Lady Kitty") Alexander to William Duer.[1] In June of 1784, Kitty's father, General William Alexander, the self-styled Lord Stirling, introduced Washington to the American-born former sheriff of the City of London, Stephen Sayre. On August 20, Sayre, a reputed adventurer, submitted a complete business proposal to Washington for a Potomac Company that aligned with the January 1784 act in public offerings. Sayre's plan included the participation of child shareholders, who would not receive dividends for at least fifteen years, "because children do not want it Sooner."

One of Washington's investments had been in the Dismal Swamp Company. North Carolina also wanted a slice of the success soon to be realized by New York and Virginia. From Annapolis on March 24, 1784, North Carolina representative to the Congress of the Confederation Hugh Williamson appealed to Washington, referring to the Dismal, on behalf of the

Lebanon Company, who own 40 or 50 thousand acres of Land on the South side of Drummonds Lake or the great Dismal . . . [they] propose to dig a canal from the head of Pasquetank into the Lake in the dismal & thence into some navigable water which leads into the Chesapeak [sic] Bay . . . The proposed Canal would be partly in Virginia & partly in Carolina . . . [and would] receive from all vessels passing through the Canal such a Toll as they may think proper to impose . . . If you should agree with the gentlemen in our state . . . I am perswaded [sic] you will not fail to recommend it in such terms that the company shall not fail in obtaining the necessary act of incorporation in the state of Virginia.

Although Washington's March 31, 1784 reply has never been found, Washington was so consistent in his longing for profit extracted from his property that a scheme that provided lucre for both his Dismal and tidewater properties undoubtedly would have pleased him. A proud Virginian, he was nonetheless an unwavering proponent of interstate cooperation and would have approved.

Unlike the missing response to Hugh Williamson, Washington's detailed March 29 reply to Thomas Jefferson's entreaties remains for posterity. It stands as a forthright encapsulation of Washington's lifelong ambitions for canal development, a recitation of the political compromises he had been forced to make in pursuit of those dreams, and a wary assessment that a good and great plan could be obstructed for a variety of reasons:

My opinion coincides perfectly with yours respecting the practicability of an easy, & short communication between the waters of the Ohio & Potomack [sic], of the advantages of that communication & the preference it has over *all* others . . . I am not so disinterested in this matter as you are . . . More than ten years ago I was struck with the importance of it, & despairing of any aid from the public, I became a principal mover of a Bill to empower a number of subscribers to undertake, at their own expence [sic] . . . the extension of the Navigation from tide water to Wills's Creek (abot 150 Miles) [sic] . . . To get this business in motion, I was obliged . . . to comprehend James River, in order to remove the jealousies which arose from the attempt to extend the Navigation of the Potomack [sic]. The plan, however, was in a tolerable train when I set out for Cambridge in 1775, and would have been in an excellent way had it not been for the difficulties which were met with in the Maryland Assembly, from the opposition which was given (according to report) by the Baltimore Merchants, who were alarmed . . . The local interest of that place [Baltimore] joined with the short sighted politics . . . the War afterwards called Mens [sic] attention to different objects—and all the money they could or would raise, were applied to other purposes . . . I am satisfied not a moment ought to be lost in recommencing this business; for I *know* the Yorkers will delay no time to remove every obstacle in the way of other communication, so soon as the posts at Oswego & Niagara are surrendered; and I shall be mistaken if they do not build Vessels for the Navigation of the Lakes, which will supercede [sic] the necessity of coasting on either side.

Washington and Jefferson were understandably anxious: despite their commiseration that the Congress of the Confederation was suffering from a lack of participation, things were moving quickly in New York State's favor. Three days after the long-awaited Virginia cession passed in the Congress of the Confederation, the Congress of the Confederation on March 4 formed a small committee to treat with the Six Nations for a peaceful relinquishment of their ancestral land in western New York State and along the Great Lakes. On March 12, New York State formed its own committee to steer state policy with the same purpose. On March 19, the Congress of the Confederation appropriated $15,000 for negotiations with the Iroquois. On March 22, Schuyler's committee approved the bill he had sketched in January called "An Act to Appoint His Excellency the Governor of this Sate or Person Administering the Government thereof for the Time Being, and the Commissioners therein designated to Superintend Indian Affairs." The bill passed with no modifications on April 6, 1784. Schuyler's resolution instructed Governor Clinton that neither the United States nor "any state of power whatsoever, [was] to hold any conference or negotiate any cession from the said Indians without the express permission of the [New York State] Legislature" because the Six Nations were residents of New York State.

Amongst the conditions of the Virginia cession, many of which were imposed with an eye on diluting New York's power, was the requirement that the western territories relinquished by Virginia would be broken into between eleven and twenty-five separate states. Sensitive to the momentum in New York's western territories, Jefferson quickly drafted a proposal that would divide the territories west of the Appalachian Mountains by longitude and latitude into fourteen states. With some geographical adjustments, on April 23, 1784, with some minor adjustments, the Congress of the Confederation, in a 22–2 vote, passed the Land Ordinance of 1784 that demarcated the United States new landholdings north of the Ohio and east of the Mississippi rivers. This ordinance, replaced in 1787, had little bite until it was formally adopted with enlarged provisions as the Northwest Ordinance in 1789 by the first Congress operating under the US Constitution.

Two days after the 1784 land ordinance passed, Thomas Jefferson wrote James Madison on April 25, 1784, that, once again, "[t]he place at which Congress should meet in Nov. has been the subject of discussion lately." Thomas Jefferson suggested an unexpected location to the Congress of the Confederation— Alexandria, Virginia. Jefferson dropped the idea of a compromise with Maryland for Georgetown. Neither did he put forth the Virginia state capital, Richmond. Instead, for the very first time, the young town of Alexandria, Virginia, the port village designed by George Washington, was offered as a possible capital city of the United States of America. Jefferson informed Madison, however, that his idea "was negatived easily." The following day, April 26, 1784, the Congress of the Confederation agreed to adjourn on June 3, 1784, until the thirtieth of October, when it would reconvene at Trenton, New Jersey. The vote was less an agreement on the permanent capital city of the new American empire than it was yet one more rebuff to Philadelphia.

Thomas Jefferson was one of the shrewdest politicians who ever lived. While pretending to be a simple country boy, he was a discriminating aesthete, and, according to the Marquis de Chastellux, an adroit Renaissance man.[2] Jefferson knew that Washington yearned for Alexandria to become America's capital of empire. Jefferson also discerned that it was important to Washington to appear to be the Virginia grandee with no tinge of the opportunist affixed to his reputation. To coax Washington to serve as a figurehead for the very projects dear to Washington's own heart, it was incumbent upon Jefferson to visibly grab the reins for advancement on Potomac development and to put forth the town of Alexandria as the seat of the federal government so that Washington, assured that his name would be disconnected from any political tussle, would then "deign" to serve the public.

Jefferson also cleverly inspired dread in Washington's mind to spur the former commander in chief into action by propagating the rumor that, based on one of those centuries-old ambiguous British charters, Maryland, lusting after Alexandria's fresh affluence, was going to seize the port town that Washington had designed. Alexandria had survived the war much intact. A cliometric analysis of pre-Revolutionary War standard of living, using courthouse documents, bills of lading, and so on, reveals that Americans were far better off than their British cousins. The average annual income in the North American British colonies was about £13.85 while in England it was roughly £10 to £12. Americans only paid about a 1–1.5 percent tax rate but in England citizens were taxed from 5–7 percent. The average net worth in the thirteen colonies was close to par with that of the wealthy European countries like Great Britain, France, and the Netherlands, and in 1774 the total physical wealth in the thirteen colonies totaled roughly £120 million. Land comprised more than half of all wealth in the thirteen colonies, resulting in a great disparity of wealth among them. The ordinary southerner was far richer than his counterparts in New England and those who lived in the middle colonies—even without the inclusion of the assessed value of slaves—however, southerners along with New Englanders had the highest debt while those who lived in the middle colonies led both of those regions in the accumulation of financial assets.[3]

With two decades of uninterrupted progress, in 1784, Alexandria, Virginia, was thriving. Regular ferry service transported goods and people across the Potomac. The Marquis de Chastellux documented his experience on the ferry and wrote of George Washington's blossoming metropolis: "This town, which stands above 200 miles from the sea . . . cannot fail of becoming one of the first cities of the new world." On February 5, 1784, the first edition of *The Virginia Journal and Alexandria Advertiser* appeared. In late spring, a regularly scheduled stagecoach business began operating between Alexandria and New York City with stops at Baltimore and Philadelphia. Alexandria's ports had also remained teeming with activity. Unlike New York Harbor, which had been under British control throughout the war and had maintained steady trading with Great Britain, about 75 percent of the trade that flowed in and out of Alexandria was to and from other American ports. Only about 12 percent of the Alexandria port wartime trade had been with European allies and about 13 percent Caribbean.

In the opinion of the Marquis de Chastellux, the inhabitants who populated the Catholic Maryland side of the Potomac River were very different from those who lived on the mostly Protestant Virginia side. Having famously ambled much of the thirteen United States of America, Chastellux offered his European reader his observations about North America that included perceptive reflections on the differing social norms. According to Chastellux, because Virginia was settled during the reigns of Elizabeth I and James I (very often by the second-born sons of the nobility), Virginians were comfortable with aristocracy. The social structure of Virginia closely followed a European hierarchical paradigm wherein leisured landowners were venerated, forming the top of a caste system that flaunted illustrious ancestors. This normative was fundamentally different from the character of Lord Baltimore's colonialists or Bostonians, for example, who had emigrated to the New World for religious freedom, and that of the industrious New Yorkers.

Growing up as a young Virginia boy, George Washington had understandably idolized the highborn Fairfax men. As a member of the Continental Congress and as the nation's commander in chief, Washington transferred that admiration to Philip Schuyler. Washington envied Schuyler's wealth and taste. Schuyler's Albany home, for example, with its English-style décor and Georgian architecture, was redolent of the residences of rich Virginians that signified patrician refinement and material ease. Philip Schuyler, his son-in-law Stephen van Rensselaer, and Washington's own brother Lawrence Washington, had indeed all eased into the role of the gentleman. George Washington, on the other hand, had to use his wiles to become a member of the landed gentry.

Washington saw himself in another of Schuyler's sons-in-law, Alexander Hamilton, who also had to make his own way in the world. Schuyler,

Washington, and Hamilton were all raised by single mothers. Schuyler's widowed mother, an heiress, was acclaimed as noble, lovely, and gracious. In contrast, George Washington and Alexander Hamilton had notorious mothers, both social pariahs. Hamilton's mother had been imprisoned for giving birth to two illegitimate sons; Mary Washington scandalized people by smoking a pipe and, even though her son supported her, Mary Washington applied to the Virginia Assembly as a pensioner. Her son George was so embarrassed by her outlandish behavior that he avoided seeing his mother as much as possible.

Washington and Hamilton were self-made men, who achieved prominence based on their talents. Throughout his life, no matter how much he read and studied, Washington remained truly awed by better-educated men like Schuyler and Hamilton, and they became indispensable to him. Schuyler would serve as counsel to both Washington and Hamilton not solely because of his fortune but because of his innate organizational and leadership skills and his empirical financial common sense.

In an exchange of letters between Philip Schuyler and George Washington in early spring 1784, Schuyler suggested to his Virginia friend that he return to New York to visit lands that were becoming open for investment. Evacuation Day in New York City had been the starter shot for the land grab of abandoned loyalist properties. There was also confidence in an imminent settlement with the Native tribes in western New York. With a surfeit of cash, Philip Schuyler went on a buying spree. His son-in-law Alexander Hamilton, now a member of the New York State bar, moved his growing family to 57 Wall Street and began practicing law. Hamilton's initial matters concerned his father-in-law's real estate transactions; Philip Schuyler purchased for his own portfolio and sometimes financed others who speculated.

This New York oligarchy, taking advantage of spoken and unspoken clan bonds, shared an agenda created by their elders, foremost that of Philip Schuyler, to turn New York into the cultural, financial, and political capital city of the American empire. Most of the men in this group had served as aides to George Washington during the war, and their wives had known the general since they were children; one of the Schuyler siblings was Washington's godchild. In essence, they were George Washington's New York circle of confidants, friends, and adopted family. Unlike his fellow Virginians, who preferred courtlier mannerisms with more artifice, Washington valued their energetic traits with which he had identified. He also admired how, even though many of the patroon families had been divided by the war, they remained loyal to one another—that, too, mirrored Washington's own sentiments about the Fairfax family.

Not every New York family, however, had reunited happily. John Jay, in London en route home after having signed the Treaty of Paris in September 1783, had no interaction whatsoever with his own brother, Sir James; further, Jay wrote that his Tory cousin William Bayard even snubbed him on the street. Bayard's son, William Jr., a patriot, chose the other side and remained in New York City. While Jay was satisfied that the Treaty of Paris had provided for clemency and parity for the sale of abandoned loyalist properties back in New York City, the New York State legislature was behaving in a contrary and retaliatory fashion. New Yorkers felt they had the right to violate the treaty, as no other city had suffered as much at the hands of the British. New Yorkers were in a punitive mood, having lived through atrocities like the regular sight of human flotsam and jetsam washing up on the East River from the British prison ships. Their churches had been desecrated, their homes had been razed, and, especially after the battle of Yorktown, their streets became growingly littered with refuse and infested with thievery.

In 1781, operating uncomfortably in exile in upstate Kingston, the New York State legislature had passed a bill that precluded Tories from practicing law in the state. On March 17, 1783, the state legislature passed the Trespass Act, a bill that allowed returning patriots to recover damages from Tories who had appropriated their homes and properties during the war. Although the signing of the Treaty of Paris later that year in September would nullify the Trespass Act, New Yorkers continued to dismiss the terms of the treaty with regard to their treatment of loyalists. In early 1784, the Sons of Liberty met on the New York City Commons and shouted for the expulsion of all Tories by May 1, and on May 12 the New York State legislature passed another law, this time precluding Tories from voting for two years—a breach of the Treaty of Paris. In the streets, Tories were tarred and feathered. While William Bayard Jr. would spend much of the 1780s after Evacuation Day building a thriving business in New York City, he would also spend a great deal of his time in court, trying to obtain payments for the "loss of property" and "damages" his father, living in England, felt were owed to him according to the Treaty of Paris. Loyalist James De Lancey, who had also fled to England, owned a large parcel of New York City land that was confiscated and sold for $234,198.75. James De Lancey's only reparation would be about £26,000 that he received from the British government for his loyalty to the Crown. Postwar New York City was a litigator's dream; even Jay knew that New York City would be the crucible for the treaty he had signed.

At the same time that Hamilton was negotiating and drafting contracts on Schuyler's behalf, the hungry young attorney accepted a controversial case that would impair the very kind of real estate deals that Schuyler had transacted to the detriment of loyalists. In *Rutgers v. Waddington*, Hamilton argued that the New York State Trespass Act, which declared all loyalist real estate holdings forfeited, was in violation of the Treaty of Paris. Already known as a fighter for a strong central government with his publication of "Vindication of Congress," Hamilton gained an immediate reputation as an unbeatable attorney and a political force. Hamilton did so well that he was able to join his father-in-law and a small group of investors in the acquisition of half a million acres in upstate New York along the St. Lawrence River; Hamilton even began keeping a separate land account entry listing within his financial records. Hamilton saw opportunity everywhere in the revitalization of New York City. On March 15, he presented a proposal that he had drafted to a group of prominent, wealthy men that included his cousins-by-marriage, William Duer, and some Livingstons. Although postwar American currency was different in every state, causing considerable chaos, by June 1784, the Bank of New York was in business. In addition to their participation in Hamilton's Bank of New York, the Livingstons patriotically began to advance seed money in a way that we now—they had no word for it then—would call either merchant or industrial banking. Postwar New Yorkers—men and "she Merchants" alike—now had easier access to money for rebuilding as well as for start-up ventures. As a member of the elite clans through marriage, William Duer would benefit from and be at the forefront of this new capitalist populism. Duer climbed stratospherically and quickly with profits from commodities like timber in ventures he had undertaken with Philip Schuyler. Duer then moved on to invest—with other people's money—in real estate (purchase and leasing), Revolutionary War debt, shipping, stocks, and bonds.

There was a secondary reason for the lust for New York City property: according to the new, liberal New York State Constitution, shaped by John Jay, for the very first time, freeholders with a very small amount of real estate and net worth were enabled to vote. The state constitution, acknowledging that city dwelling was not only more expensive but more cramped than the rest of the state, lowered the qualification even more for New York City residents. New York property, so long denied to the vast majority of average New Yorkers because of the feudal suzerains—the De Lanceys, Schuylers, van Rensselaers, Livingstons, Philipses, and van Cortlandts—now available ironically because of turncoat families like the De Lanceys and Philipses, who had abandoned their real estate and other assets. Patriots could now receive and savor the kind of tangible reward George Washington had promised his soldiers: profit as well as participation in the political process. Government would now belong to more of "the people"; enfranchisement was now a reality for many more people in post–Revolutionary War New York City. When the impounded De Lancey property in New York City came on the auction block, the Livingstons enjoyed a great deal of satisfaction at swooping in and buying large portions of it at a clearance price.

George Washington was keen on taking advantage of and increasing his New York prospects. He desperately wanted to join Schuyler and Hamilton in their investment syndicates and planned to visit with his New York friends. From Philadelphia, where Washington had been attending a meeting of the Society of the Cincinnati, Washington wrote Schuyler that it had "long been my wish, and until lately my intention to have proceeded from this meeting of the Cincinnati to the Falls of Niagara . . . I cannot but thank you . . . my good Sir, for the polite & friendly offers contained in your letters of the 6th & 12th Instt [sic]." He explained to Schuyler, however, that he had to change his plans. "[B]usiness is of such a nature that I cannot without great inconvenience, be long absent from home," wrote Washington. He assured Schuyler, however, that "if ever I should have it in my power to make an excursion of that kind nothing could add more to the pleasure of it than having you of the party."

Like Schuyler, George Washington belonged to the class of eighteenth-century agrarians who were also capitalist merchants. They saw opportunities for commerce in everything they grew, butchered, milled, and distilled. Having been precluded by the British from manufacturing many items whose very raw materials were planted or bred in the thirteen colonies, Schuyler and Washington were hungry to build their own vertical proto-conglomerates. They both favored state and federal economic policy that would assist in the development of new urban centers and ports, canal systems, and in securing favorable trade agreements to encourage postwar growth. That May, Washington decided that it was imperative to return to Virginia. Orange County representative and former representative to the Congress of the Confederation James Madison had drafted a port bill to be presented at the Assembly of the Commonwealth of Virginia that would regulate and control anchorage and tariffs. Washington had to ensure the inclusion of Alexandria as the only or one of the few chosen to conduct transatlantic business in that bill.

Before the War of Independence, Great Britain expended large amounts of money to provide naval protection for the coast of North America to safeguard her monopoly. This role and its costs would now obviously fall on Americans, but so would the benefits. With no plan for a standing United States militia, maritime patrol of ports would be the responsibility of each sovereign state. Madison, unlike Schuyler and Washington, was uncomfortable with government intervention in using natural resources for economic benefit, believing that nature should select Virginia's ports. Madison thought that legislature should only intervene in matters like taxes, trade, credit, and currency. With regard to the Port Bill, Madison viewed Norfolk as the physiographic optimum for centralizing maritime activity in Virginia, but Madison longed to be a member of Washington's inner circle. Madison could demonstrate his loyalty to Washington by supporting Alexandria in the bill.

Busy, bustling ports were good for the state only if duties, tolls, and contraband could be monitored. British merchants had for years taken advantage of colonists—with mercantilist policies that suppressed free trade, inhibited manufacturing, unfavorably manipulated credit, and indebted Americans—and were now flooding the United States with long-denied merchandise. With miles of tidewater shoreline as well as interior streams for anchorage, Virginia was a perpetual easy target for smugglers. To restrict and control "the Vessels of forreign [sic] Merchants trading to this State," Madison proposed to the Assembly of the Commonwealth of Virginia that only certain ports should provide entry, "lading and unlading—And the Revenue arising from Commerce would also thereby be more certainly collected."

George Washington's hometown, Alexandria, was also a port deep enough to accommodate massive tonnage and, with the potential of westward development of the Potomac River, would provide easy linkage between the ocean and the continental interior. Washington's known preferences, his stature, and his status had a great influence on the nominations that were presented to the state legislature on June 8, 1784. The proposed Port Bill was read on the floor of the state assembly on June 9, and, as James Madison later wrote Thomas Jefferson on July 3, 1784, a succession of heated debates went on for six days until June 15, when both Norfolk and Alexandria prevailed. Thus, Alexandria, Virginia, a town that forty years earlier had barely existed, became one of the two premier points of entry on the state's coastline.

Dissatisfied members of the legislature continued to grumble about unfair advantage, so, two days later, in homage to the great state's historicity, three more of the state's earliest ports—Bermuda Hundred, Yorktown, and Tappahannock—were added to the Port Bill to make political peace. Portsmouth, a qualifying contender as one of the deepwater ports, was negated as superfluous because it lay opposite Norfolk on the Elizabeth River. By the time Jefferson received Madison's news, Jefferson was in France as minister plenipotentiary on behalf of the United States. Jefferson's reaction to the Port Bill was one of disappointment because he felt that too many ports had been inked into it. On November 11, 1784, Jefferson rejoined: "I trust that York and Hobbs' hole [Tappahannock] will do so little that Norfolk & Alexandria will get possession of the whole."

Alexandria, Virginia, could very well have become the leading commercial center of the south. If only Virginia could have gained authority over and developed the navigation of the Potomac River. As Washington, Jefferson, and Madison well knew, the New Yorkers were many steps ahead in opening their interior channels. It was time to resume the interstate working relationship established before the War of Independence between George Washington of Virginia and now former governor of Maryland Thomas Johnson. Again, against his own prevarication that great disequilibrium would result if the government dictated Virginia's environment in favor of specialized commercial interests, James Madison nonetheless introduced on June 28, 1784, another proposal before the Virginia State Assembly that called for negotiations with the state of Maryland on the jurisdiction and development of the Potomac. Appointed to the four-man committee were Madison, General Edmund Randolph, Fairfax County (Alexandria) representative Alexander Henderson, and George Mason, co-author of the fiery 1774 Fairfax Resolves that demanded independence from the British, whose Gunston Hall plantation abutted the Potomac. Mason's Neck, much of Arlington, and Roosevelt Island were all part of Mason's Potomac River holdings. James Madison owned no Potomac River property. The resolution, his service on the committee, and his role in the creation of a statue of George Washington were all efforts exerted on Madison's part to ingratiate himself with the former commander in chief.

The Congress of the Confederation had adjourned five days before James Madison's Port Bill passed in the Virginia Assembly, but its subcommittee on Indian affairs continued working throughout the summer. This committee— which included Oliver Wolcott of Connecticut, Richard Butler of Pennsylvania, and Arthur Lee of Virginia, and was conspicuously devoid of any New Yorkers, Philip Schuyler in particular—labored throughout the summer in preparation for a meeting with the Iroquois Confederation in western New York. Schuyler received a tardy invitation to serve on the committee, which he perceived to be more of a snub than an oversight, and declined it. In addition to this federal commission, two more groups, one of them led by New York Governor Clinton, whose cross-purpose goal was to obstruct their success, and another that included Virginia Assemblyman James Madison, French chargé d'affaires François, Marquis de Barbé-Marbois, and the Marquis de Lafayette, all converged in upstate New York by the end of summer 1784.

The Marquis de Lafayette arrived in New York harbor from France on August 4 and headed south to Mount Vernon. After a short reunion with

George Washington, Lafayette reversed his course and returned north. At Baltimore, he met up with James Madison. The duo proceeded to New York City, where James Duane greeted them with four days of "feasting." Madison and Lafayette sailed up the Hudson River to Albany and reconnoitered with the Marquis de Barbé-Marbois on September 23, 1784. It then took the trio six days to travel from Albany to Fort Stanwix. When they arrived at Fort Stanwix, they were surprised to learn that Governor Clinton, Peter Schuyler (a relative of Philip Schuyler), and an interpreter had already been there for nearly two weeks (August 31–September 10) negotiating a treaty between New York State and the Iroquois Confederation.

Barbé-Marbois documented the group's colorful travels amongst the Native tribes in his letters. His "Journey to the Oneidas" titillated the European audience with stories of the indigenous peoples and their customs. On the group's return to Albany through the Mohawk Valley they encountered an increasing number of chiefs and warriors, who were en route to meet with the federal commissioners. Butler, Lee, and Wolcott, facing manmade (Governor Clinton) and natural hurdles (twenty-six degrees Fahrenheit temperature) finally arrived at Fort Stanwix on October 3, 1784. Madison, Lafayette, and Barbé-Marbois, traveling in the opposite direction, arrived in Albany on October 7, 1784. In Albany, they learned from the Schuyler family that, whilst they were on their journey into the wilderness, Betsey Schuyler Hamilton had given birth to her first daughter. On October 8, from Albany, Lafayette wrote Hamilton:

> With all the warmth of my long and tender friendship I Congratu-
> late You Upon the Birth of Your daughter, and Beg leave to present
> Mrs Hamilton With my most Affectionate Respects. Several delays
> Have Retarded the Oppening [sic] of the treaty and When I was
> Upon the Ground, it Has Been found that my influence with the
> Indians Both friendly and Hostile tribes, was much Greater than
> the Commissioners and Even myself Had Conceived—so that I was
> Requested, Even By Every one of *those* to Speak to *those* Nations.
> There were Some, more or less, from Each Tribe. I stayed as long as
> the Commissioners thought I could do them some Good, and that

Has Rather Cramped my private plans of Visits . . . about the twentieth of Next Month I Hope to Be Again With You in New York.

Lafayette believed that he had prepared the way for a seamless transaction;
however, when Lee, Butler, and Wolcott arrived at Fort Stanwix, they were in for
more surprises. New York Governor Clinton had purposefully ignored an
August 19 letter from Arthur Lee and Richard Butler, who had petitioned the
New York governor to stay out of federal matters. Clinton, who maintained
the position drafted by Philip Schuyler with which James Duane was in tacit
agreement, refused to assist Lee, Butler, and Wolcott, and, having preempted
their meeting with his own, caused them delay. Further, Clinton refused to
provide the federal commissioners with guards. Clinton had completed his own
discussions with Joseph Brant, who represented the hostile nations, but ordered
Peter Schuyler and their translator to remain at Fort Stanwix to spy on the treaty
negotiations between the nations and the representatives of the United States
of America. In defiance of the public declaration issued in Albany by Butler,
Lee, and Wolcott banning liquor from their meeting with the tribes, Clinton
slyly dispatched three wagon merchants with an enormous supply of liquor,
which Schuyler was to offer the Iroquois. The federal commissioners ordered
one of their accompanying lieutenants to confiscate the spirits. In retaliation,
the merchants went to the local sheriff and swore out a warrant for theft. The
federal commissioners were forced to intervene.

This micro-scrimmage between state and federal government was not even
resolved by the Treaty of Fort Stanwix, agreed to between the United States
commissioners and the Iroquois nation on October 22, 1784. Greatly sim-
plified, the treaty designated a firm international border with Great Britain's
Canadian territories and specified that those Native tribes that had allied with
the United States of America would retain possession of their villages with the
benediction of the Congress of the Confederation of the United States of
America. The treaty also claimed more western lands that could benefit both
(Commissioner Butler's) state of Pennsylvania and potentially New York State.
In theory, investors and settlers could now purchase legal title to, rather than
encroach on, those fertile waterside parcels as the United States of America

pressed her peripheries from the Atlantic Ocean to the Mississippi River and along the Great Lakes. On November 15, however, Virginia delegate to the Congress of the Confederation James Monroe wrote fellow Virginian and state assemblyman James Madison that there were still two great problems to surmount, both of which challenged New York State sovereignty:

> I reach'd *N. York* about eight days after you had left . . . the questions wh. Appear to me arise upon the subjects *of variance* are 1. Whether these *Indians* are to be consider'd as members of the State of *N. York*, or whether the living simply within the bounds of a State . . . while they acknowledge [sic] no obedience to its laws . . . nor enjoy the protection nor any of the rights of citizenship within it, is a situation wh. Will even in the most qualified sense, admit their being held as members of a State? 2. Whether on the other hand this is not a description of those whose manag'ment [sic] is committed by the confidation [sic] to the U.S. in Congress assembled? In either event the land held by these *Indians*, having never been ceded either by *N. York* or *Massachusetts* belongs not to the *U. States;* the only point then in wh. *N. York* can be reprehensible is, for preceding by a par-ticular [state treaty] the general Treaty. This must be attributed to a suspicion that there exists in *Congress* a design to injure her.

While the two Virginians claimed they saw "no advantages to be deriv'd" from harming the territorial claims of the citizens of New York State, there had been a clear decision made by those in Annapolis to remove Philip Schuyler from the post he had held throughout the War of Independence as commis-sioner of Indian affairs. Apparently, although Schuyler had sacrificed and served the fledgling republic, the current members of the Congress of the Confed-eration did not trust him to put his country before the territorial interests of New York State.

Schuyler had hoped that his good friend George Washington would invest with him in western New York State. In addition to their genuine camaraderie, Schuyler expected that Washington's participation would send a signal to the

New England states that their incessant battering for the territory west of the Mohawk Valley that juxtaposed the Great Lakes was a frivolous lost cause. The plan was momentarily scrapped in May 1784 when Washington explained to Schuyler that he was needed in Virginia. It was true that the pending Virginia Port Bill was extremely important to Alexandria's future; it was also true that Washington was strapped for cash and could simply not afford to invest with Schuyler. One year after Washington had invested in the Mohawk Valley, he had still not repaid Governor Clinton for his share of the purchase price.

Most of Washington's income was derived from his rental properties. The war, disputed claims, squatters, and many other reasons for delinquencies left the former commander in chief seriously short of cash in 1784. Despite the impression that he gave Schuyler that it was Mount Vernon that required his attention, Washington had no intention of staying put there. In fact, the moment he returned to Virginia, Washington began planning a voyage in another direction. He was going to visit his western lands. While his fellow Virginians Arthur Lee, James Madison, and James Monroe were perambulating the Mohawk Valley in New York State, George Washington was intent on making his sixth voyage to the Ohio Valley—this time as landlord.

On February 13, 1784, Washington had written to a real estate partner, Gilbert Simpson, demanding that Simpson produce by April 15 "a full & complete settlement of our Partnership accounts, wherein every article of debit is to be properly supported by vouchers . . . you have been much more attentive to your own interest than to mine. But I hope your Accots . . . [will show] that something more than your own emolument was intended by the partnership." Washington was completely dissatisfied with the numbers and "found it indispensably necessary to visit my Landed property west of the Apalacheon [sic] Mountains, and more especially that part of it which I held in Co-partnership with Mr. Gilbert Simpson."

On the first of September, Washington "dispatched my equipage about 9 Oclock A.M., consisting of 3 Servants & 6 horses, three of which carried my Baggage, I set out myself in company with Docter [sic] James Craik; and after dining at Mr. Sampson Trammells (abt. 2 Miles above the Falls Church) we proceeded to Difficult Bridge, and lodged at one Shepherds Tavern 25 Miles."

Thus began Washington's extraordinary journal that recorded his monthlong journey, whose purpose, he wrote, was to ascertain the correct legal filing of his deeds in local courthouses, collect delinquent rents, see what improvements could be made on his lands, and "to obtain information of the nearest and best communication between the Eastern and Western Waters; and to facilitate as much as in me lay the Inland Navigation of the Potomack [sic]." Thirty years earlier, in 1754, Washington's western travel journals made him a twenty-two-year-old sensation. During the War of Independence, Washington had employed Philip Schuyler's former secretary Richard Varick to preserve his papers for posterity. His 1784 western journal was written with a deliberate public relations goal.

Washington traveled to the Shenandoah Valley in what today would be West Virginia, met with tenants, and reunited with his brother Charles. After speaking with some of the locals, George Washington wrote that they were of the same mind as he was: they wanted to develop a water route linking tide-water Virginia with the Ohio River that circumvented Pennsylvania. Rivalry for that connection was fierce, so Washington headed toward his properties along the Monongahela to study and chart the local creeks, streams, falls, and carrying places where canals could link Virginia waters with the west without crossing the Pennsylvania border. The north and south branches of the Potomac River led to smaller tributaries with exotic names like the Great and Little Kanawhas, the Youghiogheny, the Cheat River, Paterson's Creek, Opequon Creek, and some with names like "New," "Sandy," and "the Springs." In Bath, (West Virginia), Washington visited "the situation of my lots therein, which I examined." He perused the configuration of the town and formulated a design for, "the disposition of a dwelling House, Kitchen and Stable . . . [to be] advantageously placed." Washington, the real estate developer, met with sawmill owner and contractor James Rumsey, who promised to

> undertake those Buildings, I have agreed with him to have them
> finished by the 10th of next July. The dwelling House is to be
> 36 feet by 24, with a gallery of 7 feet on each side of the House, the
> whole fronts,—under the House is to be a Cellar half the size of it,

walled with Stone, and the whole underpinned.—on the first floor are to be 3 rooms; one of them 24 by 20 feet, with a chimney at the end (middle thereof) the other two to be 12 by 16 feet with corner chimneys.—on the upper Floor there are to be two Rooms of equal sizes, with fire places; the Stair case to go up in the Gallery.—galleries above also. The Kitchen and Stable are to be of the same size—18 by 22; the first with a stone Chimney and good floor above.—the Stable is to be sunk in the ground so as that the floor above it on the North, or side next the dwelling House, shall be level with the Yard.—to have a partition therein.—the West part of which to be for a Carriage, Harness, and Saddles.—the East for Hay or Grain.—all three of the Houses to be shingled.

The fact that Washington had not only illustrated his design but wrote it out in his own journal in such great detail is telling. Washington knew that his letters and journals would be part of his legacy, and he wanted the world to see him as a builder.

Washington and Rumsey shared passions for construction and for navigation. Washington admitted being filled with wonder when Rumsey showed him a model boat that he had designed "for ascending rapid currents by mechanism." It was in this tiny West Virginia town where Washington, who wrote that he was sworn to "Secresy [sic]" about Rumsey's prototype, began a long association with this ingenious man. James Rumsey would not only assist Washington with the Potomac canal system project but he would also be a codeveloper of the steamboat.

Washington wrote of his repeated efforts to speak with local citizens to learn about where the sources and mouths of tributaries and swamps could be diverted, cleared, and drained so that he could capitalize on linking the Potomac with the Mississippi River through Virginia territories, "in order to avd. [sic] passing through the State of Pennsylvania." Whilst in Bath, Washington also met with Colonel Normand Bruce. The previous year, Bruce and a man named Charles Beatty were tasked by the Maryland state legislature to study the waters that flowed along the Maryland border and produce a report on the "opening, clearing, and making navigable the River Potomack [sic]." Bruce generously offered Washington their findings.

Crisscrossing the branches of the Potomac River, Washington visited some of his properties that contained live mines. It had been chronicled that along the Kanawha lead, iron, limestone, marble, and amethyst had been found. These minerals could make Washington very rich if managed properly. Washington also met up with "a Mr. McCraken . . . whose land joins mine—to offer mine to any who might apply for £10 the first year, £15 the next, and £25 the third—the Tenant not to remove any of the Walnut timber from off the Land; or to split it into Rails; as I should reserve that for my own use."

On the tenth of September, Washington headed northward toward the Monongahela properties he owned in Pennsylvania. Throughly disgusted with Gilbert Simpson, Washington advertised his shares of their joint property for sale. Washington noted downpours, the colorful sight of people hauling ginseng and salt to market, and the forlorn state of his own "Mill, and the several tenements on this Tract (on which Simpson lives)" and received disturbing news that made him change his travel plans. "Murders, and general dissatisfaction of the Indians . . . [made] it rather improper for me to proceed to the Kanhawa [sic] agreeably to my original intention."

His arrival at his two Pennsylvania properties, the one at Great Meadows and the one on Millers Run, caused him distress. The tenant farmer buildings at Great Meaows were in disrepair, "the Mill was quite destitute of water—the works and House appear to be in very bad condition . . . the trunk, which conveys the water to the wheel are in bad order. In a word, little Rent, or good is to be expected from the present aspect of her." His situation at Millers Run was even worse. It turned out that the lands that had been surveyed for Washington by William Crawford and purchased from Mount Vernon neighbor Captain John Posey had also been claimed by a Mr. George Croghan. Croghan sold off parcels of the property to over a dozen different men. These men and their families had lived on and farmed these lands believing they were the rightful owners. On the fourteenth of September, the group of farmers "came here to set forth their pretensions" to the land "and to enquire into my Right." After much discussion about whose deed was flawed, they all agreed to meet again in a couple of days, as Washington would be quite busy the following day.

The fifteenth of September was "the day appointed for the Sale of my moiety. Of the Co-partnership Stock—many People were gathered (more out of curiosity I believe than from other motives) but no great Sale made. My Mill I could obtain no bid for, although I offered an exemption from the payment of Rent 15 Months." Although his properties failed to provide the income stream he had hoped for, Washington noted that "[t]he Plantation on which Mr. Simpson lives rented well" for "500 Bushels of Wheat." Washington decided to follow suit and "set it up to be bid for in Wheat."

On the seventeenth of September Washington formally "close[d] my accts. [sic] with Gilbert Simpson, and put a final end to my Partnership with him." The next day, Washington and Dr. Craik set out for Millers Run to speak with the people that Washington believed were squatting on his land. Washington's diary reveals a bit of sarcasm and irritation with his task ahead: "*19th.* Being Sunday, and the People living on my Land, *apparently* very religious, it was thought best to postpone going among them till tomorrow." In other words, while Washington felt completely comfortable conducting business on a Sunday, he remained in great discomfit waiting for a showdown on Monday.

On Monday, September 20, 1784, George Washington wrote that he "went early this Morning to view my Land, and to receive the final determination of those who live upon it." First, he went to the plantation of Samuel McBride, who, with his brother, James, had served as agents for George Croghan. Washington detailed the character and quality of the properties of James McBride, Thomas Biggart, William Stewart, Matthew Hillast, Brice McGeechen, Duncan McGeechen, David Reed, John Reed Esquire, William Hillas, John Glen, and James Scott and learned the chronicle, the chain of sales, pertaining to each and every parcel. While William Crawford had built a cabin on his land to prove ownership, there had been a succession of transactions while Crawford was away at war.

Although a tradition of adverse possession laws was as old as Hammurabi and had been addressed for centuries in the British legal system, the settlers were most respectful of the fact that they were being challenged by

George Washington. Washington noted in his journal that the farmers began by inquiring

> whether I would part with the Land, and upon what terms; adding, that tho' [sic] they did not conceive they could be dispossessed, yet to avoid contention, they would be if my terms were Moderate. I told them I had no inclination to sell; however, after hearing a great deal of their hardships, their Religious principles (which had brought them together as a society of Ceceders) [Presbyterians] and unwillingness to separate or remove; I told them I would make them a last offer and this was—the whole tract at 25 S. pr. Acre, the money to be paid at 3 annual payments with Interest;—or to become Tenants upon leases of 999 years, at the annual Rent of Ten pounds pr. Ct. pr. Ann.—The former they had a long consultation upon, and asked if I wd. Take that price at a longer credit without Interest, and being answered in the Negative they then determined to stand suit for the Land.

Washington had suspicions that some of the men were being coerced, so he next called each man by name and asked him to stand and state his answer individually. "The business being thus finished," the matter would proceed to court. Washington rode to what today is Uniontown, Pennsylvania, and met with a lawyer at the Washington County Courthouse. There, the two men combed the county papers to ascertain Washington's various deeds and rights, including the parcels of land he had bought from Mount Vernon neighbor Captain John Posey. George Washington filed a lawsuit against the families whom he felt had unlawfully occupied Millers Run. In 1786, he would win the suit and evict the families from his land.

After he completed his business in Washington County, still in pursuit of a water connection that would link the Potomac River with the west, Washington headed south. "I had before been informed by others, that the West fork of the Monongahela communicates very nearly with the waters of the little Kanhawa—that the Portage does not exceed Nine Miles—and that a very good Waggon [sic] Road may be had between." Washington, of course, claimed soldier bounty land along both the Great and Little Kanawha Rivers,[4] but had already determined that it was unsafe to follow their path out toward what today would be Kentucky and Tennessee. Instead, "I resolved to return home . . . with a view to make a more minute enquiry [sic] into the Navigation of the Yohiogany [sic] Waters. My Nephew and I set out about Noon . . . for Cheat River." It was of the utmost importance to Washington to study the flows of the Monongahela and the Cheat Rivers. "The Line which divides the Commonwealths of Virginia and Pennsylvania crosses both these Rivers about two Miles up each from the point of fork." Once again, Washington learned bad news about property he believed was rightfully his:

> From the Fork to the Surveyors Office . . . is about 8 mile . . . at this Office I could obtain no information of any Surveys of Entrie [sic] made for me by Captn. Wm. Crawford; but from an examination of his books it appeared pretty evident that the 2500 acres which he (Crawford) had surveyed for and offered to me on the little Kanhawa [sic] (adjoining the large survey under the proclamation of 1754) he had entered for a Mr. Robert Rutherford—and that the other tract in the fork between the Ohio and little Kanhawa [sic] had been entered by Doctr. Briscoe and Sons.

Despite Washington's frustration with all of these betrayals or sloppiness, he was determined to continue on his mission with regard to navigation. A man named Captain Hanway suggested to Washington that he remain for a day so that he could assemble a group of men familiar with the waters. Washington did so,

> and from them I receive the following intelligence viz . . . from the fork of Monongahela and Cheat, to the Court House at Morgan Town, is by Water, about 11 Miles, and from thence to the West fork of the former is 18 More—from thence to the carrying place between it and a branch of the little Kanhawah [sic], at a place called Bulls town, is about 40 Miles by Land—more by Water—and the Navigation

good. The carrying place is nine Miles and an half between the navigable parts of the two Waters; and a good Road between; there being only one hill in the way, and that not bad—hence to ye Mo. Of the Kanhawa [sic] is 50 Miles. That from the Monongahela Court House 13 Miles along the New Road which leads to Braddock's Road, East of the winding ridge, and McCulloch's path, to one Joseph Logston's on the North branch of Potomack [sic] is about 40 Miles.

Washington's calculations go on for pages from the "Cheat River at the Dunkers bottom (25 Miles from its Mouth)" to glades of the Youghiogheny, the Kanawha, the north branch of the Potomac River, "Clarkes Town," (Clarkstown) and the falls of the"Tyger River Valley" (Tygart). "That the Cheat River where it runs through the Laurel hill is, in their opinion, so incommoded with large Rock stones, rapid and dashing water from one Rock to another, as to become impassable . . . they do not think a passage sufficient to admit a Canal can be found between the Hills and the common bed of the River." Based on his amalgamation of accounts, Washington determined that "no part of the Cheat River runs nearer to the navigable part of the No. branch of Potomack [sic] than the Dunkers bottom does." He had found what he was looking for. His voyage "left no doubt on my Mind of the practicability of opening an easy passage by Water to the Dunker bottom."

Though he had planned to travel for another three weeks, Washington heeded warnings about hostile Native Americans and reluctantly headed homeward, through property that belonged to his friend and former governor of Maryland Thomas Johnson. "A Mile before I came to Friends, I crossed the Great branch of Yohiogany . . . but then, the Yohiogany lyes [sic] altogether in the State of Pennsylvania whose inclination . . . would be opposed to the extension of this [Washington's plan] navigation, as it would be the inevitable means of withdrawing from them the trade of all their western territory." Washington also noted that he would find similar obstruction from those who wanted to link the James River in southern Virginia with central tributaries to reach the west. Washington wrote that despite the fact that "a branch of

Jackson's [Creek], which is the principal prong of James River to the Mouth of Howards Creek wch. Empties into the Greenbrier a large branch of New River abe. Great Kanhawa [sic]," he had his heart set on the Potomac as the premier waterway from the Atlantic Ocean to the Mississippi River. The Virginia Port Bill had made the intrastate competition abundantly clear; not only would he have to fight Marylanders, Pennsylvanians, and New Yorkers, but he would also have to fight fellow Virginians for primacy.

Washington intended to meet Dr. Craik at the home of Colonel Warner Washington, the former commander in chief's first cousin, who lived near Winchester. Instead, Washington proceeded to the Staunton office of Thomas Lewis to search for more papers that would further his case against the squatters at Millers Run. Washington also wanted to "obtain a more distinct acct.[sic] of the Communication between Jackson's River and the green Brier." On October 1, Washington dined with "Mr. Gabriel Jones . . . not a half mile from Mr. Lewis's, but separated by the South Fork of Shanandoah [the river]; which is between 80 and a hundred yards wide and makes a respectable appearance." Washington was very pleased with the time he spent with Mr. Jones, whose knowledge of the western Virginia waters shored up Washington's hopes that his Potomac dreams could become reality:

> I had a good deal of conversation with this Gentleman [Mr. Jones] on the Waters, and trade of the Western County; and particularly with respect to the Navigation of the Great Kanhawa [sic] and its communication with James and Roanoke Rivers.
>
> His opinion is, that the easiest and best communication between the Eastern and Western Waters is from the North branch of Potomack [sic] to Yohiogany or Cheat River; and ultimately that the Trade between the two Countries will settle in this Channel. That although [sic] James River has an easy and short Creek to the Green brier which in distance and kind of Country is exactly as Logston described them, yet that the passage of the New River, abe. Kanhawa [sic], thro' the gauly [sic] Mountain from every acct. he has had of it, now is, and ever will be attended with considerable difficulty.

On October 4, 1784, George Washington "reached home before Sun down; having travelled on the same horses since the first day of September by the computed distances 680 Miles." At Mount Vernon, Washington expanded his journal so that he could present it as a public document: "the preceeding [sic] Statement, which . . . is given from the best and most authentic Maps and papers in my possession . . . and partly from observation." His journey had only reinforced his sense of urgency to link those who were settling the wilderness before they established markets with, and turned their allegiance to, Spain or British Canada.

> And tho' I was disappointed in one of the objects which induced me to take this journey namely to examine into the situation quality and advantages of the Land which I hold upon the Ohio and Great Kanawha [sic]—and to take measures for rescuing them from the hands of Land Jobbers and Speculators—who I had been informed regardless of my legal and equitable rights, patents, &ca.; had enclosed them within other Surveys and were offering them for Sale at Philadelphia and in Europe.—I say notwithstanding this disappointment I am well pleased with my journey, as it has been the means of my obtaining a knowledge of facts . . . The more then the Navigation of Potomack [sic] is investigated, and duly considered, the greater the advantages arising from them appear . . . The Ohio River embraces this Commonwealth from its Northern, almost to its Southern limits . . . into this River French Creek, big bever Creek, Muskingham, Hockhocking, Scioto, and the two Miames [sic] (in its upper Region) and many others (in the lower) pour themselves from the westward through one of the most fertile Countries of the Globe . . . so many channels through which not only the produce of the New States contemplated by Congress, but the trade of all the lakes quite to that of the Wood [Lake of the Woods, west of Lake Superior], may be conducted according to my information, and judgment—at least by one of the Routs [sic]—thro' a shorter,

easier, and less expensive communication than either of those which are now, or have been used with Canada, New Yk. or New Orleans.

Washington affixed a table of measurements that charted all potential water routes to and from Detroit. "From Detroit to Richmond" was 840 miles. "From Detroit to Alexandria" avoiding Pennsylvania was 799 miles. "From Detroit to Albany" was 783 miles. It was another 160 miles from Albany downriver to New York City, according to Washington's table. In Washington's mind, more likely, in his hopes and dreams, Alexandria would prevail as the gateway city to the continent. Unfortunately for Washington, as he well knew, while the waterway from Albany to New York City offered smooth sailing, only a few miles upriver from Alexandria lay two sets of falls with giant boulders right across the Potomac River that would prove nearly impossible to clear.

On October 10, 1784, four days after his return, George Washington included that table of water route measurements to and from Detroit along with a letter to Virginia Governor Benjamin Harrison that in essence placed George Washington in the role of lobbyist:

I shall take the liberty now, my dear sir, to suggest a matter, which would (if I am not too short sighted [sic] a politician) mark your administration as an important oera [sic] in the Annals of this Country, if it should be recommended by you, & adopted by the Assembly.

It has been long my decided opinion, that the shortest, easiest & least expensive communication with the invaluable & extensive Country back of us, would be by one, or both of the rivers of this State which have their sources in the apalachian [sic] mountains. Nor am I singular in this opinion—Evans, in his Map and Analysis of the middle Colonies . . . And Hutchins since, in his topographical description of the Western Country . . . are decidedly of the same sentiments; as indeed are all others wo have had opportunities, & have been at the pains to investigate, & consider the subject.

Washington stated his case for the political necessity of strengthening ties with the western settlements and provided Governor Harrison with the motivation to act:

> Maryland stands upon similar ground with Virginia. Pennsylvania . . . have it in contemplation to open a communication between Toby's Creek (which empties into the Alleghany river, 95 miles above Fort Pitt) . . . they are smoothing the roads & paving the ways for the trade of that Western World. That New York will do the same so soon as the British Garrisons are removed . . . no person who knows the temper, genius & policy of those people as well as I do, can harbour [sic] the smallest doubt.

Washington assured Governor Harrison that jealousy within the state itself—"lest one part of the state should obtain an advantage over the other"—should be waved aside. Cognizant of the fact that, as the capital city of the state of New York, New York City would receive generous funding to build ports, in Washington's home state of Virginia, it was Richmond that received state largesse. Washington skillfully worked at convincing the governor that diverting funds to invest in the port of Alexandria would enhance the state with immeasurable returns. Washington, again revealing his predilection for government involvement in economic development, challenged the governor to create a "stimulas." Success, explained Washington, would "*force*" a "spirit" of cooperation that would subsume any resentment on the part of the people. Washington was not above the hard sell: Virginians will derive great benefits from, "the fur & peltry trade of the Lakes . . . & the produce of the Country . . . so soon as matters are settled with the Indians, & the terms on which Congress mean to dispose of the Land . . . [Americans will] settle faster than any other ever did, or any one would imagine." He then recopied for Harrison his journal observations about ensuring the loyalty of the western citizens, many of which would occupy lands claimed as Virginia territory. In case Harrison were to think that the rocky falls along the way were too impracticable to navigate, Washington wrote of Rumsey's miracle of design: "for working Boats against stream, by mechanical powers . . . a very fortunate invention . . . one of those circumstances which have combined to render the present epocha [sic] favourable [sic] above all others for fixing, if we are disposed to avail ourselves of them, a large portion of the trade of the Western Country in the bosom of this State irrevocably." To make the point that he was so passionate about this subject that he had "indented to have written a fuller & more digested" letter, Virginia's greatest hero closed by stating that, he was jumping back into public life with,"motives [that] are pure."

The floodgates opened. On October 15, Stephen Sayre once again wrote Washington that he could raise money in Europe for Washington's Potomac Canal Company. On October 20, George Plater, president of the Maryland State Senate, who had visited with Washington before Washington's western trip, wrote,

> Since I had the Honor of visiting you I have been revolving in my Head the Subject of our Conversation respecting the opening the Potowmack [sic], Advancing the Trade of the back & new settled Countries [in] these middle States & the more I consider it, the more I am impressed with the Utility & Advantages resulting therefrom—So much so, that I am determined to press the Measure in our Assembly, which will soon meet, & I hope we shall be joined by Virginia—To enable me to do it with more Effect, I take the Liberty to entreat the Favor of you, in some Leisure Moment, to give me as concisely as you please, some Description of the Waters in the back Country, the Land Carriage unavoidably necessary, & what other Information you may deem important.

Washington replied on October 25, the day after he received Plater's letter, with the salient points of his travel journal, which he repeated in a November 3 note to South Carolina congressman Jacob Read.

Washington was stepping up to lead with vigor. He placed an advertisement in *The Virginia Journal and Alexandria Advertiser* that appeared on November 2, 1784:

A Meeting is proposed of the Gentlemen of the States of Virginia and
Maryland, especially those who live contiguous to Potomack [sic] and
wish to see an attempt made to open and extend the navigation of that
River—The objects of this meeting will be to form a company, and
determine on the propriety of preferring a petition to their respective
Assemblies praying to be incorporated and favoured [sic] with such
immunities, as to them may seem proper for such an undertaking—
The advantages which both States must derive from the completion
of this work, are so numerous and so obvious, that it is hoped this
notice will be generally attended to, and that Gentlemen will come
prepared to offer such advice and support, as the importance of the
plan requires—The meeting is to be at Mr. Lomax's on Monday,
the 15th inst. At 10 o'clock A.M.

On November 13, Colonel Normand Bruce of Maryland, with whom Washington had met on his western journey, submitted to Washington a

Proposal, That provided the Legislatures of Virginia & Maryland will
Emit [sic] the Sum of 500,000 Dollars, which they will grant upon
Loan to the Subscribers or otherways [sic] Vest them with the Priv-
eledge [sic] of Emitting [sic] and of Circulating such a Sum for and
during the term of Ten Years from the date of the Grant or Emission—
In consideration whereof they will engage to expend the Sum of [ ]
Dollars within the Space of [ ] Years . . . The said Sum of 500,000 dollars
shall be subscribed for and divided into (either 125 or 250) Shares.

Bruce's outline went on for pages about governors, trustees, cash accounts,
and voting rights.

The most important point of Bruce's blueprint for Washington was that,
once again, Washington was gaining momentum for cooperation between
two states. *The Virginia Journal and Alexandria Advertiser* reported that the
November 15 meeting, which was attended by citizens of both Maryland and
Virginia, was successful:

On Monday the 15th Instant, at a very numerous and respectable
Meeting of the Gentlemen of this State and Maryland, convened by
public Advertisement at Mr Lomax's Tavern, to deliberate and consult
on the vast, great political and commercial Object, *the rendering navigable the River Potomack* [sic] *from Tide Water*—It was unanimously
Resolved, That every possible Effort ought to be exerted to render
these waters navigable to their utmost Sources.

On December 4, the newspaper again published an article that reinforced
interstate cooperation, stating that a canal that enabled boats to bypass the
Great Falls on the Potomac was "one of the grandest chains for preserving
the Federal Union."

Washington did not attend the November 15 meeting in Alexandria. On
November 14, the day before the summit at Mr. Lomax's tavern, Washington
arrived in Richmond, the state capital, to gain legislative support and funding
for the project. Washington was joined in Richmond by his new Potomac River
ally, state assemblyman James Madison, and the Marquis de Lafayette, both of
whom had just visited with the Schuyler family in Albany and had toured the
Mohawk Valley and the waterways of New York State. Washington expressed
his wishes for the Potomac River development to the assembly, presented a
draft of a bill to create a Potomac River Company, and then returned to Mount
Vernon with Lafayette. The French nobleman remained at Mount Vernon with
Washington for a few days at which time the pair set out together for Annapolis. Washington bid Lafayette adieu on the road to Baltimore, as the French
nobleman was scheduled to return to France from New York Harbor, which
had also been his port of arrival. From New York, Lafayette would write James
Madison: "I Have much Conferred with the General [Washington] Upon the
Pottowmack [sic] System. Many people think the Navigation of the Mississipy
[sic] is not an advantage—But it May Be the Excess of a very good thing Viz
the opening of your Rivers."[5]

George Washington remained in Annapolis. Unlike the plan envisioned
by Philip Schuyler to link the waterways within one state, the Potomac River
bordered two states—Virginia and Maryland—but was under the legal control

of the state of Maryland. All of Washington's hopes were pinned on persuading the Maryland state assembly to cooperate with Virginia in the development of the Potomac River. Sadly, Washington not only overestimated the spirit of cooperation between the two states but, as he had cautioned, the nation unified in war was now quarreling within.

The thirteen states were bickering over borders, toll collections, divergent monies, and where to locate their capital city. Though the seat of government had removed to Trenton, New Jersey, on November 1, 1784, on November 7, Virginia delegate to the Congress of the Confederation Samuel Hardy, who was still on the road to Trenton, wrote Virginia Governor Harrison: "It seems generally agreed that we shall not remain at Trenton, & as generally supposed that the remove will be either to this place, or New York." On November 12, Virginia Congressman John Francis Mercer referred to "an itinerant [sic] Congress" in a note he wrote James Madison. The body could not even summon a quorum. Representatives who bothered to attend sessions grumbled that Trenton offered insufficient space to conduct meetings for the nation's business. On November 30, after Virginian Richard Henry Lee was elected president of the Congress of the Confederation, members began to scatter.

George Washington, however, stubbornly remained in Annapolis as the Christmas holiday approached. The Maryland assembly continued to resist his project. A frustrated Washington wrote James Madison that the disobliging Maryland legislature might force him to implement an alternative plan: "if the public cannot take it up with efficient funds, & without . . . delays . . . it had better be placed in the hands of a corporate Company." On December 3, Washington again expressed his irritation with "ill-grounded jealousies" that would likely result in no money from the state of Maryland. What was needed, Washington reiterated was a "private company" with the "spirit for enterprize [sic]" comprised of "private gentlemen" who possessed "mercantile funds." On December 5, 1784, a weary George Washington wrote Henry Knox: "I am now endeavoring to stimulate my Countrymen to the extension of the inland navigation of the rivers Potomac and James . . . to connect the Western Territory by strong commercial bands . . . I hope I shall succeed." On December 11, James Madison wrote Richard Henry Lee that, although the "scheme for opening the navigation of the Potomac . . . will be favoured [sic]" by the Virginia legislature, "as the concurrence of Maryland in this scheme is necessary, some difficulties will attend its progress." There was little alleviation in the rivalry amongst the states on the topics of water rights, "resolution respecting the roads of Communication,"[6] and certainly not on the location of the nation's capital city.

On December 20, 1784, with most of the congress's members gone, New Yorker John Jay arrived at the Congress of the Confederation in Trenton. Jay was not a delegate to the Congress of the Confederation. Neither was Alexander Hamilton at that time, despite the fact that he has been persistently accused of leading the vote that December to remove the seat of government to New York City.[7] The previous July, when Jay had returned from France, he learned that he had been appointed secretary for foreign affairs. After five months, Jay had still not agreed to assume the post because, simply, he wanted to remain in New York City. Jay joined the members of the Congress of the Confederation of the United States on December 20, 1784, encamped in the damp and dingy French Arms Tavern in Trenton, New Jersey, and repeated his conditions.

The legislators listened but resolved to create a permanent seat of government in the vicinity of the "falls of Trenton." The next morning, Charles Pinckney of South Carolina introduced a motion to repeal the decree. The motion passed, and a federal government adjacent to the Trenton, New Jersey falls cascaded into oblivion. A tiny new tool known as the eraser precluded the United States Congress from making an indelible, eternal mistake. Over the next three days, Annapolis, Philadelphia, Georgetown, and Newport were all voted on and expunged, and the line remained blank. Finally, on December 24, an exasperated David Howell of Rhode Island suggested New York City. Facing inclement weather and aching to leave for Christmas, those hardiest members who had remained in Trenton voted 22–4 in favor of the motion, and without further excise congress adjourned. John Jay returned home to New York City with the news that he was now the new secretary of foreign affairs and, as of January 11, 1785, New York City would be the seat of the federal government of the United States of America.

Still in Annapolis on Christmas Eve 1784, Washington, famous for his endurance, confessed to a friend that he was completely exhausted from his lengthy meetings and burdensome work on behalf of his Potomac River project. He remained in Annapolis through Christmas, and, on December 28, 1784, George Washington wrote James Madison, "It is now near 12 at night, and I am writing with an Aching head, having been constantly employed with this business." At last, on New Year's Eve, Washington succeeded in gaining an agreement from the Maryland assembly to permit development of the Potomac River.

Washington had spent his entire life looking out over the Potomac River and her tributaries, from his small birthplace in Westmoreland County to the Mount Vernon plantation he inherited upon the death of his brother and called home. At fourteen years old, Washington had measured her shorelines and river bottoms to feed his family. As a young soldier, he journeyed northward then westward above the Great and Little Falls and southward along her interior branches that flowed along the terrestrial empire he would amass. Both Washington and Philip Schuyler gazed at the stars from America's waters and, like Pytheas, they imagined and envisioned infinite horizons—vistas that Hadley's Quadrant had yet to measure.

Washington had fought in two wars so that American men could seize control of and dominate the continent and her natural resources. At the close of 1784, George Washington, through his own exertions and doggedness, had won another revolution. It was quiet but seismic. Washington's New Year's Eve agreement would move the Virginia power base from the aristocracy in the south, whose James and York River estates had defined Virginia society for 150 years, to the upstart port town of Alexandria, drafted in the mind of a seventeen-year-old George Washington.

The rivalry for America's capital city would now narrow to a tale of two cities.

CHAPTER 8

Cousins and Climbers: New York

THE CONGRESS OF THE CONFEDERATION voted to spend no more than $100,000 to construct a capitol building in New York City. They were spared the expense because, within days of the December 1784 vote to remove the federal seat of government to New York City, an energized group of wealthy New Yorkers, with Philip Schuyler at the head of the planning committee, immediately raised $40,000 to remodel a once-grand building on Wall Street. The New York clans wanted to ensure that in New York City the congress could assemble in style and comfort. New Yorkers, unlike the residents of other places where the congress had been mistreated, were enthusiastic about hosting the congress and hoped that the federal government would remain there. New Yorkers sealed their reputation of doing it bigger, faster, and better than anyone by rebuilding and revitalizing their city so that it quickly became the most cosmopolitan metropolis of the burgeoning nation.

George Washington's departure from New York after Evacuation Day had left behind a still destabilized city. Once the victory celebrations were over, New York City got down to business with ferocity. The city's economic, social, and political renaissance was shaped and steered by five couples: Governor George Clinton and his wife, Sarah Cornelia Tappen Clinton; the newly

appointed mayor of New York City, James Duane, and his childhood sweet-
heart, Mary Livingston Duane; Alexander Hamilton and his wife, Elizabeth
"Betsey" Schuyler Hamilton; William Duer, America's first hedge-fund tycoon,
and his wife, "Lady Kitty" Alexander; and John and Sarah—"Sally"—Jay.
Mrs. Duer, Mrs. Jay, and Mrs. Duane were all first cousins. All of the wives
and John Jay were members of the *stams*, the Dutch clans whose generations
of interconnected marriages mirrored the royal houses of Europe, creating
inestimably rich families with vast landholdings embanked along New York
Harbor and the Hudson River for miles and miles.[1] The waterways northward
toward Lake Champlain, west along the Mohawk River, and south into New
York Harbor created a conduit for American products and a monopoly for
the clans. Along with their land patents and feudal system of entitlement,
these princess brides were legated doweries of wealth and education. Their
husbands, all lawyers with success stories as soldiers and statesmen, were
widely admired for their combined prodigious intelligence and forceful drive.

The John Jays, Alexander Hamiltons, William Duers, George Clintons, and
James Duanes abandoned the vast estates of their patroon parents in favor of a
more urban lifestyle. These scions of New York privilege rejected the mournful
refrains for the life of Cincinnatus, and, with contacts, cash, and an infusion
of enterprising new blood in the families, they converged on the petri dish of
New York City to contour its cultural, social, political, and economic structure.
A seven-ward local government was reestablished, and on February 5, 1784,
Governor George Clinton appointed James Duane, who was widely respected
for his logical mind and fairness, to the position of mayor of New York.

At the time, the job of mayor of New York City was an appointment and
not an elected position. Duane, who had already distinguished himself as an
eloquent member of the Congress of the Confederation, was the son of an Irish
Protestant immigrant named Anthony Duane and his wife, Althea Keteltas
of Dutch stock, who was the sister of Continental Congressman Reverend
Abraham Keteltas. Orphaned as a young boy, James Duane became the ward
of Robert Livingston, Third Lord of the Manor. In constant and close contact
with Livingston's daughter Mary, young James fell in love. His sentiments
were reciprocated, and the pair married. James Duane did not disappoint

his guardian/father-in-law. He worked alongside John Jay as a member of the Committee of Sixty, the group that had organized the revolution in New York, and again with Jay as one of the drafters of the New York State Constitution. When the British invaded New York in 1776, Duane packed up his children and wife and sent them to Livingston Manor, where they remained for the duration of the war. On Evacuation Day, James Duane got to ride in the limelight right behind General George Washington. Clinton's selection of James Duane for the position of mayor of New York City was a public acknowledgement of Duane's accomplishments as well as a signal to Mary's powerful father, who had supported Clinton's election for governor against his own cousin, Philip Schuyler.

After serving his country as minister to Spain and as signatory of the 1783 Treaty of Paris, John Jay and is wife, Sarah, the daughter of New Jersey Governor William Livingston, sailed into New York Harbor on July 24, 1784, not having seen their own little son for four and a half years. The Jays could have chosen to live on the Jay family estate on the Long Island Sound on any number of Livingston properties along the Hudson, or they could have lived an idyllic and privileged life with Sally's family at Liberty Hall in New Jersey. Instead, the Jays moved to 8 Broadway, on the east side of the street just south of Exchange Place in Lower Manhattan. Jay, described by people he passed on the street as always deep in thought and possessing the kind of pallor and serious demeanor of an intellectual, would walk to his new law office at Broad and Pearl Street to engage in the tumult of reconstructing New York City rather than indulging in the pastoral privileges of his forebears.

Eton-educated William Duer, born in England, had already had several careers by the end of the War of Independence. Once a soldier in India and a planter in the Caribbean, Duer became a wildly rich entrepreneur trading with Philip Schuyler. Duer was a patriot during the war when it suited his purpose. Considered a very shady character, who was suspected of smuggling as well as profiteering from military supply deals, Duer also headed for New York City shortly after the British evacuation, traveling with his family, "caravan" style, as his son would later describe. The Duers rode by the dismounted cannon at the Old Fort and down the west side past the "Burnt District," destroyed by a massive fire in 1776 and later acts of arson committed by the British. Duer, who wanted to improve his image, had married Lady Kitty, whose profligate father, the self-styled "Lord Stirling," essentially "sold" her to Duer after his own fortunes had crumbled during the war. Alexander Duer's trajectory would be the exact opposite of the one traveled by Alexander Hamilton: Duer had first allied himself in business with Schuyler and then married a Livingston; Hamilton was first the young mentee of New Jersey Governor William Livingston[2] and then married a Schuyler.

Unlike Theodosia Bartow Burr, the wife of Schuyler-Hamilton nemesis Aaron Burr, who was the widow of a British soldier and who, according to contemporaneous reports, "did not go out in society," and whom Burr privately derided and dismissed as dull and unintelligent, the Mesdames Duane, Hamilton, Jay, Clinton, and Duer shone with brilliance in the public arena and had an enormous impact on their city and country. The elegant Lady Kitty, with two in livery serving at her table, would arrange bank loans for her husband as he increased his holdings as well as his debts. Armed with information digested about timber, shipping contracts, leases, stocks, bonds, and Revolutionary War debt, Lady Kitty became her husband's "iron hand in the velvet glove" liaison with her Livingston investor cousins.

While it was said that John Jay preferred receding from attention, his wife, Sarah Livingston Jay, was confident being center stage. The couple was madly in love and would often exchange tender notes. As the wife of the new secretary of foreign affairs, Sally Jay was the group's stealth weapon and best ambassadress for international relations. Having lived in Spain and in Paris while her husband served as foreign minister, and having more than once been mistaken for Queen Marie Antoinette, Sarah Livingston Jay served as the perfect queen of a capital city, hosting sophisticated evenings that mirrored the courts in Europe. She was the sparkling reminder on every Tuesday evening—her "night"—that nowhere in America would any hard-working politician be better and more completely sated and amused. Every Tuesday evening, her dinners—served *à la mode française*—featured breathtaking presentations of lobster, shrimp, lamb, veal, puddings, ice creams, exotic fruits, and confections bought from Joseph Corre on Wall Street and Adam Pryor on Broadway. The wines that were served came from cases sent to them by Thomas Jefferson in Paris. Sally Jay singlehandedly established New York City as a haute cuisine destination. Her home would be the only New York City home to which the persnickety French ambassador did not bring his own chef when invited for dinner.[3] Glamorous Francophile Sarah Livingston Jay was the undisputed style doyenne of New York society. One can see her influence on the other elite female members of the clans. The portrait of "Lady Kitty" Duer depicts her with her hair in a giant poof, favored by Queen Marie Antoinette of France. The usually understated Betsey Schuyler Hamilton uncharacteristically furnished her New York City home in the ornate style of Louis XVI and, claiming Wednesday evenings as her "open house," had it all on display for *le tout* New York.

It was said at the time: "The Clintons have power; the Livingstons have numbers; and the Schuylers have Hamilton." Alexander Hamilton's wife, Betsey— aside from her obvious pedigree—was arguably indispensable to Hamilton's career. The two were opposites: he was dashing and tempestuous, she, rather plain and levelheaded; and, while he could succumb to the temptations of luxury, she remained thrifty (except for the *Louis Seize* décor). She bore several children, which gave Hamilton the stable home life he had craved as a child, and implanted him into an extended and respectable family. Her father, Philip Schuyler, became Hamilton's emotional, financial, and intellectual father figure and political rudder. At their 57 Wall Street home, Betsey would assist her husband in drafting his legal briefs, his essays bound for publication, and in some of what would become among the most important political documents in the history of the United States.

These Founding Mothers of New York City would enhance their husbands' careers, serve as the public representatives of their families, and consciously and conscientiously set the tone and pace that would characterize New York City for over two centuries: they guided social justice, health, and education charities, encouraged legal reform, and fostered European-American friendship.

On January 8, 1785, New York Governor George Clinton greeted the newly elected president of the Congress of the Confederation, Virginian Richard Henry Lee, and the delegates to the legislative body who had made the hazardous winter journey. Neither Alexander Hamilton, nor John Jay, nor James

Madison, nor John Adams, nor Benjamin Franklin, nor Thomas Jefferson were among those elected to serve in the 1785 session of the congress. When the members of the nearly bankrupt Congress of the Confederation began conducting the nation's business on January 11, 1785, to their astonishment, they were received with great respect and hailed with a lavish reception. Offered a refurbished city hall, reconstituted as Federal Hall, which was largely funded by Philip Schuyler, a number of the legislators wrote home that, having previously felt underappreciated, they now felt grateful for the largesse bestowed upon them by a community that had been war-ravaged. On the very day of the congress's opening session, Philip Schuyler wrote his son-in-law Alexander Hamilton from Albany: "Congress I hear is at New York. Will you be good enough to communicate now & then what they are about. I am not yet without hopes of making you a visit with Mrs. Schuyler."

Two days later, on January 13, 1785, New York City's Chamber of Commerce entertained the delegates at a banquet at the Coffee House. The Congressional representatives were impressed to be feted by both municipal and state dignitaries as well as foreign representatives, who had also, with no small amount of calculation, been invited to celebrate the heretofore-maligned federal government. In early February, this same Chamber of Commerce, taking full advantage of its honeymoon with the federal government, asked for special support for New York State paper currency. New Yorkers had repeatedly balked at federal interference in New York State business but, because in 1785, each state still had its own currency and would often place steep import taxes on merchandise arriving from other states, New Yorkers were hoping for a fiscal advantage. The New York merchants, who, again, had been displeased on a number of occasions when the federal government intervened, superseding local authority, petitioned the congress for yet another business intercession. Upset that the British were undercutting prices and that Americans simply could not compete, the New York Chamber of Commerce requested that the congress enforce Article IX to regulate trade. On March 28, the congress replied to the New York Chamber of Commerce concerning the paper currency that, much as it viewed New York as integral to the prosperity of the nation, "the power of relief is not within the compass of the federal resources." In other words, the congress finally behaved in accordance with what New Yorkers had previously preferred but was now contradictory: the Congress of the Confederation refused to intrude in interstate matters.

In the little more than one year since the British had evacuated Manhattan, resilient New Yorkers had torn into the rubble with vengeance, and their city literally rose from the ashes. In January 1785, New York City was teeming with renewed vitality and commotion. Ship whistles, hammers and saws, animal squeals, and street market noise created a vibrant reparation opera buffa. The older houses on the island had been made of wood, many of which had been destroyed by fire and looting during the war. In 1785, 3,340 houses would rise in the city proper. Within four years the population would approach 30,000 with 4,200 houses standing. In the small area that comprised New York City in 1785, which today is broadly termed "the Wall Street area," people could see from their windows the New Jersey, Brooklyn, and Staten Island shores and the little islands that dotted the harbor.

The years under British occupation had cut New York City off from the rest of America. After the war, New York City became a travel hub, requiring large-scale infrastructure transformation. Stagecoach companies began regular runs in order to encourage enterprise and tourism and to facilitate the journeys for the men of the congress and their families. In April 1785, a ten-year monopoly for the east side of the Hudson River was granted to the enterprising men Isaac van Wyck, Talmage Hall, and John Kinney, whose carriages left for Albany from the front of Fraunces Tavern on the southeast corner of Pearl Street. Boston stages left at three in the morning on Monday, Wednesday, and Friday. They departed from Bowery Lane, which began at St. Paul's Chapel on Broadway and went up the Post Road through Harlem and eastward. They journeyed every day until ten at night, and the trip took six days. Recurrent travel required road widening.

Regular service to Philadelphia was boosted with ferry support from Lower Manhattan to New Jersey. Today's Battery Park was underwater. Ferries transported passengers to New Jersey from what today is Greenwich Street. Then, from Paulus Hook, a stagecoach would leave twice daily, except on Saturdays and Sundays, when it would depart only once a day. In 1785, the trip to Philadelphia from Lower Manhattan took three days. In addition to the commuter boats, postwar trade activity at New York Harbor docks, which had picked up especially with the French and the West Indies, necessitated wharf improvements. The rapid pace of new construction—new ordinances demanded brick rather than wood—necessitated the organization of the Mutual Assurance Company Against Fire, whose twenty-four members signed a contract drafted by Alexander Hamilton.

The sturdy new piers brought big profits to the city's shores. In the spring of 1784, the first American ship loaded with goods for Asia set sail. Before and during the war, the British East India Company had controlled a monopoly of trade with China. Almost as if it were a sign—and people saw it that way—the *Empress of China* arrived in New York Harbor on May 19, 1785, practically simultaneously with the arrival of the Congress of the Confederation earlier in the year, with not only a $30,000 profit—a 30 percent return in a year—for its investors, but also with the assurance that the American flag aboard ship had been treated with great respect by the Chinese. The establishment of direct trade with China opened up a new world and limitless possibilities for both New Yorkers and Americans in general. Before and during the war, New Yorkers had set sail on British vessels; now the Americans began to build ships for themselves— and for the British. Another milestone occurred in the spring of 1785 when a ship laden with cotton bales sailed up the coast from South Carolina to New York Harbor. This vessel, bound for Liverpool, England, launched the cotton-trade triangle that established New York Harbor as an essential trade component to the sale of southern cotton for nearly one hundred years.[4]

Thousands of patriot soldiers and their war brides, who had amply demon-strated courage and resourcefulness during the war, poured into the streets of postwar Lower Manhattan to resurrect or seek their fortunes. They were now in a hurry to make up for years of lost time. They came from New England, from the south, and from the trenches—while a number of European sympathizers, who had come to fight the patriot cause, also decided to stay and struggle for prosperity. These New York City immigrants helped bring the population of civilians back to the 25,000 or so that New York City had enjoyed before the War of Independence.

As opposed to the abstemious and religiously homogenous towns of Boston (Puritan) or Philadelphia (Quaker), New York had been established by the Dutch as a commercial center. It had always been a tolerant melting pot where one could hear twenty different languages spoken on the streets and in the emporiums of the city. In England, all Jews—even baptized ones—were limited in their business activities, but Jews in New York had been able to enjoy complete liberty since the seventeenth century. Jews belonged to the Chamber of Commerce and were members of the Freemasons. The New York State Constitution also provided for freedom of worship to Catholics, which had been banned in other states.

The post–Revolutionary War cultural cacophony of Jewish, German, French, Italian, Spanish, Portuguese, Swedish, Dutch, and Irish vendors at the Catherine Market sold to rich and poor alike. Among the immigrant population was a twenty-one-year-old German named John Jacob Astor, who began sending furs to England, and, using his profits, famously accumulated a sizeable quantity of plots of available land in Manhattan. Eclectic emporiums like Robert Bowne's shop purveyed Madeira wines and mahogany bedsteads. New Yorkers could now enjoy the new, longer-lasting Argand oil lamps, admired by Franklin and Jefferson in Paris. Palaces of luxury began to open, like the Sign of the Rose on Pearl Street, which sold perfume, and Francis Panton, a jeweler on Wall Street. New Yorkers had shed their somber wartime costumes for silks in brighter colors, often splashed with flowers and embroideries, and trimmed with plumes. French visitor John Hector St. John de Crèvecoeur wrote home that women in New York City wore "the most brilliant silks, gauzes, hats and borrowed hair." Flashy European haute couture for both men and women, while de rigueur in New York, were looked at a bit more suspiciously by more conservative Boston and Philadelphia. As New York established itself as the fashion capital, satellite businesses such as wigmakers, hairdressers, cobblers, and palaces of luxury thrived.

Elegant dress had to be displayed in the proper setting, like the John Street Theatre, organized dances, sumptuous dinner parties with flowing liquor, and rendezvous spaces that transformed wreckage into places of delight. The old British Fort George would later be replaced by Castle Garden, a fashionable resort where New Yorkers could stroll and enjoy the sea air. New Yorkers could also choose to roam picturesque paths and marvel at artistically sculpted fountains and grottos while they savored cooling refreshments at Vauxhall's near the Hudson River at Greenwich Street. For a livelier experience, the racetrack called the Maidenhead, which opened right behind the old De Lancey property on the Lower East Side, provided another kind of temptation. Brannon's pleasure gardens stood on the southwest corner of today's Spring Street and Hudson.

The northern end of the city proper, called the "Fields," was located where City Hall now stands. The Fresh Water Pond, upon which the future King William IV of England had skated on the frozen ice (also known as Collect Pond), was Manhattan's forty-eight-acre main water supply for not only drinking but also laundry. It was not unusual to see dead animals float by. To the southeast of Collect Pond had been the Native American settlement known as Werpoes. This had been the home of the Munsee, the tribe believed to have negotiated with the Dutch for the sale of the island. To the northeast, the 110-foot-high imposing Bayard's Mount, the tallest hill in Lower Manhattan, loomed as a reminder of the Bayard family, divided by the war.

Forty percent of all households within a ten-mile radius of New York City owned slaves, which was a higher proportion than in any southern state; by the late 1780s, African Americans made up ten percent of the city's total population. Freed African Americans lived a bit north of the city hub in a quarter called "Greenwich," today known as Greenwich Village. Thousands of African Americans promised their liberty by the British nonetheless faced the constant danger of bounty hunters because the Continental Congress had guaranteed them nothing. Alarmed for the African American community by a wave of kidnapping, George Clinton, John Jay, James Duane, and Alexander Hamilton joined forces and formed the New York Manumission Society. The group held its first meeting on May 12, 1785, at the Coffee House. John Jay, who owned five slaves, became president. Clinton owned eight. Aaron Burr, who owned four or five slaves, was persuaded to join shortly thereafter. The nouveau riche William Duer and Alexander Macomb, who had twenty-five servants in his New York City mansion, each held more than ten slaves in their households. Hamilton's father-in-law, Philip Schuyler, owned twenty-seven slaves that lived between his farm at Saratoga and his Albany mansion. These numbers pale, however, in comparison with those of George Washington and Thomas Jefferson, who both owned over 200 slaves. The good intentions of the Manumission Society and high ideals of its members did not prevail, as the state legislature simply could not persuade upstate farmers to agree to abolition. Free Blacks could neither vote nor hold office, therefore they had no voice. A tremendous inroad was made, however, when the Manumission Society succeeded in obtaining the passage of a law prohibiting the sale of slaves into the state. The persistent leaders of the Manumission Society would continue to lobby, and in 1788, New York State would enact another law forbidding the purchase of any slave for export (even to another state) and permitting unprecedented trial by jury for African Americans in capital cases. With the help of their wives, Jay, Hamilton, Clinton, and Duane would establish the African Free School that same year, which, by the early 1790s, would educate both boys and girls of color.

In addition to the Manumission Society, the Jays, Hamiltons, Clintons, Duanes, and Duers all showed solidarity when it came to civic causes and philanthropy. In 1785, John Jay became a warden of Trinity Church, which had been destroyed by fire. When Betsey Schuyler Hamilton discovered that artist Ralph Earl had been locked in debtor's prison, she went there, sat for her portrait, and sent her friends so that he could pay off his creditors. Alexander Hamilton served on the Board of Regents and became a trustee of Columbia College. He worked to improve sanitation and on other very local projects that would ensure a better quality of life for his neighbors. Postwar revival of a stimulating intellectual life led Mayor James Duane to establish a lecture series and invite Noah Webster to speak at the new government building. Webster was so enthralled with New York that he remained there and began a literary magazine. The clans also worked together to rebuild the New York Society Library, which had been destroyed by the British.

Intent on receiving all of the news from New York, George Washington was apprized that congressional legislators were having a rollicking time in the rapidly rebounding city of New York. In response to a letter from Virginia delegate William Grayson, Washington advised on June 22, 1785, to refrain from prematurely introducing a bill to move the seat of government to the Potomac. Famous for avoiding battles he could not win, Washington, like Philip Schuyler, was a master at guerilla warfare and knew how to be impenetrably patient. This was not their "moment" to pounce, Washington instructed Grayson, reassuring him, however, that "the Potomac navigation proceeds under favourable [sic] auspices."

CHAPTER 9

Potomac Fever

WASHINGTON'S SIGNIFICANT NEW YEAR'S EVE victory that gained the promise of cooperation between the states of Maryland and Virginia on water rights, however, did not include the commitment from the states to share in underwriting the development scheme. It would have to be privately funded. Virginians had elected a new governor, Patrick Henry, famous for his "liberty or death" speech, who now presided in Richmond. On New Year's Day 1785, James Madison wrote Washington that, while Washington had been toiling in Annapolis, the Virginia legislature had passed some measures to forward their cause, which included opening and extending the navigation of James River and surveying both the James and Potomac Rivers. Most significant to Washington was a resolution that "passed both Houses instructing the Commissrs [sic] appd [sic] in June last to settle with Maryd [sic] Commissrs [sic] the jurisdiction & navigation of the Potowmac, to join in a representation to Pena on the subject of the Waters of the Ohio within her limits." On January 5, 1785, the Virginia Assembly passed the bills that created the Potowmack [sic] and James River Companies. These entities would be owned by private shareholder investors and would be tax exempt and free to conduct their business without any obligation to report their financials to the state of Virginia. The Virginia Act, which provided investors with the right "to receive reasonable tolls forever, in satisfaction for the money advanced by them" designated Richmond, Alexandria, and Winchester as the locations where subscriptions could be opened to the public.

On January 6, now former Virginia Governor Benjamin Harrison wrote Washington:

> It gives me great pleasure to inform that the assembly yesterday without a discenting [sic] voice complimented you with fifty shares of the potowmack company and one hundred in the James River company of which I give you this early notice to stop your subscribing on your own account. As this compliment is intended by your country in commemoration of your assiduous (cares) to promote her interest I hope you will have no scruples in accepting the present and thereby gratifying them in their earnest wishes.

On January 9, 1785, James Madison wrote Washington from Richmond with further news:

> I have not the pleasure of confirming the expectations hinted in my last concerning the result of the measures which have been favoured [sic] with your patronage. The Bill for opening the Potowmac [sic] has passed precisely on the model transmitted from Maryland, the last conditional clause in the latter being rendered absolute by a clause in the former which engages this State for fifty shares in the Company.

Madison then explained that slight variances had been made to the original proposal, "with respect to James River," which were "that the Sum to be aimed at . . . is 100,000 Dollars, only. 2. The shares are fixed at 200 Dollars and the number of public shares at 500. 3., the tolls are reduced to one half of those granted on Potowmac [sic]." In this letter, Madison added his own opinion that reinforced Jefferson's repeated entreaties to Washington. Madison assured Washington that the landmark bill that fostered cooperation between the two states was a success primarily owing to the general's involvement: "several members were honoured [sic] during your visit to Richmond." Madison wrote Thomas Jefferson on that same day that "no one had worked more vigorously" than Washington, and rather than embarrass the cash-strapped former commander in chief, the legislators determined to gift Washington shares in the company. It was a wise business and public-relations move.

On January 18, 1785, George Washington noted in his diary that the wind was "Southwardly & fresh . . . now and then dripping of rain." He had "sent the dispatches which came to me yesterday to Messrs. Fitzgerald and Harshorne who are appointed to receive Subscriptions—that they might get copies of the Act printed." Virginia Congressman William Grayson, in New York, sent Washington a package, in which was his own note, a letter from James Madison to Washington, a copy of the Potomac bill, a note to Grayson from the Virginia House Assembly clerk, several Potomac Company stock offering books, and a list of "the James River rate of Tolls."

Washington's January 19, 1785, diary entry noted that the day was "clear and fine" and that "a Mr. Watson . . . stayed all Night." Washington's visitor, Elkanah Watson, would later be credited with coordinating the Erie Canal program after Philip Schuyler's death. Watson wrote in his own memoir that he had actually spent January 23–24, 1785, with Washington at Mount Vernon and described Washington as "intently settled on the project of connecting the western waters, by canals, with his favorite Potomack [sic], and of improving the navigation of the Monongahela, and other branches of the Ohio; principally with a view, of diverting the fur trade from Detroit to Alexandria, instead of going to Montreal, as heretofore." Watson and Washington rode their horses together along the south bank of the Potomac "to examine the proposed route of the canal."

> Hearing little else for two days from the persuasive tongue of this great man, I confess completely infected me with the canal mania . . . Washington pressed me earnestly to settle on the banks

of the Potomac. At his suggestion I proceeded up the southern shore of the river, twenty-two miles from Alexandria, to examine the proposed route of the canal. The extent of this artificial navigation was designed to be about a mile respectively at the Seneca, Great, and Little Falls. Eleven miles above Alexandria occur the Lower Falls, where the river descends in curling waves thirty-six feet in a quarter of a mile. Here the contemplated canal will be a mile and a quarter, situated on the north side of the river. We reached, eleven miles further, the Great Falls, which are a stupendous exhibition of hydraulic power . . . At this place the entire fall is seventy feet, embracing a vertical descent of twenty-three feet, which adds infinitely to the imposing scene. Here existed the most serious obstacle to the execution of the work.[1]

Watson declined Washington's suggestion that he move to the Alexandria area along the Potomac.

Three-and-a-half years after his time with Washington at Mount Vernon, Elkanah Watson would visit with Philip Schuyler in upstate New York to discuss Schuyler's vision of a New York canal system. While the Potomac River had obvious obstacles that would make development nearly impossible, Watson found the New York channels to be exactly what Washington had feared: the naturally God-given best route to the west, or as John Quincy Adams, who would preside over the construction of both the Chesapeake and Ohio Canal and the Erie Canal, would call the New York conduit, a geopolitical anomaly. Like Washington, Elkanah Watson spent weeks touring the Hudson River and the Mohawk Valley. Also like Washington, Watson traveled the Hudson River to New York City. Watson's 1788 tour of upstate New York began mid-August, when he arrived at the "old Dutch city of Albany." He wandered the Mohawk Valley, which he found "a rich region under high cultivation, and adorned by luxuriant clover pastures . . . almost on a level with the river," and enjoyed the "beauty of the country, the majestic appearance of the adjacent mountains, the state of advanced agriculture . . . redolent with the perfume of clover." Once at Fort Schuyler, Watson observed with his own eyes what was clear to many others who had visited the Mohawk Valley—the rivalry between New York and Alexandria:

at the head of bateaux navigation on the Mohawk river, within one mile of Wood Creek, which runs west towards Lake Ontario, I am led to think it will in time become the emporium of commerce between Albany and the vast Western world. Wood Creek is indeed small, but it is the only water communication with the great [sic] Lakes; it empties into the Oneida Lake, the outlet of which unites with the Onondaga and Oswego, and discharges into Lake Ontario and Fort Oswego, where the British have a garrison. Should the Little Falls be ever locked, the obstructions in the Mohawk river removed, and a channel between that river and Wood Creek at this place be formed, so as to unite the waters flowing east with those running west, and other canals made, and obstructions removed to Fort Oswego—who can reasonably doubt that by such bold operations, the State of New-York has within her power, by a grand measure of policy, to divert the future trade of Lake Ontario, and the great lakes above from Alexandria and Quebec to Albany and New-York.

According to Elkanah Watson,

Albany [was] one of the most favorable positions in America . . . It may control the fur trade of the lakes; it must occupy the avenues which will penetrate into the valley of the Mohawk; and will be the depot of the produce from the luxuriant territory of the Genesee . . . Albany would become a mart of foreign commerce.[2]

In 1789, Elkanah Watson would move to Albany, New York. In 1791, he would take another tour of upstate New York, visiting the Schuyler lands at Saratoga Springs, in the company of Jeremiah van Rensselaer, Philip van Cortlandt, and Stephen Bayard. He saw "Maj. Schuyler's mills in Palatine," and wrote further observations on the Mohawk river, Oneida Lake, western canals, and Wood Creek, enjoying "in delightful anticipation the prospect of a free and open water communication from thence to the Atlantic via Albany and New-York."[3]

Though Watson did not elect to reside near Washington along the Potomac River, Elkanah Watson recalled in his memoir, that, "to have communed with" George Washington "in the bosom of his family . . . I shall always regard as one of the highest privileges and most cherished incidents of my life." Watson, Washington, Jefferson, Madison, and Monroe all knew that the waterways of New York State had a connectivity advantage over the navigability of the Potomac River and her tributaries, yet Washington and his fellow "countrymen" persisted with their illusory dream to dominate.

Watson wrote that Washington could not—or chose not to—hide his passion about the Potomac River navigation project. Washington was also seeking investors, but, as always, the former commander in chief was concerned about the appearance that his involvement in such a commercial endeavor would paint him as greedy. Washington was actually tormented about the grant awarded him by the Virginia State Assembly and vacillated about whether or not to accept the shares of stock, which amounted to 10 percent of the entire company. On March 10, 1785, William Grayson wrote Washington from New York that Washington had to accept the award. "It was talk'd [sic] of by gentlemen of the House that some mark of attention and respect (not barely complimentary) should be paid you by your native Country; that the other States in the Union knew you only as an American, but that your own knew you as an American and a Virginian." Congressman Grayson further explained that he had been told by the members of the state assembly that "the House were anxious (as you had patronized them and opened their importance to public view) that the credit of the undertaking should be ascrib'd to yourself"; however, "your being subjected to the performance of any particular service never once occurred."

Sensitive to the traditions into which they had been born, Grayson explained to Washington that the members of the Virginia legislature wanted to make it clear to the public and to Washington, "that the grant when measured by the European scale . . . was so relatively inconsiderable . . . that the act would

carry to Posterity an evidence of the part you had acted in this great undertaking, the remembrance of which would be . . . retained by your family . . .
an honorable testimonial of the gratitude & affection of your native Country."
Grayson further reassured Washington that the public would never regard to
it as "a pension" or "an annuity from the United States," which smacked of
Old World monarchial sinecure.

The Virginia and Maryland commissioners assigned to negotiate the terms
of the Potomac River canal project were scheduled to meet in Alexandria on
March 20, 1785, to flesh out agreement specifics as to lighthouses, tolls, fish-
eries, and security. Virginia commissioner George Mason had only learned of
the meeting in Alexandria two days before it was to happen when the Maryland conferees wrote asking if they could stay at Gunston Hall en route to
the summit. Despite a raging blizzard, the delegates from Maryland arrived
in Alexandria on time but were joined by only one more of their Virginia
counterparts, Alexander Henderson of Fairfax County. Conspicuously absent
were Edmund Randolph and James Madison. Two days into the negotiations,
George Washington arrived to check on the group's progress. Madison and
Randolph were still missing. Washington learned that negotiations were floun-
dering, so, he invited the group of commissioners who were present to continue
their discussions at Mount Vernon. Washington's diary entry for March 25,
1785, notes: "About One O'clock Major Jenifer, Mr. Stone, Mrs. Chase, &
Mr. Alexr. Henderson arrived here." There was still no sign of either Randolph
or Madison, the latter Washington's most dedicated minion in the Virginia
assembly with regard to the Potomac River navigation plan.

Washington had expected that Madison would be amongst the group
but Madison had never received an invitation to attend. Governor Patrick
Henry, whose role it was to extend that invitation, had deliberately with-
held it. Henry, an ardent anti-Federalist, opposed the entire project and
feared results that consolidated interstate power. It would be three months,
a full month after the official organization of the Patowmack [sic] Canal
Company and a full month after George Washington would be named its
president when Madison would learn that he had been excluded from the
meetings in Alexandria and at the home of the former commander in chief.

The second invitation, to Mount Vernon, was especially painful to Madison. Although George Washington, like his friend, Philip Schuyler, maintained an "open door" policy of hospitality, the reticent James Madison had never been presumptuous enough to invite himself to the general's door. Madison had waited for and had longed for an invitation from the great man himself and had now missed the opportunity.

The four-day meeting at Mount Vernon from March 25, 1785, to March 28, 1785, presided over by host George Washington, was a resounding success and its outcome historic. The now famous Mount Vernon Compact set an example for interstate cooperation on regulating and shaping uniform import duties, foreign currency valuation and exchange, and the Maryland cession of fishing rights to those on the south side of the Potomac River. The ugly side of the Mount Vernon Compact would be the punitive behavior on the part of both Maryland and Virginia that would enable George Washington to wrench money from his investors by means of foreclosures and liens.

In the early morning of May 17, 1785, an unusually large number of Virginia and Maryland gentry—some wealthy, some who had scraped to invest, and some who were merely curious—assembled in Alexandria to participate in the initial public offering of shares of stock in George Washington's Potomac River Canal Company. The festivities included a midday feast, which was followed by remarks by General George Washington. Washington welcomed all and assured prospective investors that they would not only glean profit beyond their wildest dreams but they would also be shaping together the future of their nation. Washington extolled the commercial project as a patriotic one.

The general subscribers of the Potomac River Company elected Articles of Confederation signer and Maryland congressman Daniel Carroll chairman of its first official meeting, at which George Washington was elected president. Other prominent shareholders included Washington's cousin Lund Washington, Washington's long time Potomac River development ally and former governor of Maryland Thomas Johnson, and David Stuart, a local businessman who had entered the Washington clan when he married Jacky Custis's widow. On that day, May 17, 1785, George Washington agreed to serve as director and president of the corporation and also became its largest single shareholder. In addition to the shares gifted to Washington, he purchased five shares from his own funds.

Even though it was a very speculative project, Washington trumpeted it as a great investment in his letters to members of his extended family, his friends, and far-flung admirers in the thirteen states and in Europe. He even had help from Thomas Jefferson in Paris, who, on May 10, completed the first printing run of 200 copies of his *Notes on the State of Virginia*, now in book form. James Madison had written Jefferson in Paris the previous January 9 of Washington's intensity in seeing the canal project through to fruition:

> The earnestness with which he expresses the undertaking is hardly to be described and shows that a mind like his, capable of great views, and which has long been occupied by them, cannot bear a vacancy, and surely he could not have chosen an occupation more worthy of succeeding to that of establishing the political rights of his country [Virginia] than the patronage of works for the extensive and lasting improvement of its natural advantages; works which will double the value of half the lands within the Commonwealth will extend its commerce and link its interest with those of the western states.

Although Jefferson was serving in France as a representative of the federal government, he was, first and foremost, a Virginian. His new book, *Notes on the State of Virginia*, filled with the calculations to the inch of every North American eastern seaboard rivulet and its meanderings, an assessment of minerals in the bowels of the American terrain, as well as the varying crops that thrived in the different regions of the thirteen states, was another topographical epic meant to champion America's greatness—but Jefferson's work was not of the poetic kind. Circulated amongst Jefferson's very rich friends, *Notes on the State of Virginia* served as a prospectus to muster investors for Washington's Potomac canal venture. Almost simultaneous with the publication of Jefferson's exhaustive catalogue, the New York State Assembly addressed a motion to improve navigation on the Mohawk River and "the speedy development of the west and unappropriated lands on the western frontier of New York." The rivalry between New York and Virginia was palpable.

Two weeks after the Potomac River Canal Company was formalized in Alexandria, Washington held another meeting at Mount Vernon for the corporation's board of directors. From May 30 to 31, 1785, Washington and his executive guests formulated overarching decisions to guide the project. At Washington's suggestion, the board agreed to portion the clearing of the great river into two different sections with Harpers Ferry as the dividing line. Washington's reasoning behind that opinion was that, since each area would require no less than fifty men, an assistant, and a general manager in order to get the project under way, it would be best to begin with the easiest segment of the entire system, as Washington explained to Lafayette. On June 5, Washington sent boat designer and contractor James Rumsey "the proceedings of the Directors of the Pawtomack [sic] navigation—I pray you to have them set up at some public place. If the manager advertised for, can come *well* recommended, liberal wages will be given him."

At the May 30–31 meeting, the minutes reveal that "four hundred and three of the five hundred Shares in the Potowmack [sic] Company have been subscribed Books are now opened at Mr William Harshornes [sic] Treasurer in Alexandria to receive the first Subscriptions that may be offered to make up the ninety seven [sic] remaining Shares." Eighty-seven of the remaining ninety-seven shares sold to three investment companies in Amsterdam. The remaining ten shares also sold out quickly. Jefferson and Madison had been correct: Washington's involvement in the canal company created a fever that actually resulted in oversubscription demand. Washington's own infectious zeal for Alexandria and the opportunities along the Potomac River persuaded Philadelphia financier Robert Morris to open a business outpost in Alexandria on the Potomac River. Owing to the tenacity of George Washington, the aspirational town of Alexandria, Virginia, was gaining momentum toward becoming a premier American city.

Washington wanted to preserve a record of his activities and, although his plans had been over twenty years in the making, what seemed to be speedy success through the conservation of his letters and diaries. The extensive cache of notes and correspondence that pertained to the Potomac River Canal Company and his grand design for its development was never meant to be secret; the documents indisputably reveal Washington's ambitious plan to create the seat of the American empire around the port of Alexandria and the Potomac River. During the summer of 1785, Washington produced and received a steady stream of letters about his burning vision and also kept a methodical account of the meetings, his visitors, and the river explorations he embarked upon, all of which pertained to his role as shareholder and president of the Potomac Canal Company.

Among those with whom he regularly corresponded at that time was Virginia Congressman William Grayson in New York. Washington's June 22 letter to Grayson offered a detailed report on the project that progressed apace:

> At the general meeting of the subscribers in May last, it appeared that upwards of 400 of the 500 shares had been engaged—Many more have been subscribed since—a Board of Directors have been chosen—proper characters & Labourers [sic] advertized [sic] for, to commence the work in the least difficult parts of the river, 'till a skillful Engineer can be engaged to undertake those which are more so; & it is expected the work will be begun by the 10th of next month.

On July 13, 1785, Thomas Johnson wrote Washington on behalf of a man who wanted a job to supervise "breakg the Rocks and removing the Fragments." On July 14, at another meeting of the board of directors, Washington's choice, James Rumsey, was named superintendent of the entire canal system, without ever having constructed one. Johnson's candidate became Rumsey's assistant manager. On August 3, Washington himself boarded a canoe and toured the Great and Seneca Falls with Rumsey and his assistant manager to assess the rapids, varying depths, clearing, the need for locks, and the possibility of ice formations and driftwood that might impede smooth sailing. On the eighth of August, Washington and the rest of the board of directors met at the Shenandoah Falls and optimistically determined that it could be cleared without locks.

On August 13 Washington wrote Edmund Randolph that he, Washington, was devoting most of his time and all of his energy to the development of the

Potomac River: "I wish to see the inland navigation of the . . . Pawtomack . . .
improved & extended . . . to connect the Western Territory with the Atlantic
States; all others, with me, are secondary." On August 22, Washington again
wrote William Grayson with another detailed update:

> We have got the Pawtomack [sic] Navigation in hand—Workmen
> are employed, and the best Manager and assistants we could obtain,
> at the Falls of Shannondoah [sic] and Seneca; I am happy to inform
> you, that upon a critical examination of them by the Directors, the
> Manager, & myself, we are unanimoustly [sic] of opinion that
> the difficulties at these two places does not exceed the expectations
> we had formed of them—and that the Navigation through them,
> may be effected without the Aid of Locks.

That same day, Washington penned an impassioned letter to shareholder and
politician Richard Henry Lee in which Washington mapped, with great fervor,
his design for continental America. There would be a "commercial connection,"
explained Washington, that would link Alexandria on the Potomac to the Great
Kanawha River, along Washington's own extensive property holdings, a blatant
choice, to the Ohio and Mississippi Rivers. On October 7, 1785, Washington
wrote James Warren, expressing, once again, that his success with the Potomac
Canal Company was meant to be two-pronged: a profitable venture that was
also for the good of the nation:

> The great Works of improving and extending the inland navigations
> of the two large Rivers Potomack [sic] & James, which interlock with
> the Western Waters, are already begun; and I have little doubt of
> their success. The consequences to the Union, in my judgment, are
> immense—& more so in a political, than in a Commercial point; for
> unless we can connect the New States, which are rising to our view
> in the Regions back of us, with those on the Atlantic by interest the
> only cement that will bring, and in this case no otherways [sic] to be
> effected than by opening such communications as will make it easier

& cheaper for them to bring the product of their labour [sic] to our Markets, instead of carrying them to the Spaniards Southwardly, or the British Northwardly, they will be quite a distinct People, and ultimately may be very troublesome neighbors to us.

Although the project was scheduled to begin with its easiest portions, Washington, as he had in war, attacked the Potomac Canal Company's most difficult problems with ferocity. He would return again and again to the Great and Little Falls. His September 22 diary entry described:

> After viewing the works we crossed to the Virginia side and proceeded to the Great Falls . . . which nature seems clearly to have marked out . . . Gilpin myself & one hand in one Canoe, and two other people in another Canoe, and proceeded down the river to the place where it is proposed to let the water again into a Canal to avoid the little Falls.
>
> The place for the Canal at the Great Falls as I have just observed is most evidently marked along a glade which runs quite from the still water above the spout . . . to the river 3/4 or a Mile below it & from appearance will not be deep to dig . . . The place at which it is proposed to take the Canal out, above the little falls, seems favourably [sic] formed for it by an Island . . . The little falls, if a Rock or two was removed might be passed without any hazard.

On October 18, Washington noted in his diary, that, after enjoying "an early breakfast at Mr. Fairfax's Govr. Johnson & I set out for the Falls (accompanied by Mr. Fairfax) where we met the other Directors and Colo. Gilpin in the operation of levelling the ground for the proposed cut or Canal from the place where it is proposed to take the Water out." Washington, the surveyor, then elaborated projections based on angles, cuts, measurements, and levels. The Great Falls, which presented the most challenging obstacle to the whole canal system along the Potomac River, would take nearly twenty years to complete and is considered to be an eighteenth-century American engineering feat.

Washington could think of little else throughout the autumn of 1785. When he was at home at Mount Vernon, his usual stream of guests reported that the Potomac River Canal Company was about the only thing the general cared to talk about. James Madison, at long last, was honored with two invitations to stay at Mount Vernon. First, from September 3 to 5; then, in October, at which time Madison observed French sculptor Jean-Antoine Houdon begin the statue of Washington that Madison's committee had commissioned.

In addition to the time spent together at Mount Vernon, Washington and Madison supplemented their conversations with an exchange of letters about the canal works. On October 20, only a few days after his departure, Madison offered Washington a suggestion that, since Washington was embarrassed by the perception that he had received improper gifts of shares in the Potomac River Canal Company, he ought to consider using any profits for the public good. Madison's thoughts prompted Washington to write Governor Henry on October 29 that he thought he should "turn the destination of the fund vested in me from my private emoluments, to objects of a public nature." That same day, Washington wrote Madison, sitting at the state assembly in Richmond, of his note to the governor. On November 11, Madison assured Washington that his proposal on the matter "was laid before" the assembly the previous day. Madison also promised his support for whatever decision the general would make with regards to the shares.

Aware of Washington's other holdings in the Dismal Swamp, Madison included with his note "two reports from the Commssrs [sic] for examining the head of James River &c. and the ground between the waters of Elizabeth River & N. Carolina." That same day, Virginia Governor Patrick Henry, who had tried to sabotage preliminary meetings between the representatives of the states of Maryland and Virginia, revealed in a note to Washington that, owing to the groundswell of popular support, he had not only gotten on board with the Potomac River project but he was also in line with the plan to develop the Dismal Swamp water. "And indeed," wrote Henry, "nothing more is necessary in this Canal Business, than giving a proper Direction to the Efforts which seem ready for Exertion." That was indeed high praise for the president of the Potomac River Canal Company from contrarian Governor Patrick Henry.

CHAPTER 10

Disunity

THOUGH WASHINGTON'S FOCUS WAS ALMOST entirely on hydraulics, he was continually updated on the workings of the Congress of the Confederation by Virginia Congressman William Grayson with news from New York City. On September 22, 1785, Massachusetts Congressman Elbridge Gerry moved to create a $100,000 fund to construct a federal government building, which was vetoed. On October 3, 1785, Grayson informed Washington that a previously authorized, "Article of 30,000 dollars for fœderal [sic] buildings at Trenton" was also "expunged." While the leaders of New York City and Alexandria, Virginia, were mounting aggressive campaigns to become international meccas of business and power, lethargy and rivalries amongst the thirteen states made their purposeful wartime unity a faded memory.

Charles Thomson, recording secretary of the Congress of the Confederation, noted poor attendance at the congress. Some days, fewer than nine states were represented at meetings, precluding a quorum, and other days, even fewer than seven states bothered to show up. This was to go on for months. Some members of congress decided that the onus of paying their way was prohibitive, others pointed to bad weather, and some others to family obligation. The plain truth was that many of the delegates knew that a strong federal government that subsumed local law was unpopular back in their own states, where the prevailing attitude was "we won the war, why bother?" Between 1785 and 1790 about 116 representatives to congress would attend sessions in New York City; however, some thirty-five who had also been chosen to serve would never appear—six of whom would be from Connecticut. The trip from Connecticut, obviously easier than from other more distant states was not the excuse; it was the contentious relationship with its neighbor—New York—that kept the Connecticut delegates from attending congressional sessions. In hope of reviving some kind of spirit in the country, the congress asked John Hancock to return to the congress as president; his term lasted from November 23, 1785, to June 5, 1786, much of that in absentia. While the congress was seated in New York City, there were five other presidents between 1785 and 1788; many months of that time period the congress was either without quorum or in recess.

New York State, home of the new federal capital, was no different from any other state that continued to behave contrary to the good of the union, and, in fact, was one of the worst irritants in the Confederation. As of 1786 New York State had still not ratified the revenue agreement of 1783 and continued to antagonize neighboring states, placing high import taxes on products from Connecticut and New Jersey. So angry were the delegates from those states that the Congress of the Confederation had to intervene or, as Nathaniel Gorham of Massachusetts wrote, "bloodshed would very quickly be the consequence." Members of the congress—like Gorham, who would serve as president of the Congress of the Confederation from June 6, 1786, to November 3, 1786; James Monroe of Virginia; Rufus King, also of Massachusetts; past president of the Congress of the Confederation Richard Henry Lee of Virginia; and Charles Pinckney of South Carolina—were among the most able of men, yet they seemed to be fighting a losing battle. Interstate wrangling, often fought out on the congressional floor, became the nation's business. When one state got angry with another, that state sometimes took its grievances out on the federal government, often withholding payments owed the US Treasury; some states would merely override federal agreements with their own elaborate conditions, which resulted in the same outcome—empty treasury coffers. Just ten years after the Declaration of Independence, while New York City, having reaped large benefits from the sale of Tory property, was booming as the nation's new capital city, the nation was falling apart.

By day, statesmen faced stifling governmental inertia; however, the rich social life in New York City afforded them the opportunity to cement relationships that would come in handy in shaping the republic. Though no political parties had yet been established, there were disagreements and filibusters. Enemies by day openly mingled with gusto in the evening as New York City's fortunes and cultural life amplified. Future president and ambassador John Quincy Adams, a visitor between Europe and his Harvard education, reported on a sumptuous supper at Secretary Henry Knox's estate four miles outside of New York City proper, and dinners with the Jays, Governor Clinton, Elbridge Gerry, historian David Ramsay, foreign ministers from Spain and the Netherlands, and fellow New Englander, Rufus King, who had married a New York City girl. Although the Adams family was forever squarely on the side of their home "country" in her battles with New York City, the family of John and Abigail Adams adored living in New York City and amongst New Yorkers. So desirable was life in New York City in those years that, when John and Abigail Adams's daughter, Abigail "Nabby," married and committed family treachery by moving to New York, her parents, whom others feared would cry "traitor!" when Nabby emigrated from their beloved Boston, actually relished the letters she wrote with her hearsay stories of the political haggling going on in the smoke-filled rooms in New York's popular coffee houses. Abigail mère, who arrived in New York City to meet her first grandchild and stayed with the Jays, made it clear to all that she did not want to leave. Virginian St. George Tucker, most acutely aware of the rivalry between his home state and New York, nevertheless admitted in his diary: "I confess I like the hurly burly and bustle" of Manhattan, where he would "see as great a variety of faces, figures and Characters as Hogarth . . . ever drew." His diary reflects the colorful life he witnessed and experienced from the "Gentlemen in . . . pea Green silk" to his utter enjoyment at passing time in "Mr. Rivington's shop." Post–Revolutionary War New York City welcomed everyone regardless of religion, fashion preferences, or political opinion.

The Jays, the Hamiltons, the Duanes, the Duers, and the Clintons were joined by other generous hosts like the Temples (Lady Temple was the daughter

of Governor James Bowdoin of Massachusetts), the Rufus Kings, and the Beekmans, who all had regular evenings in their homes. They offered novelties such
as lemon trees that made the table's lemonade and, in the case of the Beekmans,
the china and silver that became a conversation piece: the Beekmans had buried
it when the British invaded and the family unearthed it unscathed after the war.
At that time, most American hostesses relied on menus prescribed by Hannah
Glasse in *The Art of Cookery Made Plain and Easy*, first published in 1747, with
many subsequent editions, the most recent at the time in 1784. United by food
in the kitchens from South Carolina to New England, the nation, however, was
falling apart at its very delicate seams.

Washington, Madison, Philip Schuyler, Alexander Hamilton, and John Jay
all communicated with urgency amongst one another about the need for the
standardization of laws and economic regulations for the nation to survive, and
all foresaw an empire that reached from the Atlantic beyond the Mississippi
River. Yet they, too, were not immune from sectional rivalry. The Virginia–New
York rivalry for a navigable water system to the interior that would flow to a
port town, presumably America's primary city, created one divide amongst this
likeminded, collegial group. The 1785–86 negotiations between John Jay and
Spanish Ambassador Gardoqui spotlighted the competitiveness.

Encompassed in the territory ceded by Great Britain at the end of the War
of Independence was a southern swath of land that included the Natchez,
Mississippi, area and terrain to latitude 31° north in Florida. Georgia claimed
some of that land; so did Spain.

It was imperative for the young United States, in its quest for prosperity
and empire status, to resolve trade, land disputes, and use of the Mississippi
River with Spain. John Jay spent one year trying to resolve those concerns.
The treaty he presented to the Congress of the Confederation in 1786 would
have guaranteed exclusive navigational rights to Spain for twenty-five years
in exchange for a commercial treaty that granted American fishermen (mostly in
the northeast) commercial access to the Spanish market. On May 31, 1786,
Virginia Congressman James Monroe wrote James Madison with bitterness
that Rufus King, who had married a New York heiress, would benefit from
the agreement but there was no benefit for Virginia. Virginians, like George

Washington, who had invested in the southwest, found a twenty-five-year delay in the ability to transport their goods on the Mississippi River intolerable. Madison would become a delegate to the Congress of the Confederation, and among his most pressing missions would be the defeat of the Jay-Gardoqui Treaty. The New York–Virginia rivalry was so contentious that, though a neighbor of John Jay in Lower Manhattan, Madison would avoid speaking with the American foreign minister about the pending bill; instead, Madison would call on the Spanish ambassador to learn the inner workings of the deal.

Although Madison, Washington, Philip Schuyler, Alexander Hamilton, and John Jay were guilty of the sectional partisanship they denounced, they also left an extensive paper trail lamenting the imminent possibility that the Confederation was teetering on collapse. If unity completely disintegrated, so, too, would their dreams. On November 30, 1785, George Washington wrote Madison:

> We are either a United people or we are not. If the former, let us, in all matters of general concern act as a nation, which have national objects to promote, and a National character to support—If we are not, let us no longer act a farce by pretending to it. for [sic] whilst we are playing a dble [sic] game or playing a game between the two we never shall be consistent or respectable—but *may* be the dupes of some powers and, most assuredly, the contempt of all. In any case it behoves [sic] us to provide good Militia Laws, and look well to the execution of them—but, if we mean by our conduct that the States shall act independently of each other it becomes *indispensably* necessary—for therein will consist our strength and respectability in the Union.

Washington could point to his March 1785 landmark Mount Vernon Compact as the inspiration for the further inclusion of Pennsylvania and Delaware in multilateral discussions on the land and water trade routes. He had hoped to turn jealous competitors into productive partners, which was also the intent of a multistate conference scheduled to be held in September 1786 at Annapolis,

Maryland. The ineffectual four-day September 11–14, 1786, Annapolis Convention, to which only five states sent representatives,[1] and the many months when the congress could not summon a quorum, caused Washington and the rest of his Federalist sympathizers dismay.

George Washington did not attend the Annapolis Convention but he did attend the annual meeting of the Potomac River Canal directors that was held in Alexandria on August 7, 1786. The Potomac River Canal Company, begun with such optimism, was already in dire need of money—the money pledged by its subscribers.[2] There also had been an unusual amount of rain, so, on October 2, 1786, the company petitioned the state legislatures for a three-year extension to complete the work agreed upon between the Great Falls and Cumberland, Maryland. The directors began sending notices to delinquent shareholders. Some paid their obligations; however, fifty-five shares were publicly advertised for sale.

The Potomac River Canal Company concerns weighed greatly on its president, and, although he liked to pretend that he was too busy with his project to pay much attention to the federal government, the Cincinnatus posturing was patently disingenuous. On August 15, 1786, Washington wrote Theodorick Bland Jr., who was in New York as a newly elected Virginia delegate to the Congress of the Confederation: "Sequestered as I am, from the . . . intrigues of the world . . . I can hardly flatter myself with being able to give much light or assistance, to those who may be engag'd [sic] in passing thro' [sic] the dark & thorny paths of politics." Besides, added Washington, "my sentiments respecting foederal [sic] measures, in general, are so well known that it is unnecessary to reiterate them." In case anyone might believe that Washington had abandoned all concern for the future of the United States of America, that same day, Washington wrote Lafayette that "there will assuredly come a day when this country will have some weight in the scale of Empires." Washington's diaries also reflect that James Madison arrived at Mount Vernon on Monday evening, October 23, 1786, and spent three days with Washington to discuss what had transpired at the Annapolis Convention.

In February 1787, James Madison arrived in Lower Manhattan after a nearly one-month-long arduous winter journey by horseback. Madison moved in to

Dorothy Elsworth's boarding house at 19 Maiden Lane. A second convention to improve the Articles of Confederation was called, and, this time, Madison wanted to ensure that a Federalist synergy propelled the conversation. He found a sympathetic ear in Alexander Hamilton. Eyewitness accounts recall seeing Madison and Hamilton walking the streets of lower Broadway, deep in conversation: the elegant, fashionably dressed Hamilton, and the diminutive, always-dressed-in-black Madison. James Madison supplemented his conversations with Hamilton by reading the classics of history and political theory that arrived in crates sent to him from Paris by Thomas Jefferson. Hamilton relied on Philip Schuyler, with whom he outlined a proposal for a new federal government that would abolish states altogether.

It was going to be an uphill battle to revamp the failing government. Twenty of the fifty delegates appointed to this second convention, to be held in the Philadelphia State House in May, were also delegates to the Congress of the Confederation. Many of them had horrendous memories of that fateful day in June 1783 when they were nearly assassinated by the mutinous Pennsylvania battalion. Twenty of the fifty delegates expected to attend the convention would never bother to appear.

New York Governor George Clinton, opposed to stronger federal control, had enough sway in the New York State legislature to obtain the appointment of two of his own likeminded minions as delegates to the Philadelphia convention. The third, again forcefully pushed upon by Philip Schuyler, was Alexander Hamilton. Clinton's designees understood that their role was to dilute any Federalist proposals made by Alexander Hamilton. In an anonymously written article for the *Daily Advertiser*, Hamilton excoriated Clinton for undermining the good efforts intended to redress the weaknesses in the federal government all agreed upon by Hamilton, Jay, Schuyler, Madison, and Washington. Hamilton accused Clinton of having "greater attachment to his own *power* than to the *public* good."

On the twenty-first of March, Madison wrote George Washington with some news of the pending Philadelphia convention. On March 31, 1787, Washington replied, "I am glad to find that Congress have recommended to the States to appear in the Convention proposed to be holden in Philadelphia in May." Washington did not, however, inform Madison that three days earlier he had written to Governor Edmund Randolph, agreeing to serve as a Virginia delegate to the convention. Washington did, however, rail against the Jay-Gardoqui Treaty and criticize the state of New York, "which used to be foremost in all federal measures, should now turn her face against them in almost every instance." Washington remained not only Hamilton's champion against the George Clinton faction but also a steadfast Federalist.

On April 16, Madison responded to Washington's note that he found "much pleasure that your views of the reform which ought to be paused by the Convention, give a sanction to those which I have entertained." Madison revealed that he had "formed in my mind some outlines of a new system," which he took "the liberty of submitting . . . without apology, to your eye." This early proposal comprised "the ground-work . . . in the principle of representation." Madison foresaw that an imbalance in population amongst the states needed could cause some states to be too powerful; the only way to ensure uniformity was to guarantee equal voice for every citizen. Madison also suggested expanded "national supremacy" that would supersede state sovereignty in some judiciary matters and understood that there would be conflicts with already-existing state constitutions. For that reason, Madison insisted that, to "give a new System its proper validity and energy, a ratification must be obtained from the people, and not merely from the ordinary authority of the Legislature."

In this same note, Madison also reported to Washington on a matter before the congress that Madison knew would be of great personal interest to Washington, the real estate developer: the Congress of the Confederation had authorized the surveyance of some 700,000 acres of western lands that it was preparing to sell to replenish the Treasury coffers. Madison and Washington also exchanged their satisfaction that Vermont and New York State were inching closer to resolving their border disputes, both of them aware that it was Philip Schuyler whose negotiations and whose own private real estate empire were central to any agreement. Philip Schuyler's imprimatur was also notably behind a new bill that was introduced to the New York State Assembly for the improved navigation of the Mohawk River, "extending the same, if practicable to Lake Erie."

That kind of pressure on the president of the Potomac River Canal Project was intensified when, instead of the expected five days at the Philadelphia State House, this more serious effort at unifying a fractious young nation lasted from May to September 1787. As a courtesy to Washington while he presided over the Philadelphia business, the Potomac River Canal Company postponed its annual August meeting to November.[3] Other news traveled to Philadelphia from New York, where the Congress of the Confederation was still in session (despite the absence of many delegates in attendance at the Philadelphia convention), that the Congress of the Confederation had passed the Northwest Ordinance, a plan to shape and to admit new states to the union.

The Philadelphia Convention did not amend the Articles of Confederation. Instead, over the four-month period, a new document—the US Constitution— was drafted. James Madison, the document's scribe, knew how essential it was for Washington's Virginia investors to establish the capital city of empire on the Potomac. Madison wanted to put the subject of a permanent seat of government on the table but Washington advised against it. Fearful that too many arguments would cause the convention to disintegrate into chaos, the former commander in chief and president of the Potomac Company counseled once again to a fellow Virginian that the moment was inopportune.

James Madison's August 1, 1787, notes on the permanent location of the seat of government reflect the discussions amongst the members of the Committee of Detail. The committee, which was established on July 24 to draft the new constitution, did, in fact undertake the debate, and Madison's own notes reveal that he ignored Washington's instructions. According to what transpired in committee sessions, Madison was a vociferous proponent for legally memorializing the location of a permanent seat of government into the new US Constitution that he was drafting. Desperate to remove the capital from New York City, Madison nonetheless couched his argument as a good-faith attempt at fairness:

> Mr. Madison supposed that a central place for the seat of Govt . . .
> wd. be . . . insisted on by the H. of Representatives, that though a
> law should be made requisite for the purpose, it could & would be

obtained. The necessity of a central residence of the Govt. wd. Be much greater under the new than old Govt. The members of the new Govt. wd. be more numerous. They would be taken more from the interior parts of the States; they wd. not like members of the present Congs. Come so often from the distant States by water. As the powers & objects of the new Govt. would be far greater than heretofore, most private individuals wd. have business calling them to the seat of it, and it was more necessary that the Govt. should be in that position from which it could contemplate with the most equal eye, and sympathize most equally with, every part of the nation. These considerations he supposed would extort a removal even if a law were made necessary.

James Madison was folding a bicameral legislature into the new US Constitution and wanted preemptory action to force consensus: "in order to quiet suspicions both within & without doors, it might not be amiss to authorize the 2 Houses by a concurrent vote to adjourn at their first meeting to the most proper place, and to require thereafter, the sanction of a law to their removal." Congressman Rufus King of Massachusetts supported Madison's proposal for the seat of government to be written into the new constitution. North Carolina congressman Richard Dobbs Spaight, aware that King had just married a New York girl and that the couple wished to remain there, strenuously objected. As Washington had anticipated, the topic of the location of the permanent seat of government would lead to a second failed convention.

The wider meetings in Philadelphia reflected the ongoing contention. Debate on the location of the seat of the new federal government exploded several times on the convention floor. Philadelphia financier Robert Morris had a bitter dispute with New York's Gouverneur Morris, who, with the June 1783 Philadelphia mutiny in mind, thought that a capital city at either Newburgh or New Windsor on the Hudson River would provide, as it had for Washington during the war, a fortress-like protection for the legislators. George Mason of Virginia insisted that the constitution must outline a law that prohibited the seat of the federal government from being located in any state capital. Elbridge Gerry of Massachusetts agreed and amplified the conditions to include all commercial cities. Hugh Williamson of North Carolina and Gouverneur Morris of New York teamed up to argue that no prohibitions should be included in the document, and they succeeded in getting Mason to withdraw his motion. Virginians William Grayson and James Monroe fought for a capital city on the Potomac River, and said they would oppose any constitution that stated otherwise. Heated disagreements led to a variety of unripe suggestions like an adjournment without ever passing a law, the revival of a transient congress, and the introduction by James Madison that the executive under the new constitution should decide where he would like the seat of government to be.

While a fixed location for America's seat of government was not determined at the four-month-long 1787 Constitutional Convention, a secure and self-governing federal capital city was so important to the Founding Fathers that they prioritized the matter in the very first constitutional article: Article I, Section 8 of the Constitution provides for a seat of government that would function independently in its own jurisdiction.

Madison and Hamilton together, in homage to George Washington and Philip Schuyler respectively, proposed an "interior improvements" clause to the convention that would empower the congress to fund the construction of canals. Both Madison and Hamilton, albeit with some self-interest, argued that canals would bolster economic success for the entire debt-ridden nation. Their motion was voted down. Navigation development would be left to individual states or to private corporations like Washington's Potomac Company. While Washington had personally and tenaciously unified two states and had arm-twisted investors, Schuyler would be more fortunate. The rivers that inspired his dreams were all within one state, and he would enjoy the complete support from the New York State Assembly for funding a canal system. Washington's Sisyphean task could only be made easier with government backing: if he could wrangle the permanent capital to the Potomac, the federal government would be compelled to disgorge dollars to make navigable its abutting waterways. That would be a local, community obligation.

It is important to understand what Hamilton and Madison tried to accomplish on behalf of the canal dreams but did not. The US Constitution did endow the Congress with the right to regulate interstate commerce but did not grant the Congress the authority to fund interior improvements. What would become an ongoing demand for the Congress to allocate money for infrastructure improvement would rely on the evolution of custom rather than law. The Erie Canal, whose channels were within the borders of New York State, would be funded by that state, while George Washington's dream to make the Potomac River navigable was a multistate venture, which, at the time of the writing of the Constitution, was a privately held corporation. The Potomac Canal Company would ultimately fail; however, after the completion of the Erie Canal, the fifth president of the United States, Virginian James Monroe, would sign a bill in 1825 to fund the Chesapeake & Ohio Canal, essentially another name for George Washington's unprofitable Potomac Canal Company, using federal money. Under the auspices of Article I, Section 8 of the US Constitution that gave the federal government the right to regulate interstate commerce, President Monroe effectively declared that interstate connectivity was an essential component of interstate commerce. More than one hundred years and many federally funded infrastructure projects later, President Franklin Delano Roosevelt's massive New Deal public works program put a nation back to work. To this day, however, according to the specified powers granted to the Congress by the US Constitution, it is essentially not legally the purview of the Congress to fund infrastructure. Latitude has been granted to such endeavors if the projects reflect that they are indispensable to either interstate commerce or the US armed forces, as in the construction of military bases, also specifically regulated by the federal government in the US Constitution.

The Constitution of the United States was ratified on September 17, 1787, but the battle for its legal passage would just begin. Alexander Hamilton was the only delegate from New York State who voted for and signed the document; the other two—the Clinton surrogates—departed the assembly in a huff. As the convention attendees returned either to their home states or to New York City, where the sessions of the Congress of the Confederation were scheduled to resume, these crafters of the future of an empire knew that the battle for the document's legal ratification was just beginning.

The crusade to ratify the US Constitution mirrored the battle between the New Yorkers and the Virginians for the capital city of empire. The process toward ratification of the US Constitution required consent from nine states. Virginia and New York State assemblies stubbornly refused to pass it, both convinced that withholding confirmation would provide them with the leverage to reshape articles in the document to their benefit. Each of those state's assemblies wanted to wield the most power by dominating the other twelve states.

Washington was well aware of the anti-Federalist factions in his own state and knew who the antagonists would be. On October 22, 1787, he wrote Madison that for the moment he could only report on the sentiments of those in his "circle of Alexandria." It did not take long for Washington to learn that the movement to quash ratification in Virginia was swelling statewide. On November 5, Washington forwarded to Madison an "extract of a letter from Doctr Stuart," which reported on the "avowed opposition of Mr Henry." Stuart's note contained evidence "that an attempt would be made . . . that would convey to the people an unfavourable [sic] impression of the opinion of the House, with respect to the Constitution: And this was accordingly attempted."

In New York State, Governor Clinton waged a similar smear campaign against the new US Constitution—and most pointedly against Alexander Hamilton. Newspapers like the *Independent Journal* and the *New York Daily Advertiser* churned out the unfolding drama as ratification began to play out. Hamilton, John Jay, and James Madison met at the Jay house over tea and cakes served by Sally Jay to discuss a mission: they wanted to ensure the ratification of the US Constitution, and they needed to undo the damage caused by men like Governor George Clinton. The trio decided to use the power of their pens and collaborate on a series of articles. Published pseudonymously under a single name, "Publius," *The Federalist Papers* was actually a collaboration written by all three. Before publication, the group, of course, sought approval from both George Washington and Philip Schuyler. Schuyler would mobilize pro-Federalist forces in the New York State Senate. Washington similarly would circulate copies of *The Federalist Papers* in Virginia to sway opinion. On December 22, 1787, Washington wrote David Stuart, "I have sent you Seven numbers of the Foederalist [sic], under the signature of Publius. The subsequent numbers that have come to my hands, I herewith enclose." That thought was immediately followed by his two other pressing concerns: "Have you received a letter from me, enclosing one for my Nephew Bushrod Washington; containing queries respecting my land? . . . PS A number of Certificates [shares in the Potomac Canal Company] were sent to you a few days ago—have these been received by you from me?"

One by one the states began to ratify the US Constitution at their state conventions: on December 7, 1787, Delaware became the first by a vote of 30–0; Pennsylvania followed on December 12, 1787, by a vote of 46–23; New Jersey ratified on December 18, 1787 by a vote of 38–0; on January 2, 1788, Georgia ratified the US Constitution by a 26–0 vote; on January 9, 1788, Connecticut ratified the US Constitution by a 128-40 vote; and Massachusetts followed on February 6, 1788.

On Sunday, April 13, 1788, John Jay, who had written numbers 2–5 and 64 of *The Federalist Papers*, was critically injured, putting an end to his contributions. The episode, one of New York City's most violent since the War of Independence, rocked the nation. It began as a prank, when a group of boys obtained a ladder and climbed up and peered through the windows at the City Hospital located on Duane and Anthony Streets. To their surprise, they saw an assembly of doctors performing surgery on cadavers. The boys alerted their fathers, who broke into the building. The doctors escaped, fleeing to the city jail, where City Hall now stands, for protection. By evening, a mob surrounded the jail, threatening to hang the doctors. Jay, Clinton, Duane, Hamilton, and Baron von Steuben arrived to quiet the crowd. The rabble, unimpressed, grew even more belligerent. Jay was attacked, suffering head injuries. Von Steuben was also hit in the head. He was carried to the Duers' house, where Lady Kitty—as all of the surgeons were still hiding out in the city jail—had to stitch his head. Soldiers fired on the crowd, killing five and wounding eight.

In addition to the "Doctors' Riot," several other pockets of civil disobedience and escalating regional unrest made it apparent to citizens and officials alike that the United States, which now had an army of less than seven hundred, was failing. On April 28, Maryland became the seventh state to ratify the

Constitution; on May 23, South Carolina became the eighth state to ratify the Constitution of the United States.

With only one state still needed for formal ratification, Governor Clinton of New York scheduled the New York State ratification convention for June 17, 1788. Clinton, who wanted to remove the ratification debate away from downstate pro-Federalist influence, believed that he now held an extraordinary amount of power in the hands of New Yorkers. John Jay, recovering from his injury, along with Robert R. Livingston—known as "the Chancellor"—Alexander Hamilton, and James Duane embarked on the Hudson River on June 14 with cannons roaring and crowds waving them on. Westchester County sent Philip Livingston to their group. Governor Clinton and his brother, James, represented Ulster County. As a courtesy, the convention named Clinton its chairman, but the argument between the two factions for or against ratification was heated, at the very least. John Jay wrote letters home to Sally chronicling the infighting. She knew all the players: it would be the Livingstons and the Schuyler clans united against the Clinton faction. In *The Federalist Papers* number 77, Hamilton charged that Clinton maintained, "a despicable and dangerous system of personal influence," and, while Clinton stubbornly stood his ground, on June 21, 1788, New Hampshire became the all-important ninth state to ratify the US Constitution.

The intransigence of both the Virginia and New York legislatures had backfired, and Virginia relented, becoming the tenth state to ratify the Constitution four days later on June 25, 1788. As the necessary quorum of states was attained without New York State, Governor Clinton had basically reduced New York State to impotence; still, the anti-Federalists stalled. New Yorkers were rightfully worried about losing the seat of government. Article I, Section 8 of the Constitution provided for a federal seat of government but had neither specified its location nor the rights and responsibilities of its citizenry.

On July 15, Alexander Hamilton made a fiery speech at the New York State Ratification Convention addressing the federal district delineated in the new Constitution of the United States. This subject was of the utmost concern to anxious New Yorkers. That same day, George Washington wrote Samuel Holden Parsons that the Potomac River Canal project was going well. Parsons was a New England lawyer and Revolutionary War brigadier general who had moved to Marietta, Ohio, in the spring of 1788 to serve as registrar and probate clerk for the Northwest Territories. Parsons was also a director of the Ohio Land Company, an entity that had purchased a million acres of land from the congress after the passage of the Northwest Ordinance in 1787. One of the primary functions of the corporation was to purchase soldiers' pay certificates at a depressed price and exchange them for parcels of western land. Among the investors in the Ohio Land Company would be Alexander Hamilton, who had also recently purchased land along the St. Lawrence River in upstate New York, James Madison, and a number of representatives to the congress. Washington reassured Parsons that the Potomac River Canal project was going to ensure a thriving society and enrich those clever enough to have a stake in either the land or canal projects from Alexandria to the western waters:

> It is with sincer [sic] pleasure I can inform you, that the navigation of the Potowmac [sic], so interesting in its consequence to the welfare of your Establishment as well as to the emolument of this Country, is in a fair way of being opened in as short a time and in as beneficial a manner as could have been expected. In order to meet the Directors of the Potowmac [sic] Company on business, I have lately been obliged to make a visit to the Great falls, the Seneca and the Shenandoah; and, therefore, give you this information from my own knowledge. Indeed, I may venture to conjecture, from the enormous quantity of labour [sic] already established by the Legislatures of Virginia and Maryland to obtain the Subscription Money, that, instead of ten years which the Company is allowed for opening the navigation, it will be made passable in little more than half the time.

Hamilton's investment in the Ohio Land Company was negligible compared to his family's interests in New York State. For the moment, New York City retained the seat of government, and he needed to sway New York voters to pressure their representatives by assuaging voters' fears—intentionally implanted and promulgated by Governor Clinton—that federal sovereignty would be dangerous. Hamilton's July 15 speech on the seat of the federal government was staged as a prelude to the July 16 publication of number 84 of *The Federalist Papers*. In number 84, Hamilton offered an array of reasons for why the US Constitution had ordained a jurisdictionally separate seat of government that would benefit the American citizen more than the legislator: an independent federal district would protect American citizens from their own legislators, and it would inhibit corruption. Should a lawmaker face prosecution, cronyism in his home state could result in an improper adjudication. Was Hamilton being disingenuous in his belief or naïve in his position that a one-industry jurisdiction filled with self-interested politicians could function impartially?

Americans also wanted to know what rights and privileges would be extended to those lawmakers living outside the boundary of state and city law. On July 22, Hamilton made a motion on the floor of the New York Ratifying Convention that New York State would seek to impose an amendment to Article I, Section 8 of the Constitution refining its parameters. The federal city

> shall not be exercised as to exempt the Inhabitants of such District from paying the like Taxes Imposts Duties and Excises as shall be imposed on the other Inhabitants of the State in which such District may be; and that no person shall be priviledged [sic] within the said District from Arrest for Crimes Committed or Debts contracted out of the said District and that the Inhabitants of the said District shall be entitled to the like essential Rights as the other Inhabitants of the United States in general.

Impatient and outraged at having lost the glory of having been the deciding ratification vote and irritated with Clinton that he might cost New York the federal seat of government, the citizens of New York City, to spite the governor and his ego, went ahead with a great parade on Wednesday, July 23, to celebrate the new Constitution. The most impressive feature of the pageant was a twenty-seven-foot-long, thirty-two-gun frigate named the Federal Ship *Hamilton*. Three days after the New York City spectacle, the New York State convention, essentially pressured and embarrassed into doing so, ratified the US Constitution with a vote of 30–27, the narrowest margin of any state to ratify.

There was an emotional dissent upstate, suspected to have been ignited by Governor Clinton. There was rioting in the streets in Albany, near the Philip Schuyler mansion, and a public burning of the Constitution. Conversely, in New York City, the state and federal capital city, there was an outpouring of joy: cannons fired, bells rang, and the citizenry celebrated in the streets. James Madison wrote George Washington that the ratification of the Constitution by New York State was undoubtedly and inextricably linked to the location of the seat of the federal government in New York City.

New Yorkers were concerned that they would be punished for Clinton's contrarianism. The seat of government was at stake, and George Clinton had played politics. On August 18, 1788, Philip Schuyler anxiously wrote "the Chancellor" Robert R. Livingston that he had received a "letter from Colo. Hamilton . . . on his . . . way to Fort Schuyler . . . The blank for the place at which the new Congress are to meet was not yet filled on Wednesday last, the last vote was in favor of New York. Hamilton's letter which was of the 10th says, 'It is still critical but we are the strongest.'"

Nine states—the necessary quorum—voted to keep New York City as the nation's capital city for the time being. The energized New York clans together contributed some $40,000 to transform New York City's City Hall building into a dignified monument that would symbolize the new empire. They hired French architect Pierre L'Enfant to redesign the building, which would also be renamed "Federal Hall." L'Enfant's "Federal Hall" would initiate and set the standard for what would become known as the Federal style. Federal style, one of America's most preeminent contributions to architectural design history, was born in New York City.

Two contrapuntal forces were at work to erode the momentum in favor of New York City as the permanent seat of government or capital city of the United States of America. One was understandable: George Washington and his coterie were intent on grabbing the honor for Alexandria. The second was completely irrational: with reckless disregard for his own constituents, disgruntled, ungrateful George Clinton and his surrogates engineered a counterproductive and increasingly opaque political quagmire meant to stall the advancement of federal sovereignty in New York State. The Clinton faction spent weeks and weeks hypothesizing and thrashing out their own bill of rights, which would be respectfully considered by Congress, and they delayed the formation of an electoral college, condemning New York State for eternity with the singular stigma of being the state of the twelve states that had ratified the US Constitution[4] that did not participate in the election of the first president of the United States.

CHAPTER 11

The Calm Before
the Storm

THE PLEASANT AUTUMN OF 1788 in New York City turned into a frosty winter. A chill had also set in amongst the New York clans. The Hamiltons, Jays, Schuylers, Livingstons, Duanes, and Duers had struck a deal to support Philip Schuyler and James Duane for the first US Senate under the new Constitution. Hamilton, afraid that Clinton would use the opportunity to insert a puppet New York City mayor once Duane left office, became a rogue operator, throwing his support behind thirty-four-year-old Massachusetts-born-and-raised Rufus King.[1] General Schuyler won his Senate seat; Duane did not. Hamilton not only breached the *sous-entendu* understanding amongst the clans but he also nudged Governor Clinton and his new protégé, Aaron Burr, from the realm of political adversary to one of personal enmity.

Blizzards blasted the thirteen states during the 1788–89 winter. The electoral college was called to convene the first Wednesday of February of 1789 to choose the first president of the United States. Two months before his expected election, George Washington, nestled at Mount Vernon, had already begun drafting his inauguration speech. That early version—a florid, seventy-five-page piece of drivel—was tossed out and revised by James Madison. Madison would also pen the reply to Washington's speech on behalf of the House of Representatives.

Washington, however, was most eloquent about the Potomac River developments. On February 13, 1789, he wrote Thomas Jefferson, still in Paris, with an update about the exciting developments along the Potomac River: "Mr Milne . . . was at my House this week." James Milne's father, who in the 1780s had moved from England to France, had invented a flour-dressing machine and had devised revolutionary methods of cotton carding and spinning wool. Both Benjamin Franklin and Jefferson had met with the Milnes. The opportunity of establishing mills along the Potomac River that utilized their innovations would result in cheaper cloth and greater employment in the area. Washington also reported that a

factory of Glass is established, upon a large scale on Monocasy [Monocacy along the Great Wagon Road], near Frederick-Town in Maryld [sic]. I am informed it will this year produce Glass of various kinds, nearly to the amount of ten thousand pounds value. This factory will be essentially benefitted, by having the navigation of the Potomac completely opened. But the total benefits of that Navigation will not be confined to narrower limits, than the extent of the western territory of the U: States.

You have been made acquainted, my dear Sir, with my ideas of the practicability, importance & extent of that navigation, as they have been occasionally, though fully expressed, in my several letters to you . . .

I am going on Monday next to visit works, as far as the Seneca Falls. Could I have delayed writing this letter untill [sic] my return . . . I might have been more particular in my account of the state of the several works, & especially of the situation of the Land adjoining to the Canal at Great Falls. Whensoever the produce of those parts of the Country bordering on the sources of the Potomac & contiguous to the long rivers that run into it (particularly the Shanandoah [sic] & the South Branch) shall be waterborne down to Tide-water for exportation, I conceive this place must become very valuable . . . I cannot entertain a doubt of the establishment of a Town in that place . . . Mill Seats, I well know, have long been considered as very valuable ones.

The glass factory of which Washington wrote became the legendary New Bremen Glass Manufactory. Washington's prediction about a town at the Great Falls came to fruition the following year when the Virginia State Assembly chartered Matildaville (today within the Great Falls National Park), located right near Washington's Difficult Run property. He also owned, as Jefferson well knew, thousands of acres "contiguous" to those tributary rivers that he believed destined to become "very valuable."

The opening of the new government under the US Constitution in New York City was delayed owing to winter storms that left roads difficult to travel upon. No quorum was reached until April 1, 1789. The bleakness of that harsh winter mirrored Washington's own feelings about his financial situation. He wrote his business agent, "I have never before felt the want to cash so severely as at present." The previous summer, Washington confessed to his personal physician and friend, Dr. James Craik, that, "with much truth, I can say I have never felt the want of money so sensibly since I was a boy of 15 years old." There is a plethora of letters from Washington to craftsmen and merchants in which he declared himself poverty-stricken. When, at last, Washington was able to depart Mount Vernon for New York City on April 16, 1789, he traveled on borrowed money. The Congress, many of whose members had operated the accounts payable to Washington's exorbitant wartime expense tally, this time established a firm salary—$25,000 per annum—a generous remuneration, nonetheless an inflexible one.

En route to New York to swear his oath of loyalty to the United States as its first president, Washington made a very public stop in Alexandria to bid farewell to his neighbors, many of whom were, like himself, financially dependent on agriculture and cash-strapped. Exacerbating the situation was the fact that a number of them drained liquidity by investing in the Potomac Company. Mayor Dennis Ramsay addressed Washington on behalf of the citizenry of Alexandria:

> [Y]our neighbors and friends now address you . . . The first and
> best of citizens must leave us . . . our agriculture its improver; our
> commerce its friend; our infant academy its protector; our poor their
> benefactor; and the interior navigation of the Potowmack (an event

replete with the most extensive utility, already, by your unremitted exertions, brought into partial use) its institutor and promoter.

Sharing their pangs and longings for financial ease and their hopes that Alexandria would become America's capital city, Washington swore a separate oath of loyalty to them, professing "attachment to yourselves, and regard for your interests . . . the whole tenor of my life . . . and my past actions . . . must be the pledge of my future conduct."

After Alexandria, every city, small town, and farm regaled him with poems, songs, and cheers on his way, and he would politely alight his carriage to acknowledge their greetings. When he reached the west side of the mighty Hudson River a flotilla awaited to transport him from New Jersey to the southern tip of Manhattan Island, where he disembarked at Murray's Wharf to further fanfare. Both his arrival and the general gaiety of the week between April 23 and April 30, 1789, that led up to Washington's inauguration are so well documented with eyewitness accounts that cannons, bells, fireworks, and ladies' fashion offer a cinematic intimacy with the epic week. Many New Yorkers kept diaries and letters that effusively prologued the antici-pated solemn-but-joyful inauguration of the first president of the United States, which, in their eyes, would be a testament to the hard-earned battle for nationhood.

On Thursday, April 30, 1789, a small, hand-selected group of dignitaries, a pantheon of America's Founding Fathers, convened at 3 Cherry Street at Franklin Square, Washington's new home, located on what had been a cherry orchard planted by a wealthy seventeenth-century Dutch merchant. The house itself, built by Walter Franklin, had been redecorated for the president of the United States to much acclaim by Lady Kitty Duer.[2] George Washington was ushered to the newly reconfigured Federal Hall. Sculpted into the pediment above the front balcony was the symbolic American bald eagle. There were rooms for the House and Senate and a portico so that the public could witness Washington swear his oath of allegiance, "to preserve, protect, and defend the Constitution of the United States," as prescribed by the document itself. When "the Chancellor" Robert R. Livingston administered the oath of office,

Washington, speaking softly and meaningfully, added his own epilogue: "So help me, God!"—which every US president has uttered since.[3]

Washington dressed in domestic broadcloth to set the tone for his administration. It was also symbolic of his mission to encourage American enterprise. For weeks, the Congress had worked to establish etiquette and protocol to befit a republic. Some wanted no ceremony. Others, like John Adams, who had lived in Europe and had envisioned his family a New World dynastic aristocracy, wanted elaborate titles. Adams had suggested to the Congress, believing that he would undoubtedly be next in line for the presidency, that "His Highness" would be the appropriate designation for America's executive-in-chief. The Congress would determine the president's social obligations, his fixed salary and a limited expense account. The president of the United States would have at his disposal a cream-colored state coach ornamented with cupids and festooned with flowers. It would be driven by six horses when he was on official business or four when he used the carriage for personal reasons.

Philip Schuyler missed the inauguration, as the New York State elections had begun on April 28. For at least a month, Schuyler would poll and canvas voters in order to convince them to place Federalists into office. On May 2, Schuyler wrote his friend George Washington that "we were advised of Your Excellenys [sic] arrival at New York, and If a variety of incidents did not concur to prevent me, I should have the honor in person to congratulate you, on the gratitude and confidence, which you so eminently experience from united America." Schuyler expressed his commiseration with Washington that the previous malfunctioning system of government "was a constant, and a painful reflection to every patriot" who had fought for a united nation. "Anxiety is now at an end, the impending clouds are dispelled . . . Let me Join my wish to the universal one, that health, happiness and every blessing may be your portion. I am Dear Sir with affectionate and sincere Esteem." Schuyler's son-in-law Alexander Hamilton, to be Washington's secretary of the treasury, was in New York City and reported to his father-in-law on both the goings-on amongst the federal representatives as well as the vote-jockeying "in the Southern district."

Washington's cabinet—his inner circle—was heavily populated by his New York family. He offered the position of secretary of state to John Jay, who turned it down in favor of becoming the first chief justice of the United States. Washington selected Alexander Hamilton to head the Treasury department fully cognizant and in agreement with Hamilton's fiscal vision for America. Hamilton would undertake his job leading the Treasury department with ferocity and unequaled genius. His breadth of understanding of the most modern concepts available in economics guided him in implementing an English-inspired sinking fund, unified customs and tariffs that facilitated international and interstate trade, and a system of taxation on commodities and real estate. America would become a creditworthy capitalist empire because of Alexander Hamilton.

It was only after John Jay turned down the post of secretary of state that Washington would offer the position to his fellow Virginian Thomas Jefferson. Washington chose another Virginian, Edmund Randolph, for the post of attorney general. Washington did not offer a cabinet post to James Madison. Unlike Madison, whom Washington could easily manipulate, Philip Schuyler would remain among Washington's closest confidantes and a man with whom Washington would never trifle.

On Thursday, May 7, 1789, the first inaugural ball was held at the Assembly Room on the east side of Broadway slightly north of Wall Street. Washington, Adams, members of the Congress, foreign ambassadors, and preeminent members of New York society attended. Mrs. Washington, in her late fifties at the time, had not yet arrived, and many of those who were present noted her husband's predilections for dancing and the ladies. The much younger Betsey Hamilton, who danced with Washington, recalled with amusement that the aging man's style was to step the sequence but not really dance. On May 19, Mrs. Washington, accompanied by her grandchildren Eleanor and George, set off from Mount Vernon to join her husband in New York City. On the day after her arrival, her husband, the president of the United States, hosted his own dinner party in her honor. Proving himself to be not only a great general but also a consummate politician, Washington invited both Vice President Adams, still sullen about his own low vote count against Washington's resoundingly popular election, and the enemy of the Federalist cause, Governor George Clinton.

The Washingtons were, of course, invited everywhere. Public amusements included a wax museum, theatricals, and staged fights, considered too undignified by the Congress for the president's entertainment. Alexander Hamilton advised Washington that it would be too cumbersome for Washington to accept private invitations, as everyone would want a home visit and courtesy would leave Washington no time to do anything else. On May 29, Mrs. Washington hosted the first of many subsequent social events. Although these receptions were held in the evening from eight to ten, they were mistakenly called "levees," after the French morning gatherings called *levées*. In an effort to suggest a folksy atmosphere, Washington would appear without hat or sword. Mrs. Washington's "levees" for women were held on Fridays, at which time she served ice cream and lemonade. Among the usual attendees were Mrs. John Adams, Mrs. Henry Knox, Kitty Duer, Mary Duane, Betsey Hamilton, Sally Jay, Sara Cornelia Clinton, Mrs. Philip Schuyler, and a number of other Livingston, Schuyler, and van Rensselaer cousins.

The Washingtons maintained a staff of twenty in help, seven of them slaves, all of them in livery. Washington's diaries reveal that throughout his residence in New York City, the John Jays, the Philip Schuylers, and the Alexander Hamiltons were among his most frequent guests. Senator William Maclay of Pennsylvania grumbled in his own diaries that Washington's parties were pretentious and that invitations were only extended to those in the highest circles of government and society. Maclay, who, nonetheless, was invited to 3 Cherry Street on a few occasions, complained further that Washington would look at his watch, decide he had had enough, and simply leave the table.

The oxymoronic splendor of a republican court was concentrated in a very small geographic area and elicited contradictory feelings. Administration officials attended spectacular parties at the foreign embassies, giving American politicians like Washington and James Madison—who, unlike Jefferson, Adams, or Monroe, would never live abroad—an opportunity to socialize among the diplomatic corps. Some charged that the New York City encounters with foreign representatives would impact and bias foreign policy for years to come. Europeans, accustomed to older and more expansive capital cities with awe-inspiring kings and castles, pointed to Washington as a country bumpkin. Republican idealists criticized the new elite: Washington behaved too like a monarch, riding around in his "kingly" coach, sitting for portrait artists as if he were a reigning sovereign, appearing in public to "The President's March," whose melody was the tune of "God Save the King." Mrs. Washington, addressed as "Lady Washington," did return social calls, shepherded by a footman. Although the Washington's were suffering a cash shortfall, Washington asked Robert Morris to ship him expensive mirrors from Philadelphia that would reflect the table silver with blazes of light.

There is an old adage that states: "living well is the best revenge." There is no better example of that aphorism than the decision by President George Washington to also host very elegant picnics, to which he would invite America's most important people and the representatives of Europe's kings, at the abandoned former home of British Colonel Roger Morris. Morris's wife, née Mary (Polly) Philipse , had declined a young, unimportant, practically impoverished George Washington's offer of marriage. On more than a few Sundays, the most elegant liveried carriages would ride in a flamboyant cavalcade up Broadway at the behest of President George Washington to join him on the hilltop with the panoramic view that bore the shadow of the girl who had rejected him.

Washington invited both friends and those critical of him to his home, to his box at the theater, and to worship alongside him at St. Paul's Chapel (Trinity Church was under construction until the following spring, at which time Washington would have his own elegantly adorned, canopied pew there), as he thought it was imperative to establish the appearance of harmony and stability in his government.

On July 4, 1789, the Tariff Act went into effect, pointing the nation's commerce in a unified direction. In a gesture to promote American commerce that was also redolent with symbolism—that, as he advised his soldiers, a southerner could embrace a northerner for the good of the nation—Washington set out on a tour of the New England—or "Eastern" states, as he referred to them—in late summer. He visited the Hartford Woolen Manufactory in Connecticut, where his inaugural costume had been produced. In Massachusetts, Washington, the entrepreneur, observed with pride "the new Invented Carding and Spinning Machines at the Beverly Cotton Manufactury [sic]." Rhode Island was not yet a state in the autumn of 1789, but, a year later, when it did join the union, Washington would make the inclusive gesture of attending worship services at a synagogue in Newport, Rhode

Island. Washington also advocated for the first national holiday—Thanksgiving, which was celebrated for the first time on November 26, 1789—and, to set the tone of tolerance and neighborliness, Washington incorporated the Dutch tradition of New Year's Day open house at his 3 Cherry Street residence.

New Yorkers willingly disposed of their own history when, in the summer of 1789, with the full consent of the United States Congress, the old Dutch English fort on the Battery was decimated so that construction could begin on Government House. The enormous three-story brick building with its own waterfront promenade and prime harbor views was meant to accommodate a growing federal government. The Congress of the United States was giving every indication that it was in New York City to stay.

Americans were buoyant following Washington's inauguration. Washington himself set a tone of consonance. Congress enjoyed steady quorums in the summer of 1789 as it operated under the new United States Constitution with New York City as the convivial backdrop. It was in August, however, when Americans got word of the storming of the Bastille prison in France, that an old and simmering argument resurfaced in Lower Manhattan. It began with some behind-the-scenes lobbying and an alliance formed between delegates from the states of Pennsylvania and Maryland.

In December 1788, the Maryland State Assembly had passed a resolution to offer a large parcel of land to the federal government for the federal seat of government. On August 27, 1789, the representatives from Maryland to the House of Representatives made a motion to enter into the record that "a permanent residence ought to be fixed for the general government of the United States, at some convenient place, as near the center of wealth, population, and extent of territory, as may be consistent with convenience to the navigation of the Atlantic ocean, and having due regard to the particular situation of the western country." On September 11, 1789, Federal Hall architect Pierre L'Enfant wrote President Washington:

> The late determination of Congress to lay the Foundation of a City which is to become the Capital of this vast Empire, offer so great an occasion of acquiring reputation, to whoever may be appointed

to conduct the execution of the business, that your Excellency will not be surprised that my Embition [sic] and the desire I have of becoming a usefull [sic] Citizen should lead me to wish a share in the Undertaking.

No nation perhaps had Ever before the opportunity offered them of deliberately deciding on the spot where their Capital city Should be fixed, or of Combining Every necessary consideration in the choice of Situation . . . the plan Shuld be drawn on such a Scale as to leave room for that aggrandizement & embellishment which the increase of the wealth of the Nation will permit it to pursue.

Factions amongst the members of the House were not about to leave the location of the permanent seat of government to chance. On September 7, a second resolution was put forth, stating that the permanent seat of government should be located "at some convenient place on the east bank of the river Susquehanna, in the state of Pennsylvania, and that until the necessary buildings be erected for the purpose, the seat of government ought to continue at the city of New-York." Ten days later, on September 17, Virginia Congressman Richard Bland Lee, who represented Alexandria, moved to replace "on the east bank of the river Susquehanna" with "on the banks of the Potomac." Warning that southerners would lose faith in the union if the capital city were placed in Pennsylvania, Richard Bland Lee forced a vote on his revision, which was defeated 29–21. A series of subsequent challenges called for the "Potowmac [sic], Susquehanna, or Delaware," "on the banks of either side of the river Delaware, not more than eight miles above or below the lower falls of Delaware," and the replacement of Maryland for Pennsylvania. On September 23, 1789, Vice President John Adams wrote in his diary: "We are about founding a City which will be one of the first in the World, and We are governed by local and partial Motives."

The Pennsylvania contingent fought hard for Philadelphia but there were too many members of the Congress who would not forget the mutiny of June 1783. With that option less likely, Pennsylvania's alliance with Maryland for a capital city on the Susquehanna River was a less distasteful measure to push.

By mid-September 1789, the House of Representatives passed a resolution that "the President of the United States be authorised [sic] to appoint three commissioners to examine and report to him the most eligible situation on the banks of the Susquehanna, in the state of Pennsylvania, for the permanent seat of the government of the United States." The commission, with President Washington's direction, would authorize monies and construction "within four years, suitable buildings for the Congress," providing that the states of Pennsylvania and Maryland remove all obstructions in the river between the mouth of the river and the location of the seat of government.

This latest proviso—that the reward of hosting the capital city would require a state to ensure navigable waters—did not go unnoticed by Washington and his other canal company investors. The very patriotic Washington was still consumed with personal profit. The annual shareholders and directors meeting of the Potomac River Canal Company took place without him in late summer. The project was in dire need of the money that shareholders had pledged but had not contributed. The Potomac River Canal Company directors, without Washington's participation but with his agreement, placed penalties on outstanding monies owed and accelerated condemnation proceedings on the properties owned by delinquent shareholders. Washington had not relinquished his holdings in the commercial venture upon assuming the office of the president of the United States. In fact, most members of the administration and of both houses of the Congress continued to receive outside income from sources other than their government salary. Many had purchased public securities from Revolutionary War soldiers, who had still not been remunerated for their wartime service. About the only one who seemed to take financial conflict of interest seriously was Alexander Hamilton, who forwent any salary from his legal practice for the duration of his tenure as secretary of the treasury. In addition, according to Alexander Hamilton's third son, James, Alexander Hamilton also asked his father-in-law, Philip Schuyler, to keep his own son from making new purchases of public securities and to refrain from putting any in the Hamilton family accounts lest it appear that the secretary of the treasury was providing insider information to his family.

Land speculators who served in Congress and the president of the United States kept a watchful eye on the September 1789 bill that would locate a capital city on the banks of the Susquehanna River. The bill progressed from the House to the Senate. On a September 25, the Senate added a clause to the bill that specified a ten-square-mile capital district in the area of Germantown, Pennsylvania. That bill and addendum were reviewed in the Senate on September 26 and returned to the House. On September 28, the House agreed to the Senate's addendum and returned the bill to the Senate, at which time the Senate decided to postpone a vote on the bill until the next session in January 1790. That would give the members of the Senate nearly four months to campaign for the bill's rejection, overturn it, and send it back to the House for yet more haggling and revision.

President Washington remained in New York City between the two sessions. His diaries reflect frequent dinners throughout the autumn and Christmas season with "Genl. Schuyler, his Lady," and Schuyler's married daughters and their husbands, the Hamiltons and the Stephen van Rensselaers (Peggy Schuyler). Virginia representatives James Madison and William Grayson, on the other hand, returned to Virginia. On October 7, 1789, Grayson wrote Madison from Philadelphia that dissension and further lobbying for a different seat of government had simply relocated there. Financier and US Senator from Pennsylvania Robert Morris buttonholed Grayson on the street on behalf of Philadelphia. Grayson told Morris that, as New York and New Jersey were especially against Philadelphia, it was unlikely; Grayson shared with Morris that New York and New Jersey might, however, agree to a location in western Pennsylvania, as had been written in the bill pending before the Senate. Grayson informed Madison that the ongoing jockeying and shifting alliances were dizzying.

Grayson wrote Madison that there was favorable news concerning a capital city on the Potomac River, which, along with western Pennsylvania and New York City, were the three most talked-about locations amongst the Virginians, the Pennsylvanians, and the Carolinians. Representative Thomas Scott from Pennsylvania believed, according to Grayson, "that a majority of the delegation are so irrietated [sic] as to go unconditionally to the Potowmack [sic] by way of spiting N. York." Scott admitted to Grayson, who reassured Madison that, "our contest about the Potowmack [sic] has been of infinite consequence; she is gaining friends daily."

On November 20, 1789, back home in Orange County, James Madison wrote George Washington a recap of his own experiences in Philadelphia, where, he had also stopped en route to Virginia. Madison

> fell in with Mr. Morris. He broke the subject of the residence of Congs. [sic] and made observations which betrayed his dislike of the upshot of the business at N. York, and his desire to keep alive a "Southern project"—"an arrangement"—a cabal—with Pennsylvania: I reminded him of the conduct of his State [the June 1783 mutiny] . . . His answer implied that Congress must not continue at New York . . . the E. States . . . refusal to take up the bill and pass it as it went to the Senate, he should renounce all confidence in that quarter, and speak seriously to the S. States. I told him . . . after what had passed, if Penna expected them to listen to her, that indeed there was probably an end to further intercourse on the subject.

Madison retold Grayson's stories and suggested probable strategies:

> an attempt will first be made to alarm N. York and the Eastern States into the plan postponed, by holding out the Potowmac [sic] & Philada [sic] as the alternative, and if the attempt should not succeed, the alternative will then be held out to the Southern members. On the other hand N.Y. and the E. States [New England], will enforce their policy of delay, by threatening the S. States as heretofore, with German Town or Trenton or at least Susquehanna, and will no doubt carry the threat into execution if they can, rather than suffer an arrangement to take place between Pena [sic] & the S. States.

While the Congress was on its hiatus, Americans received more unsettling news from France that would amplify and intensify the conversation on where to locate the American seat of government. In 1682, King Louis XIV of France famously declared, "*L'État, c'est moi!*"—"I am the State!"—and, exercising his divine right, amputated his court from the nation's capital city of Paris to his favorite countryside chateau, the Palace of Versailles. In 1789, when George Washington was inaugurated as first president of the United States, the Palace of Versailles had served as the political and cultural nexus of France for one hundred years. Louis XIV's great-great-grandson, King Louis XVI, had been America's greatest European patron in its struggle for independence from Great Britain. In October 1789, King Louis XVI was forced from the Palace of Versailles to Paris with his queen and two children.

Although the notion of the shining city on a hill, an isolated, corruption-free government, appealed to the inherently idealistic nature of an American people dreaming of liberty and equal rights, the dramatic events in France highlighted the consequences of a government that was inaccessible to the people. Should the seat of government of any nation be removed from that nation's social and financial heartbeat? Shoring up its own alliance with the state of Maryland, on December 3, 1789, the Virginia Assembly voted to donate a portion of Fairfax County on the Potomac River adjacent to Maryland acreage to form the new federal district. This designated territory was located in Virginia Congressman Alexander White's district and did not include Alexandria.

Synchronized with the Virginia cession was a propaganda brochure published by Washington's stepson-in-law David Stuart that extolled the virtues and marvels of Alexandria, Virginia. Stuart submitted it to Washington for his approval. Once endorsed by Washington, the pamphlet was disseminated. Washington especially hoped that rich New Yorkers and New England shipbuilders would relocate. Reportage on the contents of the brochure appeared in newspapers like the *Massachusetts Centinel*, the *Worcester Gazette*, and the *Gazette of the United States*. In casual conversations with congressional representatives from the northern states, Washington would recommend the more temperate climate of Alexandria as conducive to greater ease and more productivity. The president was also continuously informed of every meeting in Alexandria that recapped results from the publication of the brochure.

Washington felt that momentum was in his favor when the *Maryland Journal and Baltimore Advertiser* featured a glowing story on the brochure. He advised his Virginia representatives to caucus with the Maryland and

Pennsylvania delegations and remind them that a seat of government on the Potomac River would benefit all three states. Washington wanted them to form solid voting bloc.

Washington's tactic, allowing them all to infer that the location of the permanent seat of government would be at the Northern Neck so designated by the Virginia resolution, was a smokescreen solely for negotiation purposes. The federal bill gave him authority to select the ten-square-mile location within a wider parameter. Pennsylvania representatives were offered an additional concession: while the new capital was under construction, the Congress would remain in Philadelphia for ten years. The Pennsylvania contingent was convinced that once the Congress resumed its familiarity with the wonders of the City of Brotherly Love, where their members had nearly been assassinated, legislators would surely vote to abandon the notion of a government on a swamp, and would, instead, choose to remain on the Schuylkill River.

While George Washington's brochure had made waves, his ongoing machinations to remove the seat of government were subterranean. The president's protégé, Alexander Hamilton, on the other hand, was intent on causing a tsunami.

CHAPTER 12

Toward Duopoly

BY JANUARY 1790, LIKE A phoenix that had risen literally from ashes, New York City had become the nation's seat of government and its financial and cultural capital. On January 8, George Washington delivered his first State of the Union address. In it, he brought up a subject that Alexander Hamilton had been hammering persistently at with him and with the members of the Congress: the government debt needed to be addressed. Washington agreed with Hamilton that in order to buoy an empire, a unified plan for solvency was essential. Six days after Washington's State of the Union message, Hamilton gave his "First Report on Public Credit" to the Congress on January 14th. The Hamilton plan is important to the true story behind the Great Compromise of 1790 because George Washington cleverly packaged it as the quid for the quo in a swap deal for his capital city on the Potomac River.

Hamilton's proposal was revolutionary. He boldly urged the Congress to reckon with its fiscal liabilities: US foreign and domestic debt had now expanded to some $54 million, and outstanding state debt totaled another $25 million. The nascent republic was saddled with a nearly $80 million deficit.[1] Hamilton put forward the creation of a national bank to pay back this enormous amount, including the full value of all Revolutionary War bonds.

Most of the Continental soldiers had still had not been paid. If the federal government did not unify its house and assume the states' war debt, Hamilton argued, the nation would never succeed. Most economists agree. Without Alexander Hamilton's plan, the United States would never have been able to issue bonds, borrow money, and fully participate in the international flow of commerce, finance defense, or effect cohesive interstate industry.

Virginians were unhappy with the plan. Their state had whittled down a good deal of their debt. Other states like Massachusetts had been far less responsible, scoffed the Virginians. Some historians argue that the debate reflected a clear-cut north-south divide but, in fact, South Carolina, a state that still had mountains of debt, was for Hamilton's plan. While the Virginia delegation haggled in Federal Hall, Washington watched from the sidelines. He was in a difficult situation. He had to support his fellow Virginians but he also agreed with Hamilton.

To appear presidential, impartial, and a friend to both sides, Washington made a show of hosting frequent dinners for his fellow Virginians as well as the Hamiltons and the Schuylers. On January 27, 1790, Washington entertained Alexander Hamilton, Philip Schuyler, and James Madison along with Pennsylvania senator and financier Robert Morris, South Carolina senators Ralph Izard and Pierce Butler, Massachusetts senator Tristram Dalton, and representatives Michael Jenifer Stone (Maryland), Theodore Sedgwick (Massachusetts), James Schureman (New Jersey), Thomas Fitzsimons (Pennsylvania), and William Loughton Smith (South Carolina). Washington also made a point of being seen in public with his New York family, accompanying them to the theater and to church. Again, on March 2, 1790, Washington recorded in his journal that New York Senators Philip Schuyler and Rufus King, Robert Morris of Philadelphia, and "The Vice-Presidt." were among those who joined him for dinner. On Thursday, March 25, 1790, Washington listed his dinner guests as:

> The Chief Justice Jay & his Lady Genl. Schuyler & his Lady, the Secretary of the Treasury [Hamilton] and his Lady, the Secretary of War & his Lady & Mrs. Greent The Secretary of State (Mr. Jefferson) Mr. Carroll [of Maryland] & Mr. Hanry of the Senate Judge Wilson,

Messrs. Madison & Page of the Ho. Of Representatives, and Colo. Smith Marshall of the District.

Washington's dinners forced a conversation on seemingly insurmountable problems that had been tabled for years that Hamilton's report had addressed. One of the most vociferously expressed concerns was what to do about those still unpaid Continental Army soldiers. Many of them had received government IOUs, and, in desperate straits, had sold their certificates to speculators. Even thrifty Abigail Adams had invested in the scripts. A debate in the Congress and amongst the general public included reflections on questions such as: Who should and how should certificate holders be able to redeem funds, and at what interest? Should there be a differing interest payment for the soldier versus the speculator, who, according to some, had taken advantage of the destitute freedom fighters? James Madison reasoned that since the original owners had sold their bonds for very little money, it would be unethical for opportunists to profit. He proposed tracing the bonds to their original patriotic owners.

Senator Maclay noted in his journal that concern for ethos was mere pretense: some of the very members of the Congress voting on this bill would enjoy big returns if Hamilton's bill passed. Of the twenty-six members of the Senate, at least sixteen were security holders at the time. Elbridge Gerry of Massachusetts owned federal certificates valued at $32,900 and Massachusetts state continental securities valued at $16,180; Roger Sherman and Jeremiah Wadsworth, both of Connecticut, owned $7,700 and $21,500 certificates respectively; former president of the Congress of the Confederation Elias Boudinot of New Jersey owned a face value of $49,500 in federal certificates; George Clymer of Pennsylvania, $12,500; William Loughton Smith of South Carolina held $11,900 worth of certificates; and many more owned a smaller number of the financial instruments.[2] Secretary of War General Henry Knox began aggressively purchasing government securities in the spring of 1790, amassing some $60,000 worth of federal certificates. Those who charged Philip Schuyler of self-interest were incorrect, as Schuyler's certificates dated back to 1782, and, at Alexander Hamilton's request, neither he nor his family engaged in purchasing continental securities once Hamilton became secretary of the treasury.

Also serving in the Congress were members who owned shares in George Washington's Potomac Canal Company. Although they were aching to remove the capital to the Potomac, it seemed very unlikely to these investors that the seat of government would leave New York City in 1790. Government House was beginning to rise, reflecting a commitment to New York City as the seat of the federal government. Philip Schuyler and his circle continued to endow improvements for the Washington administration with the tacit understanding that their largesse was an outlay for the permanent seat of government. Schuyler and other New Yorkers had designed a presidential box at the John Street Theatre, a distinguished pew for the president of the United States at Trinity Church, and other amenities with a long-term view in mind.

On February 23—the day after the new republic celebrated the president's birthday—President and Mrs. Washington moved into the fabulous Macomb mansion on lower Broadway. Washington commenced pouring money into freshening the new and very grand presidential palace, whose grounds rolled toward the Hudson River. Even in cold weather, from time to time Washington could be seen at the shore's edge with a fishing rod in his hands. In his diary, which Washington consciously made available for posterity, his March 25 entry commemorated attendance at the consecration of Trinity Church, "where a Pew was constructed and set apart for the President of the United Sts," followed by another small dinner with "Lady Genl. Schuyler & his Lady, the Secretary of the Treasury & Lady [Hamilton]." Presidential landmarks indicated that New Yorkers, at the very least, were convinced that New York City would remain the seat of government.

The only reversal that spring was a lethal influenza epidemic that attacked and stalled the city. Only days after his excursion to Trinity Church, Washington became gravely ill; the prognosis was not good, and it became necessary for the other members of the executive branch to step forward in the president's stead. Alexander Hamilton became de facto head of state, and his usual critics bitterly hurled epithets of abuse, like referring to the capital city as "Hamiltonopolis."

Jealousy, however, surfaced from a surprising source. After five years in Paris, Thomas Jefferson returned to the United States during the winter of 1789–90 to assume the position of secretary of state. Jefferson busied himself unpacking crates of furniture, paintings, porcelain, silver, clothing, and books, along with 288 bottles of wine and the sacks of rice seed he had smuggled illegally out of Italy (punishment for that was death). There were also eighty-six crates of cooking utensils, packages of olives, which he adored, Maille mustard, and his daughter Patsy's gorgeous harpsichord. As had Washington, Jefferson also stopped in Alexandria en route to New York City for a dinner in his honor on March 10, at which time Mayor Will Hunter firmly reminded Jefferson that Alexandrians had invested in the Potomac Canal Company, and they expected results.

Jefferson arrived in New York City on March 20, 1790, and began customizing his shabby New York City Maiden Lane residence at great expense, which would seem to indicate that he, too, thought the seat of government would not remove from New York City. It was while Jefferson had been living in Europe that the much younger Alexander Hamilton's reputation had begun to skyrocket, and although they had never met, the Hamiltons hosted a welcome dinner for Jefferson upon his arrival. Jefferson wore very expensive French couture—an elegant blue coat and crimson knee-britches—to the party. Throughout his life, Thomas Jefferson spent with wanton recklessness, and, by the time of his death, his unrestrained expenditures would leave him and his estate so in debt that his home in Virginia would be parceled off, and his descendants were so reduced in circumstances that they would be forced to turn to all connections, including later presidents and their families, for handouts.

There was no doubt that Thomas Jefferson was fiscally irresponsible, yet, when he whispered in Madison's ear that a national bank would put too much power in too few hands, Madison, originally for the Federal Bank, as had been written in *Federalist* 44, suddenly reversed his position. A longtime Washington minion, Madison was the surrogate who had fought for Washington's ownership in and leadership of the Potomac Canal Company. In what Washington would later call an act of treachery, Madison not only began to lobby hard against Hamilton's plan but also, with Washington presumably on his deathbed, Madison called for a House vote to sink the bill. Anti-Federalist Massachusetts representatives, who viewed Madison's volte-face with suspicion, nonetheless needed the Assumption Bill to pass because their state was deeply in debt. Most of the southern states did not support assumption of state debts except for South Carolina, another state still deeply in debt. Two of Virginia's three representatives were against assumption, as were three of the New York Clintonian delegates to the House of Representatives. Philip Schuyler blasted those representatives with a warning that New York City would lose the seat of government because of their anti-Federalist actions.

On April 12, Madison shepherded the bill's 31–29 defeat. The vote revealed interesting alliances: Maryland, Georgia, North Carolina, and Virginia voted against assumption; South Carolina, Connecticut, Massachusetts, and Delaware voted for Hamilton's plan. New Jersey and Pennsylvania split their votes, signaling that their delegations could be lobbied with the right inducement. In fact, Robert Morris began threatening both sides of the assumption argument that Pennsylvania would vote with the opposing bloc if the Congress did not declare Philadelphia the permanent seat of government. Virginia representative Richard Bland Lee confided to friends back in Alexandria that secret backroom wrangling about the seat of government was afoot.

President Washington learned of Madison's public betrayal and was enraged. Some blamed Madison's disloyalty for Washington's worsening health. For nearly two months, Washington lay near death. His protracted frailty was of such concern that the streets around his house were closed to traffic so that the president could rest undisturbed. Despite that, ordinary citizens strolled by the new presidential residence and stopped to pray. Ignoring the possibility of contagion, Washington's loyal friends visited his chamber, sincerely believing that Washington's final days were imminent.

While Washington lingered near death, and having learned that Madison had acted out of concert, Washington experienced an epiphany: his power, along with his own life, could dissolve in an instant—and his tenure as president offered him a very limited window of influence. Vice President John Adams would be the next president. Adams had little interest in a seat of government on the Potomac River. Slowly, Washington began to recover, and, with new appreciation, he realized that if he dawdled, his potential windfall could evaporate. Although he admired his New York friends, their goals, their devotion, and their financial commitment to the republic, Washington was now implacable: the time was *now*. He had to gamble: he would bundle Hamilton's bill to deliver solvency for the nation with the seat of government to ensure his own comfort.

On May 22, Philip Schuyler shared wonderful news: the president was, at long last, able "to traverse his room a dozen times." Now that Washington was on the mend, James Madison apologized to the president, expressing great remorse for his errant behavior and unreliability. Washington knew that Jefferson had been behind Madison's act of untrustworthiness. Jefferson was on board with the seat of government in Alexandria but Jefferson was most definitely for states' rights above a strong federal government. He did not agree with Washington, Madison, and their New York friends. Although Washington knew that Jefferson had incited Madison to move against Hamilton's bill, the president could and would make Madison pay for his perfidy. Washington calculated how Madison was going to redeem himself. He was going to become the president's point man in securing both the reintroduction and passage of Hamilton's bill as well as the removal of the capital city to the Potomac. The two Virginians would work closely and clandestinely on strategy, reviewing every vote, every weakness, and every possibility for a presidential "win-win." Washington viewed Jefferson as counterproductive and preferred keeping Jefferson out of their conversations unless he became useful.

On May 24, South Carolina representative William Loughton Smith reported to South Carolina state legislator Edward Rutledge that the assumption component of Hamilton's bill had been excised in order to pass the rest of it:

> We have taken up the Funding Bill & have nearly got thro [sic] it in a Committee of the whole . . . if the measure is lost, it will not be for its demerits, but thro [sic] some out-of-door management—I am pretty sure the removal to Philadelphia is to be connected with it . . . the Assumption must be kept back till the close of the Session & then we shall be made to understand that unless we vote for Philadelphia, the State debts will not be provided for.

On that same day, May 24, Robert Morris made a motion in the Senate to remove Congress to Philadelphia for its next session as a temporary seat of government. Debate continued for two days, at which time New York Senator Rufus King and Pierce Butler of South Carolina made a motion to postpone the debate. Postponement won 13–11.

By the end of May, the voting blocs would change. On May 29, 1790, Rhode Island became the thirteenth state. The reappearance of New England representation meant that a southern seat of government would be harder to obtain. Things needed to escalate before the arrival of those delegates from Rhode Island. On May 31, Pennsylvania representative Thomas Fitzsimons introduced another bill in the House to remove from New York. Fierce arguments ensued but the bill passed 38–22. Fitzsimons's bill went to the Senate, where Vice President John Adams broke a tie vote. The bill went to a committee chaired by South Carolina senator Pierce Butler, who stalled the bill for a week in anticipation of the arrival of the delegation from Rhode Island. Butler, himself, introduced a bill for a permanent seat of government leaving the location blank.

On June 2, 1790, the House passed Hamilton's funding bill without the assumption ingredient. Completely independent from a southern bloc were the South Carolinians. They needed Hamilton's funding and were going to vote for assumption. They also liked the sophistication and fun of New York City. On June 7, a bill was introduced in the Senate for a permanent seat of government on the east bank of the Potomac with a temporary seat of government filled in upon agreement. That evening, all eleven senators agreed to remove to Philadelphia temporarily, but they would not agree on a permanent seat of government. The Senate voted on Fitsimons's bill, which was defeated 13–11. Butler's vote to build a capital city on the Potomac River did not receive enough support, and the men adjourned.

It would now come down to a three-state bloc of Virginia, Maryland, and Pennsylvania to approach affirmative votes for both a residence and assumption bill. Their swing votes on Hamilton's bill, unpopular in Virginia and Maryland, could ensure its passage. Washington instructed Madison to dangle once again the Fairfax, Virginia, cession before the representatives of the area and the adjacent Maryland counties. To violate the will of their voters on the fiscal measures would bring reward with the removal of the seat of government to the northern Potomac. Madison broached the subject quietly with the appropriate delegates to form the tristate voting bloc.

The members of Washington's hoped-for three-state cabal vociferously resumed their tussle on the floor of the Congress: Maryland insisted on Annapolis or Baltimore as the ideal choices for a permanent seat of government. Philadelphians harangued about their city's role in independence. New Yorkers pointed to their own claims of being first in liberty: on May 1, 1690, the first intercolonial convention was held in New York City; in 1754, the Albany Plan to unite the colonies was devised in Albany, New York, in the vicinity where the Hudson River meets the Mohawk; in 1765, the Sons of Liberty first met in New York City—*not* in Boston, as commonly believed. New Yorkers also reminded the Congress of the great trouble and expense they had gone to to welcome the US government. Debate got so discombobulated that a representative from Rhode Island stood up and declared that since it was a foregone conclusion that Canada would at some point join the union, Providence would be the exact center of empire on the North American continent and should, therefore, be the empire city.

Philip Schuyler was understandably upset with this melee after all he had done to fund the new capital for the federal government. Congressional members as well as the executive branch seemed mighty ungrateful, according to Schuyler, who wrote with concern to son-in-law Stephen van Rensselaer, the largest single landowner in New York State: "if the assumption is not carried, that the South Carolinians (in order to obtain an object which is so important to them) negotiate with those who wish the removal." Schuyler knew who wanted that removal more than anyone. He also recognized the game plan, one guerilla fighter to another. Neither he nor Washington was going to go down without a fight, but Schuyler became increasingly agitated with Washington for ill-using Alexander Hamilton as a presidential pawn.

While Washington's New York family had understandably soured on their longstanding affection for the president, Washington's Alexandrian neighbors still trusted him. His Potomac Canal Company allies reassured their congressman, Richard Bland Lee, that his vote for the Hamilton Assumption Bill, though unpopular, must be the sacrifice he had to make to ensure the removal of the capital city to Alexandria. The still contrite James Madison, acting as the president's field marshall in the center of the New York City theater of operation, had stumped against the Hamilton plan but now found himself, on instructions from Washington, prodding Congressman Alexander White of northern Virginia, Maryland Senator Charles Carroll, and Maryland representatives Daniel Carroll and George Gale to vote against their own constituents and for the Assumption Bill. Every single one of these legislators was misled by the representation from President George Washington, through Madison, that the seat of government would be located on the northern branch of the Potomac River where their three states converged. On June 26, however, Richard Bland Lee wrote his brother Theodorick Lee, in Virginia, with great confidence that "the place to be selected will be left to the discretion of the President . . . the bill will be so formed as to admit Alexandria if it should be deemed proper into the ten mile [sic] square."

Maryland Senator Charles Carroll, representatives Daniel Carroll and George Gale, as well as Virginia Congressmen Richard Bland Lee and Alexander White were all shareholders in the Potomac Canal Company. Virginia judge and politician Edmund Pendleton, in a letter to James Madison, expressed the opinion of many when he wrote: "I hazard some serious reflections which have occurred on hearing of the late enormous Sepeculations in b[ank] & Ch[annel/Canal] stock . . . a question—whether a Member of Congress ought to be a . . . Director?" President Washington, who was still the Potomac Company's largest shareholder, was not mentioned in that query.

There is no doubt that it was President George Washington who shaped the so-called Great Compromise of 1790. Thomas Jefferson was an exogenous figure who inserted himself into the story to enhance his own importance. Jefferson's dinner-party story was merely meringue on mud. According to Jefferson, his legendary dinner party was held on June 20, 1790. The Congressional Record itself debunks Jefferson's self-congratulatory avowal. On June 29, Massachusetts senators Tristram Dalton and Caleb Strong softened their position on removal from New York City in Senate proceedings in order to obtain passage of the

Assumption Bill. A deal was struck between the two states that would provide Virginia with extra financial considerations. The following day, on June 30, Pennsylvania senator William Maclay, who had been strong-armed to join the tristate voting bloc, expressed disgust in his diary that ongoing political haggling seemed endless. Significantly, he also accused President Washington of driving the matter of removal, which, to Maclay, was apparently not yet settled. Maclay's June 30 diary entry reads: "It is, in fact, the interest of the President of the United States that pushes the Potomac. He [Washington], by means of Jefferson, Madison, Carrol [sic], and others" were urging the matter. On July 6, the members of the House of Representatives were still bickering over the location of the permanent seat of government. Richard Bland Lee spent his day on the floor reassuring worried New Englanders, who were fearful that a southern capital would be too far to travel to, that the president would place the new seat of government a long way upriver from Alexandria. Lee even offered to insert a phrase that suggested proximity to Baltimore, which was more palatable to the delegates from the northern states. A skeptical Massachusetts representative, Elbridge Gerry, challenged Lee and demanded that "Baltimore" be inserted into the bill.

On July 15, nearly a month after Jefferson's grand dinner compromise, Pennsylvania senator Maclay reflected in his journal that the entire barter was a byzantine affair, engineered by Washington: "The President of the United states has (in my opinion) had a great influence in this business. The game was played by him and his adherents of Virginia and Maryland . . . Alas, that the affection—nay, almost adoration—of the people should meet so unworthy a return! Here are the best interests sacrificed to the vain whim of fixing Congress . . . on the Potomac." To Maclay, Jefferson and Madison had minor roles.[3]

The outcome of Washington's back-parlor politics resulted in the conflation of two seemingly disparate issues and bills. Hamilton's Assumption Bill was approved by one vote in the Senate—that of Charles Carroll of Maryland—and by one vote in the House of Representatives—that of Alexander White of northern Virginia. Per their agreement, James Madison was allowed to vote against assumption. On July 16, 1790, the Residence Act was signed, removing the capital city to a swamp on the Potomac River somewhere between the

Conococheague Creek, a tributary of the Potomac River that has its source in
western Pennsylvania and joins the Potomac in western Maryland at Williams-
port, and no farther south than the Anacostia River. This designation rewarded
all of the tristate legislators in league with Washington.

The exact location and design of America's capital city, however, would be
selected and supervised by the president of the United States. Although the bill
for Washington's dream city was intentionally vague about the exact location of
the permanent seat of government, it did specifically state that the empire city was
to be along the Potomac River no farther south than the Anacostia River. Alexandria, Virginia, is south of the Anacostia River. When Washington selected the
parameters of his federal seat of government, Alexandria, Virginia was within
the ten-square-mile designated capital city of the United States of America. In
charge from the shadows, George Washington clearly misled Maryland representative Alexander White, the Maryland senators, and members of the Congress
who anticipated a capital city farther north. Washington did, however, keep his
word to the Pennsylvanians about removing the capital to Philadelphia for ten
years while the permanent seat of government rose to grandeur.

Contemporaneous reaction to the congressional evacuation of New York
City shows great displeasure on the part of government employees as well as
their families. Maclay complained about taking "leave of New York . . . whose
allurements are more than ten to two compared with Philadelphia . . . I know
no such unsocial city as Philadelphia." Abigail Adams also wrote disparagingly
of the forced move and mourned that Philadelphia "would not be Broadway."
The Congressional Record provides documentation that more than a few legislators were outspokenly critical of the president.

New Yorkers were irate. They spat on the members of the Pennsylvania
delegation on the street. *The New York Advertiser* published scathing editorials.
A plethora of articles and unflattering illustrations reflected the outrage of the
community. One cartoon depicted a "Ship of State" wherein Washington was
charged with "self-gratification" and was captioned, "To the Conochegue by
way of Philadelphia." Another derisive cartoon, no longer extant, is alluded to
among the Horatio Gates papers. Gates, a nemesis to both Washington and
Schuyler during the Revolutionary War, noted with glee a profane caricature

called "The Entry," which depicted Washington "mounted on an Ass" led by his secretary, David Humphreys. The legend read: "The glorious time has come to pass / When David shall conduct an Ass."

Philip Schuyler was indignant about Washington's behavior toward his entire family and openly berated the members of the Congress for abusing the citizens of New York City. Schuyler denounced the vote swap as, "a want to decency which was due a city whose citizens made very capital exertions for the accommodation of Congress."[4]

On August 12, 1790, the Congress convened in New York City for the last time, and when George Washington departed on August 30, there was pointedly little fanfare—a striking difference from the customary tribute to the commander in chief.

Washington arrived in Georgetown, then in the state of Maryland, by eight o'clock in the morning on September 11, 1790, and, even before heading home to Mount Vernon, the president summoned a Potomac Canal Company business meeting at John Suter's tavern. His priorities were clear, and throughout the autumn, Washington busied himself planning his new federal seat.

When the government gathered in Philadelphia in early 1791, the president arrived prepared. He presented location survey and blueprint to the Congress for the new federal city. The ten square miles of land included the tidal Potomac port town of Alexandria, Virginia. When members of Congress balked, Washington vowed to retaliate and got his seat of government where he wanted it. He intentionally placed the nucleus of his federal government not far from the Great and Small Falls, which presented the most expensive obstructions to streamline on the Potomac River. Clearing the falls for navigation presented such a difficult challenge for engineers that many refused to accept the task. Once again, Washington acted for the benefit of the Potomac Canal Company shareholders. Unrelenting, he petitioned Congress for funding to unclog the falls, arguing that since they were to be in the very heart of the capital, it was the legislators' obligation to cover the cost of making the falls passable. Washington pressured and strong-armed local, state, and federal legislators in what can only be understood as an effort to enlarge the value of his own real estate portfolio.

Washington's charter remains documentary evidence that he had intentionally been deceitful. He never had any intention of abiding by the parameters of the Residence Act of 1790. He had duped Congressman Alexander White of northern Virginia, who would lose his congressional seat in shame. As repayment for the intentional infliction of the damage he had caused to White, Washington, ironically, would appoint White to the planning board commission for the new capital city. George Gale and Daniel Carroll of Maryland would also lose their reelection bids for voting in the affirmative on the Assumption Bill. Washington would also compensate them with appointments.

Philip Schuyler and George Washington maintained infrequent but cordial correspondence for a few years but never saw each other again. Schuyler was re-elected to the US Senate in 1797 and would have seen Washington at the March 4, 1797 inauguration of John Adams in Philadelphia but for an open and inflamed wound in his thigh that made it uncomfortable to travel.

Philip Schuyler turned his anger with Washington into energy and action. Schuyler prompted the New York State Assembly to request a report "to examine . . . what obstructions in the Hudson and Mohawk rivers will be proper to be removed, and to report thereon with their opinion of the most eligible mode for effecting the same, and defraying the expense thereof." Schuyler then drafted the first New York State canal law to promote "inland navigation," which was passed on March 24, 1791. "And to be it further enacted . . . the necessary survey made, of the ground situated between the Mohawk river . . . also between the Hudson river and the Wood creek . . . to cause an estimate to be made of the probable expense that will attend the making canals, sufficient for loaded boats to pass."

The next year, in 1792, Philip Schuyler became president of the Western Inland Lock Navigation Company and the Northern Inland Lock Navigation Company, both of which entities underwrote dams, locks, short canal segments, and drainage systems. Philip Schuyler was en route toward creating the Erie Canal, the most expansive and successful canal project in US history that would link the New York City Atlantic port with the interior of the United States.

George Washington was elected to a second term. If imitation is the highest form of flattery, Washington, in what also could be seen as one more slap in the face to the New York contingent, hired architect Pierre L'Enfant, Schuyler's choice to design Federal Hall in Lower Manhattan, to plan the new empire city. In addition to supervising L'Enfant to ensure the proper degree of grandeur, President Washington was engulfed in lawsuits in both the Virginia and Maryland Assemblies in an attempt to force Potomac Company shareholders to pay up. Washington spent wantonly to create his empire city, costing the young republic millions of dollars. As part of his scheme, he muscled out many property owners, mowing over their hard- won rights. The evidence for these tactics is exhibited on M Street plaques in Georgetown and in historical maps that demonstrate the chronological destruction of houses. To develop navigation along the Potomac was not only a byzantine political endeavor but it was also a geological nightmare.

Unfortunately for Washington, by the time the federal government settled into "Washington City," the Potomac Canal Company was financially insolvent. The cost of creating Washington, DC, was scandalously incalculable. A chilling insight into Washington's *modus operandi* can be found in his personal copy of the 1789 Acts of Congress, recently auctioned at Christie's for $10 million. The 106-page leather-bound volume, annotated with margin notes by Washington, contained his copy of the Constitution, the Bill of Rights, and the acts creating the State and Treasury Departments. Marked on its title page, signed by Washington, was a line that he claimed to be his personal motto: "*Mindexitus acta probat*,"—"the ends justify the means."

For 220 years, Thomas Jefferson's pablum has upstaged the truth that George Washington clearly attempted to profit from his office. Jefferson created his Dinner Table Bargain farrago for a quartet of reasons, all of which stemmed from the need to create an origin mythology for the United States. Instead of hailing George Washington as the American Pericles, Jefferson engineered a tale that made himself the hero. John Adams, Thomas Jefferson, James Madison, Alexander Hamilton, and John Jay were among the most educated men in history. All trained lawyers, they read history, literature, material on scientific methods, navigation and exploration, the principles of mathematics,

architecture, and the history of art. They were multilingual men of let-
ters who had studied the Bible, Sparta and Athens, the republics of Rome,
Carthage, and Venice; they read Plato and Aristotle, James Harrington's
Commonwealth, Machiavelli, and Montesquieu. While Adams, Jefferson,
Madison, Hamilton, and Jay often published their arguments on political
theory pseudonymously using Roman pen names, they exchanged tens of
thousands of letters among themselves that they preserved for posterity. Our
Founding Fathers were aware that they were writing history.

The first reason for Jefferson's fictional account about the alleged deal that
removed the capital city from New York to an undeveloped swamp along the
Potomac River was to insert himself into the trio from which he had been
excluded so that posterity would believe that he was the nation's great mediator.
(More than once, John Adams accused Jefferson of making up stories.) The
second reason for the tale was so that Jefferson could substitute the Christian
leitmotif of a "shining city on a hill" that painted a civilization free of taint for
the Realpolitik that Washington, DC, was not only created from a physical
swamp but also a moral morass. Jefferson's third intent, similar to the cherry-
tree allegory, was meant to burnish a hallowed legacy for our nation's first
president, who, in truth, co-opted the seat of government from New York
through trickery.

Thomas Jefferson's fourth reason was to make Alexander Hamilton a
villain. The rivalry for America's capital city charts two competing dreams
and the ruthless competition between two dear friends and American
statesmen—George Washington and Philip Schuyler. The collateral damage
caused by Jefferson's fabrication was lasting ignominy for the young man—
Alexander Hamilton—both called son. Alexander Hamilton would never
have "sold New York down the river"; he would never have betrayed the
New York clans. Jefferson's vengeful version of events, which was never
corroborated by James Madison, George Washington, or Alexander Hamilton,
and which is contradicted by factual records, made Alexander Hamilton a
convenient scapegoat. Jefferson's abuse of Hamilton, which marked the end
of their friendship, intensified over the years. Clearly unconcerned about
destabilizing Hamilton's relationship with Philip Schuyler, Jefferson also

demonstrated callous disregard for Betsey when he spitefully publicized Hamilton's private indiscretion with Maria Reynolds, causing a very public scandal. Despite Jefferson's persistent malevolent attacks against Hamilton, both George Washington and Philip Schuyler remained steadfastly loyal to Hamilton.

In 1792, at the same time that Jefferson first scribbled his tale, Aaron Burr, with the help of George Washington's real estate financier New York Governor Clinton, defeated Philip Schuyler for the New York Senate seat that Schuyler had held. Burr then became an enemy to both Schuyler and his son-in-law. Schuyler died in 1804. That same year, his son-in-law Alexander Hamilton also died. Mortally wounded in a duel with Burr, Hamilton, to the end of his life, remained loyal to Schuyler and to the people of New York.

Over time, George Washington's neighbors grew unhappy under the jurisdiction of the federal city. Among their list of dissatisfactions was the worry that their slave trade would be interrupted. The citizens of Alexandria voted and subsequently petitioned the US Congress to retrocede the city t o Virginia, which occurred on July 9, 1846.

The rivalry for America's capital city, in fact, resulted in a nation with two capitals—a symbiotic and inseverable duopoly: New York City, founded as a Dutch trading post after one of history's most legendary real estate deals, remains the financial and cultural heartbeat of the country; and Washington, DC, created from a swamp on the Potomac River, is the seat of government. Wall Street depends on a friendly federal government; political victories are, in turn, oxygenated by New York City money. The inadvertent adoption of duopoly from the United Provinces of the Netherlands by the United States of America caused a reverberation throughout the world. In addition to emulating the Constitution of the United States of America in the formation of new republics, countries like Australia, Brazil, Canada, New Zealand, and South Africa, with an eye on America, purposefully separated their seats of government from their financial and cultural capital cities. What began as a challenge between two men, two rivers, and two port towns has resulted in a tectonic shift in the very structure of modern nations and in redirecting the course of international relations.

ACKNOWLEDGMENTS

THIS BOOK COULD NOT HAVE been written without the love and support of Jon and Hadley Nagel. My most profound thanks to publisher Claiborne Hancock, to Jessica Case, and to the entire Pegasus team including Maria Fernandez, Peter Kranitz, Dan O'Conner, and Richard "Rick" Britton. My deepest thanks to bibliophile and very wise and talented Don Fehr. I owe a debt of gratitude, also, to those who have labored to digitize and annotate the letters and journals that comprise the University of Virginia Rotunda Collections. I salute the entire staff, in particular Holly Shulman and John Stagg, who have become friends, and Ted Crackel and his colleagues Ed Lengel and Benjamin Lee Huggins. Another big thank you to Kenneth Bowling, Charlene Bickford, Chuck di Giacomantonio, and Helen Veit at George Washington University's First Federal Congress Project for generously allowing me to spend days with the material it has taken them over thirty years to lovingly and expertly compile and preserve. It is my fervent hope that more of our universities, libraries, and historical societies use Rotunda and the First Federal Congress Project as paradigms for encouraging scholarship.

A book like this truly takes a village.

Thank you to the New York Historical Society's indefatigable Louise Mirrer and Jim Basker at the Gilder Lehrman Institute. Thank you to Valery Paley, Jean Ashton, Edward "Ted" O'Reilly, Tammy Kiter, Joe Festa, Michael Ryan, Marilyn Kushner, Debra Schmidt Bach, Jill Reichenbach, and Wendy Ikemoto for their unparalleled knowledge and passion for my subject.

Enormous thanks to Jessica Serfilippi at the Schuyler Mansion State Historic Site in Albany, New York, who never lost her patience with my millions of questions. Jessica, you are a rock star! Thank you also to her boss, Heidi Hill, for an absorbing and very factual tour of The Pastures. A thank-you to Christine Valosin at the Saratoga National Historical Park and to Doug McComb at the Albany Institute of History & Art. Thank you also to Hilary Anderson Stelling and Maureen Harper at the Scottish Rite Masonic Museum & Library for allowing me to use their wonderful painting that portrays and poeticizes the very first meeting between George Washington and a young soldier named Alexander Hamilton.

At the Library of Congress: Thank you to Steven J. Herman, Jeffrey M. Flannery, Bruce Kirby, Teresa Sierra, and Travis Westly—all expert at guiding authors and the public through our cherished national treasures. At the National Archives: Thank you to Jane Fitzgerald, William H. Davis, and Brenda Kepley.

Retired New York Public Library uber librarian David Smith, known affectionately by many as "Librarian to the Stars," can find anything and can locate anyone pertinent to any topic. He is a good friend and rounded up Thomas Lannon, Ermino D'Onofrio, Vincenzo "Vinny" Rutigliano, and Sachiko "Sachi" Clayton in the Milstein Collection, all at the New York Public Library, to come to my assistance. Thank you to Mark Bartlett, Carolyn Waters, and Barbara Bieck of the New York Society Library. At Mount Vernon: Samantha Snyder, Amanda Isaac, and Dawn Bonner. Thank you to Lindsay Turley and Lauren Robinson at the Museum of the City of New York. And thank you to Daniel Prebutt at the Federal Hall National Memorial, who loves New York City as I do. Thank you to Steve Lansdale at Heritage Auctions in Texas for digging and digging until we found Lady Kitty.

At the Columbia University Libraries: Jennifer Steenshorne, associate editor of the John Jay papers, and Stephen Paul Davis, director of the digital program. Eric Novotny of Penn State University Library. Heather Iannucci and her colleagues Arthur Benware, Andrea Cerbie, Wendy Ross, and Allan Weinreb at the John Jay Homestead in Katonah, New York. At the Society of the Cincinnati in Washington, DC: Rachel Jirka. At the University of Virginia Library: C. Jared Loewenstein. At Gunston Hall: Mark Whatford. At the Fred W. Smith National Library for the Study of George Washington at Mount Vernon: Mark Santangelo and Corby O'Connor. At the Yale University Jonathan Edwards Center: Kenneth Minkema.

Thank you to my friends and "FBC" (family by choice): Claxton Edmonds Allen, III , aka "Ed Allen;" Betsy Smith and John Barrie; Christine Biddle; Carla and Henry Darlington; Marc de Gontaut-Biron; Steven Hill; Tom and Colleen Hills; Kathy and Rick Hilton; Roberta and Arthur Houghton; free-spirited world travelers Jeanne and Stephanie Lawrence; HRH, Prince Charles-Henri de Lobkowicz; Cathy Michaelson; SuSu, Jeff, Blaise and Pierce Miller; Christa Percopo; Mitzi Perdue; Alexandra Stafford Rathlé; Peter Schweizer; Marc G. and Lindsay Smith; Kari Tiedemann; my *Causeries du Lundi* compatriots in culture; Jordon Carroll; Thomas Collier; Wendy Carduner, for giving me an oasis; Stuart Vander Schauw and Evelyn Scheffer, for keeping me in Antica Tostatura espresso.

One day, when I was a sophomore at Mount Holyoke College, my neighbor in Safford Hall, Mary Macmanus, went running down the hall screaming, "Joe Ellis is a GOD!" She may be right. One of the biggest regrets of my life is that I never took a class with Joe while I was at Mount Holyoke, not having an interest in those days for battles, dates, and dead guys. Joe, however, has become Professor of Life and friend to the entire Nagel family; another thank-you to Joe's wife, Ellen, for understanding Joe's great heart and for allowing us to intrude into your lives.

BIBLIOGRAPHY

A Century of Lawmaking for a New Nation: U.S. Congressional Documents and Debates, 1774–1875. http://memory.loc.gov/ammem/amlaw/lwac.html. https://memory.loc.gov/ammem/amlaw/.

Abbott, Carl. "The Neighborhoods of New York, 1760–1775." *New York History,* vol. 55, no. 1 (1974), 35–54.

Achenbach, Joel. *The Grand Idea: George Washington's Potomac and the Race to the West.* New York: Simon & Schuster, 2004.

Adams, Herbert Baxter. "George Washington's Interest in Western Lands." *Johns Hopkins University Studies in Historical and Political Science,* Third Series, vol. 3 (1995), 55–77.

———. "Washington's Interest in the Potomac Company." *Johns Hopkins University Studies in Historical and Political Science,* Third Series, vol. 3, 79–91.

Albion, Robert Greenhalgh. "New York Port in the New Republic, 1783–1793." *New York History,* vol. 21, no. 4 (1940), 388–403.

Alexander, Edward P. *A Revolutionary Conservative: James Duane of New York.* New York: Columbia University Press, 1938.

Allen, Stephen. *Memoirs.* New York: New York Society Library, 1927. (Not published, but edited and donated by John C. Travis, a great-grandson of Mr. Allen.)

Allgor, Catherine. *Parlor Politics.* Charlottesville, VA: University of Virginia Press, 2000.

Ambler, Charles Henry. *George Washington and the West.* New York: Russell & Russell, 1936.

Amory, Thomas Coffin, editor. "Centennial Memoir of Major-General John Sullivan (1740–1795)." *The Pennsylvania Magazine of History and Biography,* 1876.

Arendt, Hannah. *On Revolution.* New York: The Viking Press, 1963.

Asher, G. M. *Henry Hudson: The Navigator*. London: The Hakluyt Society, 1860.

Bacon-Foster, Cora. *Early Chapters in the Development of Patomac Route to the West*. Washington, DC: Columbia Historical Society, 1912.

Baldwin, Leland D. "The American Quest for the City of God: Errand into the Wilderness." *Western Pennsylvania Historical Magazine*, vol. 59, no. 2 (April 1976), 185–213.

Barck, Oscar Theodore. *New York City During the War for Independence*. Port Washington, NY: Ira J. Friedman, Inc., 1966 (first published by Columbia University Press, 1931).

Baxter, Katherine Schuyler. *A Godchild of Washington*. London, NY: F. Tennyson Neely, 1897.

Bayard-Campbell-Pearsall Collection, Manuscripts and Archives Division, Research Libraries, New York Public Library.

Beard, Charles A. *An Economic Interpretation of the Constitution of the United States*. New York: The Macmillan Company, 1921.

Beeman, Richard, Stephen Botein, and Edward C. Carter II, editors. *Beyond Confederation: Origins of the Constitution and American National Identity*. Chapel Hill, NC: University of North Carolina Press for the Williamsburg, Virginia, Institute of Early American History, 1987.

Berkin, Carol. *A Brilliant Solution*. New York: Harvest Books, 2003.

Bickford, Charlene B., Kenneth R. Bowling, William Charles diGiacomantonio, and Helen E. Veit, editors. *The Documentary History of the First Federal Congress of the United States of America, March 4, 1789–March 3, 1791, vols. I–XX*. Baltimore: The Johns Hopkins University Press, 1972–2012.

Bond, Beverley W., Jr. "The Quit-Rent System in the American Colonies." *The American Historical Review*, vol. 17, no. 3 (April 1912), 496–516.

Booth, Mary L. *History of the City of New York from Its Earliest Settlement to the Present Time*. New York: W. R. C. Clark & Meeker, 1859.

Bordewich, Fergus M. *Washington: How Slaves, Idealists, and Scoundrels Created the Nation's Capital*. New York: Amistad, 2009.

Botero, Giovanni. *The Greatness of Cities*. London: Robert Peterson, 1606.

Boucher, Jonathan. *Letters to George Washington*. Edited by Worthington Chauncey Ford. Brooklyn, NY: Historical Printing Club,1899.

Bowen, Catherine Drinker. *Miracle at Philadelphia*. New York: Little, Brown & Company, 1966.

Bowling, Kenneth R. "A Place to Which Tribute is Brought: The Contest for the Federal Capital in 1783." *Prologue,* vol. 8, no. 3 (Fall 1976), 129–139.

———. "Dinner at Jefferson's: A Note on Jacob E. Cooke's 'The Compromise of 1790.'" *The William and Mary Quarterly,* Third Series, vol. 28, no. 4 (October 1971), 629–648.

———. "New Light on the Philadelphia Mutiny of 1783: Federal-State Confrontation at the Close of the War for Independence." *The Pennsylvania Magazine of History and Biography,* vol. 101, no. 4 (October 1977), 419–450.

———. "The Bank Bill, The Capital City and President Washington." *Capitol Studies,* vol. 1 (1972), 59–71.

———. *The Creation of Washington D.C.: The Idea and Location of the American Capital.* Fairfax, VA: George Mason University Press, 1991.

Brissot de Warville, Jacques-Pierre. *New Travels in the United States of America: Including the Commerce of America with Europe; Particularly with France and Great Britain.* London: J. S. Jordan, 1794.

Broadwater, Jeff. *James Madison: A Son of Virginia & A Founder of the Nation.* Chapel Hill, NC: The University of North Carolina Press, 2012.

Brookhiser, Richard. *James Madison.* New York: Basic Books, 2011.

Brooks, Geraldine. *Dames and Daughters of Colonial Days.* New York: Thomas Y. Crowell & Co., vol. I, 1900, and vol. II, 1901.

Brunhouse, Robert L. *The Counter-Revolution in Pennsylvania, 1776–1790.* Harrisburg, PA: Pennsylvania Historical Commission, 1942.

Burrows, Edwin G., and Mike Wallace. *Gotham: A History of New York City To 1898.* New York: Oxford University Press, 1999.

Burstein, Andrew, and Nancy Isenberg. *Madison and Jefferson.* New York: Random House, 2010.

Caldwell, Mark. *New York Night.* New York: Scribner, 2005.

Campbell, William J. *Negotiating at the Oneida Carry.* Bloomington, IN: Organizations of American Historians (National Park Services), May 2017.

Carpenter, Theresa, editor. *New York Diaries, 1609–2009*. New York: Modern Library, 2012.

Carroll, Charles. *Unpublished Letters of Charles Carroll of Carrollton and his father Charles Carrollton of Doughoregun*. New York: The United States Catholic Society, 1902.

de Chastellux, François-Jean. *Voyages Dans l'Amérique Septentrionale Dans les années 1780, 1781 & 1782*. Paris: Chez Prault, 1786.

Chernow, Ron. *Alexander Hamilton*. New York: The Penguin Press, 2004.

———. *Washington: A Life*. New York: The Penguin Press, 2010.

Cleland, Hugh. *George Washington in the Ohio Valley*. Pittsburgh: University of Pittsburgh Press, 1955.

Clinton Family Papers, 1776–1806, Peter Force Collection, Library of Congress.

Condorcet, Marie-Jean-Antoine-Nicolas de Caritat, Marquis de. *De l'Influence de la Révolution d'Amérique sur l'Europe*. Paris, 1786.

Constantelos, Demetrios J. "American Philhellenism, parts I & II." *Greek-American Review*, (2002).

Conway, Moncure Daniel. *Barons of the Potomack and the Rappahannock*. New York: The Grolier Club, 1892.

Cooke, Jacob E. "The Compromise of 1790." *The William and Mary Quarterly*, Third Series, vol. 27, no. 4 (October 1970), 523–545.

Countryman, Edward. *A People in Revolution: The American Revolution and Political Society in New York, 1760–1790*. Baltimore: The Johns Hopkins University Press, 1981.

———. *The American Revolution*. New York: Hill and Wang, 2003 (revised edition).

———. "The Uses of Capital in Revolutionary America: The Case of the New York Loyalist Merchants." *The William and Mary Quarterly*, Third Series, vol. 49, no. 1 (January 1992), 3–28.

Craughwell, Thomas J. *Thomas Jefferson's Crème Brûlée*. Philadelphia: Quirk Books, 2012.

Crawford, Mary Caroline. *Romantic Days in the Early Republic*. Boston: Little, Brown, and Company, 1912.

Cress, Lawrence Delbert. "Whither Columbia? Congressional Residence and the Politics of the New Nation, 1776–1787." *The William and Mary Quarterly*, Third Series, vol. 32, no. 4 (October 1975), 581–600.

Cresswell, Donald H., editor. *The American Revolution in Drawings and Prints; A Checklist of 1765–1790 Graphics in the Library of Congress*. Washington, DC: For sale by the Supt. of Docs., US Govt. Print. Off., 1975.

Custis, George Washington Parke. *Recollections and Private Memoirs of Washington by his Adopted Son*. Philadelphia: J. W. Bradley, 1861.

The Custis-Lee Family Papers, Washington, DC, Manuscript Division, Library of Congress.

Dawson, Henry B. *The Sons of Liberty In New York*. New York: Arno Press & The New York Times, 1969.

Desmond, Alice Curtis. *Alexander Hamilton's Wife*. New York: Dodd, Mead & Company, 1952.

DeVoe, Thomas F. *The Market Book*. New York: Burt Franklin, 1969 (first published in 1862).

DeWitt, Dave. *The Founding Foodies: How Washington, Jefferson, and Franklin Revolutionized American Cuisine*. Naperville, IL: Sourcebooks, 2010.

Duer, William Alexander. *New York as It Was, During the Latter Part of the Last Century: An Anniversary Address Delivered Before the St. Nicholas Society, of the City of New-York, December 1st, 1848*. New York: Stanford and Swords, 1849.

Dunlap, William. *History of the American Theatre*. London: Richard Bentley, 1833.

Duyckinck, Evert A. "New York After the Revolution: The First Seat of Government Under the Constitution." *Frank Leslie's Popular Monthly*, vol. 18, no. 3 (September 1884), 339–353.

Elkins, Stanley, and Eric McKitrick. *The Age of Federalism: The Early American Republic, 1788–1800*. New York: Oxford University Press, 1993.

Eller, Ernest McNeill, editor. *Chesapeake Bay in the American Revolution*. Centreville, Maryland: Tidewater Publishers, 1981.

Ellet, E. F. *Court Circles of the Republic*. Hartford: Hartford Publishing Co., 1869.

Ellis, Joseph J. *After The Revolution: Profiles of Early American Culture*. New York: W. W. Norton & Company, 1979.

———. *American Creation: Triumphs and Tragedies at the Founding of the Republic*. New York: Alfred A. Knopf, 2007.

———. *American Sphinx: The Character of Thomas Jefferson*. New York: Alfred A. Knopf, 1997.

———. *First Family: Abigail and John Adams*. New York: Alfred A. Knopf, 2010.

———. *Founding Brothers: The Revolutionary Generation*. New York: Alfred A. Knopf, 2005.

———. *His Excellency, George Washington*. New York: Alfred A. Knopf, 2004.

Evans, Lewis. *Geographical, Historical, Political, Philosophical and Mechanical Essays, Number II [1754]*. Philadelphia: L. H. Gipson, 1939.

Featherstonhaugh Collection, New York Historical Society.

Ferling, John E. *The First of Men: A Life of George Washington*. New York: Oxford University Press, 2010.

Fish, Hamilton. *New York State: The Battleground of the Revolutionary War*. New York: Vantage Press, 1976.

Fiske, John. *The Critical Period of American History: 1783–1789*. Cambridge: The Riverside Press, 1895.

Fleischacker, Samuel. "Adam Smith's Reception among the American Founders, 1776–1790." *The William and Mary Quarterly*, Third Series, vol. 59, no. 4 (October 2002), 897–924.

Flexner, James Thomas. *George Washington: The Forge of Experience (1732–1775)*. Boston: Little, Brown and Company, 1965.

———. *George Washington and the New Nation*. Boston: Little, Brown and Company, 1969.

———. *George Washington In the American Revolution*. Boston: Little, Brown and Company, 1967.

Fontaine, James, et al. *Memoirs of a Huguenot Family*. Translated and compiled by Ann Maury. New York: G. P. Putnam, 1853.

Ford, Paul Leicester. *The Journals of Hugh Gaine, Printer*. New York: Dodd, Mead Company, 1902.

————. *The True George Washington*. Philadelphia: The Lippincott Company, 1896.

Forsyth, Mary Isabella. *The Beginnings of New York*. Boston: The Gorham Press, 1909.

Founders Online. National Historical Publications and Records Commission, National Archives and Records Administration, United States Government. www.founders.archives.gov.

Freeman, Douglas Southall. *George Washington: A Biography*. Fairfield, NJ: Augustus M. Kelley, 1981 (first published by Scribner in 1952).

Freeman, Linda, Louise V. North, and Janet M. Wedge, editors. *Selected Letters of John Jay and Sarah Livingston Jay: Correspondence by or to the First Chief Justice of the United States and His Wife*. Jefferson, NC: McFarland & Company, 2005.

Fripp, Charles Bowles. "Statistics of the City of New York." *Journal of the Statistical Society of London*, vol. 2, no. 1 (February 1839), 1–25.

Gawalt, Gerard W., and Ann G. Gawalt, editors. *First Daughters*. New York: Black Dog & Leventhal, in association with the Library of Congress, 2004.

Gerlach, Don R. *Proud Patriot: Philip Schuyler and the War of Independence, 1775–1783*. Syracuse, NY: Syracuse University Press, 1987.

Gilchrist, Agnes Addison. "John McComb, Sr. and Jr., in New York, 1784–1799." *Journal of the Society of Architectural Historians*, vol. 31, no. 1 (1972), 10–21.

Gilje, Paul A. "Culture of Conflict: The Impact of Commercialization on New York Workingmen, 1787–1829." In *New York and the Rise of American Capitalism*, edited by William Pencak and Conrad Edick Wright. New York: New York Historical Society, 1989.

Graymont, Barbara. "New York State Indian Policy After the Revolution." *New York History*, vol. 57, no. 4 (October 1976), 438–474.

Greene, Everts Boutell. *A History of American Life in Twelve Volumes, vol. 4: The Revolutionary Generation, 1763–1790*. Edited by Arthur M. Schlesinger and Dixon Ryan Fox. New York: The Macmillan Company, 1943.

Griswold, Rufus Wilmot. *The Republican Court or American Society in the Days of Washington*. New York: D. Appleton and Company, 1855.

Grunwald, Lisa, and Stephen J. Adler, editors. *Women's Letters: America from the Revolutionary War to the Present*. New York: The Dial Press, 2005.

Gutheim, Frederick. *The Potomac*. New York: Holt, Rinehart and Winston, 1949.

Hakluyt, Richard. *The Navigations Voyages Traffiques & Discoveries of the English Nation*. Glasgow: James MacLehose and Sons, 1905.

Hamilton, Allan McLane. *The Intimate Life of Alexander Hamilton*. New York: Charles Scribner's Sons, 1911.

Hamilton, James A. *Reminiscences of James A. Hamilton*. New York: Charles Scribner & Co., 1869.

Hamm, Margherita Arlina. *Famous Families of New York (vols. I & II)*. New York: G. P. Putnam's Sons, 1902.

Harrington, James. *The Common-Wealth of Oceana*. London: J. Streater for Livewell Chapman, 1656.

Hazard, Ebenezer. Letter to Theodore Morse, December 29, 1788. Manuscript Division, Library of Congress.

Henderson, Helen W. *A Loiterer In New York*. New York: George H. Doran Company, 1917.

Hess, Stephen. *America's Political Dynasties: From Adams to Kennedy*. Garden City, NY: Doubleday & Company, Inc., 1966.

Hitchens, Christopher. *Thomas Jefferson*. New York: Atlas Books/HarperCollins, 2005.

Hixton, Ada Hope, and William Reid Cubban. "George Washington Land Speculator." *Journal of the Illinois State Historical Society*, vol. 11, no. 4 (January 1919), 566–575.

Hobart, Lois. *Patriot's Lady: The Life of Sarah Livingston Jay*. New York: Funk & Wagnalls Company, Inc., 1960.

Hobbes, Thomas. *Leviathan*. London: Andrew Crooke, 1651.

Hofstadter, Richard. *The Idea of a Party System: The Rise of Legitimate Opposition in the United States, 1789–1840*. Berkeley, CA: University of California Press, 1969.

Holliday, Carl. *Woman's Life in Colonial Days*. Boston: The Cornhill Publishing Co., 1922.

Holmes, David L. *The Religion of the Founding Fathers*. Charlottesville, VA: Ash-Lawn Highland and The Clements Library (University of Michigan), 2003.

Holton, Woody. "Abigail Adams, Bond Speculator." *The William and Mary Quarterly*, Third Series, vol. 64, no. 4 (October 2007), 821–838.

Homberger, Eric. *The Historical Atlas of New York City: A Visual Celebration of 400 Years of New York City's History—Revised and Updated*. New York: Henry Holt and Company, 2005 (first published 1994).

Hood, Clifton. "An Unusable Past: Urban Elites, New York City's Evacuation Day, and the Transformations of Memory Culture." *Journal of Social History*, vol. 37, no. 4 (Summer 2004), 883–913.

Hopkinson, Francis. *The Miscellaneous Essays and Occasional Writings, vol. I*. Philadelphia: T. Dobson, 1792.

Humphrey, Thomas J. *Land and Liberty: Hudson Valley Riots in the Age of Revolution*. DeKalb, IL: Northern Illinois Press, 2004.

Irving, Washington. *A History of New York by "Diedrich Knickerbocker."* Philadelphia: Inskeep and Bradford, 1809.

———. *Salmagundi; or The Whim-Whams and Opinions of Launcelot Langstaff, Esq. & Others*. Written with William Irving and James Kirke Paulding. New York: David Longworth, 1807–1808.

———. *The Complete Works, vols. 19–21, Life of George Washington*. Edited by Allen Guttmann and James A. Sappenfield. Boston: Twayne Publishers, 1982.

Jackson, Kenneth T., and David S. Dunbar, editors. *Empire City: New York Through the Centuries*. New York: Columbia University Press, 2002.

Jea, John. *The Life, History, and Unparalleled Sufferings of John Jea, the African Preacher. Compiled and Written by Himself*. Portsea, England: John Jea, 1811.

Jefferson, Thomas. *A Summary View of the Rights of British America*. Williamsburg, VA: Clementina Rind, 1774.

———. *Notes on the State of Virginia*. London: John Stockdale, 1787.

Jensen, Merrill. *The New Nation: A History of the United States During the Confederation 1781–1789*. New York: Alfred A. Knopf, 1950.

Johnson, Paul. *George Washington: The Founding Father*. New York: HarperCollins, 2005.

Johnston, Henry P., editor. *The Correspondence and Public Papers of John Jay, vol. III (1782–1793).* New York: G. P. Putnam's Sons, 1891.

———. "New York After the Revolution." *Magazine of American History,* vol. 29, no. 4 (April 1893), 305–331.

Jones, Alice Hanson. "Wealth and Growth of the Thirteen Colonies: Some Implications." *The Journal of Economic History,* vol. 44, no. 2 (June 1984), 239–254.

Jones, Robert F. *"The King of the Alley" William Duer: Politician, Entrepreneur, and Speculator.* Philadelphia: American Philosophical Society, 1992.

Journal of the Votes and Proceedings of the General Assembly of the Colony of New York from 1766–1776. New York: J. Buel Printers, 1820.

Kendall, Joshua. *The Forgotten Founding Father: Noah Webster's Obsession and the Creation of an American Culture.* New York: G. P. Putnam's Sons, 2011.

Ketcham, Ralph. *James Madison.* Charlottesville, VA: University of Virginia Press, 1990.

Ketcham, Ralph, editor. *The Anti-Federalist Papers and the Constitutional Convention Debates.* New York: Signet Classic, 2003.

Kilmeade, Brian, and Don Yaeger. *George Washington's Secret Six: The Spy Ring That Saved the American Revolution.* New York: Sentinel, 2013.

Kitman, Marvin. *George Washington's Expense Account.* New York: Simon and Schuster, 1970.

Kroessler, Jeffrey A. *New York Year by Year: A Chronology of the Great Metropolis.* New York: New York University Press, 2002.

Kurlansky, Mark. *The Big Oyster.* New York: Random House, 2007.

Lamb, Martha J. *History of the City of New York: Its Origin, Rise, and Progress.* New York: A. S. Barnes and Company, 1877.

Larson, Edward J. *A Magnificent Catastrophe.* New York: Free Press, 2007.

———. *The Return of George Washington: 1783–1789.* New York: William Morrow, 2014.

Leibiger, Stuart. *Founding Friendship: George Washington, James Madison, and the Creation of the American Republic.* Charlottesville, VA: University of Virginia Press, 1999.

Lewis, Tom. *The Hudson: A History.* New Haven: Yale University Press, 2005.

Littlefield, Douglas R. "The Potomac Company: A Misadventure in Financing an Early American Internal Improvement Project." *The Business History Review*, vol. 58, no. 4 (Winter 1984), 562–595.

Livingston, John Henry. "The Livingston Manor." Address written for the New York branch of the Order of Colonial Lords of Manors in America, New York, 1916.

Loeb, John L. Jr., et al. editors. *An American Experience: Adeline Moses Loeb (1876–1953) and Her Early American Jewish Ancestry*. New York: Sons of the Revolution in the State of New York, 2009.

Loftin, T. L. *Contest for a Capital: George Washington, Robert Morris, and Congress, 1783–1791 Contenders*. Washington, DC: Tee Loftin Publishers, Inc., 1989.

Longacre, James Barton, and James Herring, editors. *The National Portrait Gallery of Distinguished Americans*. Philadelphia: Henry Perkins, 1834–1839.

Lopez, Claude-Anne. *Mon Cher Papa: Franklin and the Ladies of Paris)*. New Haven: Yale University Press, 1990.

Lossing, Benson John, editor. *The Diary of George Washington, from 1789–1791*. New York: Charles B. Richardson & Co., 1860.

———. *The Life & Times of Philip Schuyler, vols. I & II*. New York: Sheldon & Company, 1872.

Lundberg, David, and Henry F. May. "The Enlightened Reader in America." *American Quarterly*, vol. 82, no. 2 (Summer 1976), 262–293.

Maclay, William. *The Journal of William Maclay (United States Senator from Pennsylvania, 1789–1791)*. New York: Albert & Charles Boni, 1927.

Manzo, Bettina, editor. "A Virginian in New York: The Diary of St. George Tucker (July–August 1786)." *New York History*, vol. 67, no. 2 (April 1986), 177–197.

Marcus, Maeva, editor. *The Documentary History of the Supreme Court of the United States, 1789–1800: Suits Against States (Van Staphorst v. Maryland)*, vol. 5. New York: Columbia University Press, 1994.

Matson, Cathy. "Public Vices, Private Benefit: William Duer and His Circle, 1776–1792." In *New York and the Rise of American Capitalism*, edited by William Pencak and Conrad Edick Wright. New York: New York Historical Society, 1989.

McCraw, Thomas K. *The Founders and Finance: How Hamilton, Gallatin, and Other Immigrants Forged a New Economy*. Cambridge, MA: The Belknap Press, 2012.

McCullough, David. *John Adams*. New York: Simon & Schuster, 2001.

McDonald, Forrest. *Alexander Hamilton: A Biography*. New York: W. W. Norton & Company, 1982.

———. *E Pluribus Unum: The Formation of the American Republic 1776–1790*. Indianapolis: Liberty Fund, 1965.

———. *The Presidency of George Washington*. Lawrence, KS: University Press of Kansas, 1974.

Miller, John Chester. *Alexander Hamilton: Portrait in Paradox*. New York: Harper & Brothers, 1959.

Mitchell, Broadus. *Alexander Hamilton: Youth to Maturity (1755–1788)*. New York: The Macmillan Company, 1957.

Monaghan, Frank, and Marvin Lowenthal. *This Was New York: The Nation's Capital in 1789*. Garden City, NY: Doubleday, Doran & Co., Inc., 1943.

Montross, Lynn. *The Reluctant Rebels: The Story of the Continental Congress 1774–1789*. New York: Harper & Brothers, 1950.

Morgan, Edmund S. *The Meaning of Independence*. Charlottesville, VA: University of Virginia Press, 1976.

Nadeau, Jean-Benoît, and Julie Barlow. *Sixty Million Frenchmen Can't Be Wrong*. London: Robson Books, 2004.

Nagel, Hadley. "The Pen and the Sword: The Friendship Between James Madison and George Washington (1786–1789)." Senior thesis, Johns Hopkins University, 2012.

North, Louise V. "Sarah Jay's Invitations to Dinner/Supper 1787–1788." *The Hudson River Valley Review* (Spring 2005), 68–79.

Norton, Mary Beth. *Liberty's Daughters: The Revolutionary Experience of American Women, 1750–1800*. Boston: Little, Brown & Co., 1980.

Nute, Grace L., editor. "Washington and the Potomac: Manuscripts of the Minnesota Historical Society," pt. I, *American Historical Review*, vol. 28 (1922–23), 503–18.

Nye, Russel Blaine. *The Cultural Life of the New Nation 1776–1830*. New York: Harper & Row, 1960.

Paine, Lincoln. *The Sea & Civilization: A Maritime History of the World*. New York: Alfred A. Knopf, 2013.

Paine, Thomas. *A Letter Addressed to the Abbé Raynal, on the Affairs of North America; In which the Mistakes of the Abbé's Account of the Revolution of America Are Corrected and Cleared Up*. Philadelphia: Melchoir Steiner, 1782.

———. *Common Sense*. Philadelphia: Robert Bell, January 10, 1776.

Papenfuse, Edward C. *In Pursuit of Profit: The Annapolis Merchants in the Era of the American Revolution, 1763–1805*. Baltimore: The Johns Hopkins University Press, 1975.

Pencak, William. "'Faithful Portraits of Our Hearts': Images of the Jay Family, 1725–1814." *Early American Studies*, vol. 7, no. 1 (Spring 2009), 82–108.

——— and Conrad Edick Wright, editors. *New York and the Rise of American Capitalism*. New York: New York Historical Society, 1989.

Peskin, Lawrence A. "Protection to Encouragement: Manufacturing and Mercantilism in New York City's Public Sphere, 1783–1795." *Journal of the Early Republic*, vol. 18, no. 4 (Winter 1998), 589–615.

Pomerantz, Sidney I. *New York, An American City: 1783–1803*. Port Washington, NY: Ira J. Friedman, Inc., 1965.

Pope, Michael Lee. *Hidden History of Alexandria, D.C.* Charleston, SC: The History Press, 2011.

Rackove, Jack N. *Revolutionaries: A New History of the Invention of America*. New York: Houghton Mifflin Harcourt, 2010.

———. *The Beginnings of National Politics: An Interpretive History of the Continental Congress*. New York: Alfred A. Knopf, 1979.

Raleigh, Sir Walter. *The Causes of the Magnificency and Opulency of Cities*. London: W. Bentley, 1651.

Ramsay, David. *The History of the American Revolution*. Philadelphia: R. Aitken & Son, 1789.

Riker, James. *"Evacuation Day," 1783: Its Many Stirring Events With Recollections of Capt. John Van Arsdale*. New York: Printed for the Author, 1883.

Roberts, Cokie. *Founding Mothers*. New York: HarperCollins, 2004.

Roberts, Warren. *A Place in History: Albany in the Age of Revolution, 1775–1825*. Albany, NY: State University of New York Press, 2010.

Romney, Susanah Shaw. "Intimate Networks and Children's Survival in New Netherland in the Seventeenth Century." *Early American Studies*, vol. 7, no. 2 (2009), 270–308.

Roth, Eric J. "From Protestant International to Hudson Valley Provincial: A Case Study of Language Use and Ethnicity in New Paltz, 1678–1834." *The Hudson River Valley Review*, vol. 21, no. 2 (2005), 40–55.

Sale, Edith Tunis. *Old Time Belles and Cavaliers*. Philadelphia: J. B. Lippincott Co., 1912.

Saunt, Claudio. *West of the Revolution: An Uncommon History of 1776*. New York: W. W. Norton and Company, 2014.

Scharf, J. Thomas, and Thompson Westcott. *History of Philadelphia 1609–1884*. Philadelphia: L. H. Everts & Co., 1884.

Schaukirk, Ewald Gustav. "Occupation of New York City by the British." *Pennsylvania Magazine of History and Biography*, vol. 10, no. 4 (January 1887), 418–445.

Schechter, Stephen L., and Wendell Tripp, editors. *World of the Founders: New York Communities in the Federal Period*. Albany, New York: New York State Commission on the Bicentennial of the United States Constitution, 1990.

Schecter, Barnet. *George Washington's America: A Biography Through His Maps*. New York: Walker & Company, 2010.

———. *The Battle For New York: The City at the Heart of the American Revolution*. New York: Walker & Company, 2002.

Schutz, John A., and Douglass Adair, editors. *The Spur of Fame: Dialogues of John Adams and Benjamin Rush 1805–1813*. Indianapolis: Liberty Fund, 1966.

Schuyler, George Washington. *Colonial New York: Philip Schuyler and his Family*. New York: Charles Scribner's Sons, 1885.

Seelye, John. *Beautiful Machine: Rivers and the Republican Plan 1755–1825*. New York: Oxford University Press, 1991.

———. *Prophetic Waters: The River in Early American Life and Literature*. New York: Oxford University Press, 1977.

Shomette, Donald G. *Maritime Alexandria: The Rise and Fall of an American Entrepôt*. Westminster, MD: Heritage Books, 2008.

Singleton, Esther. *Social New York Under the Georges 1714–1776*. Port Washington, NY: Ira J. Friedman, Inc., 1969 (first published 1902).

Smith, Abigail Adams. *Journal and Correspondence*. New York: Wiley and Putnam, 1841.

Smith, Adam. *An Inquiry into the Nature and Causes of the Wealth of Nations*. London: W. Strahan and T. Cadell, 1776.

Smith, Thomas E. V. *The City of New York in the Year of Washington's Inauguration, 1789*. New York: A. D. F. Randolph, 1889.

Smith, William Loughton. *Journal of William Loughton Smith 1790–1791*. Edited by Albert Matthews. Cambridge, Massachusetts: The University Press, 1917.

———. "Letters of William Loughton Smith to Edward Rutledge." *The South Carolina Historical Magazine*, vol. 69, issue 2 (April 1968), 101–139.

Spaulding, E. Wilder. *New York in the Critical Period, 1783–1789*. Port Washington, NY: Ira J. Friedman, Inc., 1963 (formerly published as *New York State Historical Association Series – Empire State Historical Publication XIX*, New York: Columbia University Press, 1932).

Stahr, Walter. *John Jay: Founding Father*. New York: Hambledon and London, 2005.

Stewart, Andrew, and United States Congress (House). *Chesapeake and Ohio Canal*. Washington, DC: United States Congressional Report 228 (House, First Session, 19th Congress), May 22, 1826.

Sutherland, Arthur. E. "Tenantry on the New York Manors." *Cornell Law Review*, vol. 41, no. 4 (Summer 1956), 620–639.

Sweig, Donald. "A Capital on the Potomac: A 1789 Broadside and Alexandria's Attempts to Capture the Cherished Prize." *The Virginia Magazine of History and Biography*, vol. 87, no. 1 (January 1979), 74–104.

Sylla, Richard, David J. Cowen, and Robert E. Wright. "The U.S. Panic of 1792: Financial Crisis Management and the Lender of Last Resort." Delivered at the NBER DAE Summer Institute, July 2006, and XIV International Economic History Congress, Session 20, "Capital Market Anomalies

in Economica History," Helsinki, August 2006. http://public.econ.duke
.edu/~staff/wrkshop_papers/2006-07Papers/Sylla.pdf.

Tebbel, John William. *George Washington's America*. New York: E. P. Dutton
and Company, Inc., 1954.

The Papers of Alexander Hamilton Digital Edition. Edited by Harold C. Syrett.
Charlottesville, VA: University of Virginia Press, Rotunda, 2011.

The Papers of James Madison, Digital Edition. Edited by J. C. A. Stagg. Charlottesville, VA: University of Virginia Press, Rotunda, 2010.

The Papers of George Mason. Edited by Robert Rutland. Chapel Hill, NC:
University of North Carolina Press, 1970.

The Papers of George Washington, Digital Edition. Edited by Theodore J. Crackel
and Edward G. Lengel. Charlottesville, VA: University of Virginia Press,
Rotunda, 2008.

The Papers of (Major General) William Alexander, "Lord Stirling" (1767–
1782), New York Historical Society.

The Papers of Nicholas Fish, Peter Force Collection, Library of Congress.

The Papers of Thomas Jefferson, Digital Edition. Edited by James P. McClure
and J. Jefferson Looney. Charlottesville, VA: University of Virginia Press,
Rotunda, 2009.

The Philip Church Papers, 1779–1861, New York Historical Society.

The Robert R. Livingston Papers (1658–1888), New York Historical Society.

The William Duer Papers, New York Historical Society.

Thomson, Hannah. "The Letters of Hannah Thomson, 1785–1788." *The Pennsylvania Magazine of History and Biography*, vol. 14, no. 1 (April 1890), 28–40.

Tilghman, Tench. *The Memoir of Lieut. Col. Tench Tilghman*. Albany, NY:
J. Munsell, 1876.

Virga, Vincent. *Cartographia*. New York: Little Brown and Company, 2007.

"Visit to Washington (diary extract of an Englishman Mr. Hunter)." *West
Virginia Historical Magazine Quarterly*, vol. 1, (1901), 60–64.

Warren, Mercy Otis. *History of the Rise, Progress, and Termination of the American Revolution*. Boston: Manning and Loring, 1805.

———. *Observations on the new Constitution, and the Federal and State Conventions. By a Columbian patriot. Sic transit Gloria Americana*. Boston, 1788.

Washington, George. *The Journal of Major George Washington*. Williamsburg, VA: William Hunter, 1754. http://digitalcommons.unl.edu/etas/33. https://digitalcommons.unl.edu/cgi/viewcontentcgi?article=1033&context=etas.

Watson, Elkanah. *Men and Times of the Revolution or Memoirs of Elkanah Watson*. New York: Dana and Company, 1856.

Webster, Noah. "General Description of New York." *The American Magazine*, no. 4 (March 1788).

Wharton, Anne Hollingsworth. *Salons Colonial and Republican*. New York: J. B. Lippinott Company, 1900.

———. *Social Life in the Early Republic*. New York: Benjamin Blom, 1902.

White, Philip L. *The Beekmans of New York In Politics and Commerce 1647–1877*. Baltimore, MD: Waverly Press, 1956.

Wilentz, Sean. *Chants Democratic*. Oxford: Oxford University Press, 2004 (twentieth anniversary edition).

———. *The Rise of American Democracy*. New York: W. W. Norton & Company, 2005.

Wilson Woodrow. *George Washington*. New York: Harper & Brothers, 1896.

Winchester, Simon. *The Men Who United the States*. New York: Harper Collins, 2013.

Wood, Gordon S. *Revolutionary Characters*. New York: The Penguin Press, 2006.

Wright, Robert E., and David J. Cowen. *Financial Founding Fathers: The Men Who Made America Rich*. Chicago: University of Chicago Press, 2006.

ENDNOTES

CHAPTER 1: THE RACE FOR A NEW WORLD CAPITAL OF EMPIRE

1   One earlier attempt occurred in mid eleventh-century England when an Anglo-Saxon king, known as Edward the Confessor, who was famous for being pious, built Westminster Palace, removing his government from commercial London. Westminster and London quickly grew together, however, creating the great metropolis and capital city. The economic and geopolitical tradition of one financial and legislative capital city dates back several millenia. In the ancient world, Eridu is considered the first capital city of Sumer. As the Mesopotamian empire expanded, the royal seat of ruler Gilgamesh (about 2900 b.c.e), called Uruk, became the empire's capital. During Sumer's Golden Age, its population was estimated to be around 50,000–80,000 people. The entire population of the country was about 1.5 million. The world population at that time was about 27 million. Similarly, for the Israelites, their capital city was Jerusalem; the Old Kingdom in Egypt (3000 B.C.E.) located its capital city at Memphis, which was subsequently supplanted during the New Kingdom (1500 B.C.E.) by Thebes. Carthage for the Phoenicians, Beijing, Athens, Rome, Byzantium, which became Constantinople under the Ottomans, London, Paris, Madrid, and Vienna are further examples of historic capital cities that served—and, in some cases, still serve—as both the financial and political nexus of their respective nation-empires.

CHAPTER 3: PARALLEL LIVES: GEORGE WASHINGTON AND PHILIP SCHUYLER

1   The Schuyler children were all christened with Dutch names. Elizabeth was known as "Betsey" until she was nearly forty years old, when her husband began calling her "Eliza." Both "Betsey" and "Angelica" ("Engeltje"—"little angel"—after her maternal grandmother, Engeltje Livingston van Rensselaer) spent part of their teenage years in New York City at the home of a Livingston cousin, where they were privately tutored. There were two branches of Livingstons—the Manor and the Clermont—and both hated the DeLanceys. The Livingstons claimed they were descendants of Robert the Bruce, thus, there were many Livingstons named Robert, including Robert, Third Lord of the Manor, and Robert R. of the Clermont line, who was John Jay's law partner and became known as "The Chancellor."

CHAPTER 4: A CHAIN, A COMPASS, AND A TOMAHAWK

1   Fontaine, *Memoirs of a Huguenot Family,* 388.
2   Among them were the powerful Iroquois, the Erie, Shawnee, Delaware, and Cherokee.

3   Among the parcels of property brought into the Custis-Washington clan were two
    large sections of two of three famous Claiborne family plantations near Williamsburg
    in aristocratic King William County. In 1752, Daniel Parke Custis purchased the
    2,800-acre "Claiborne Plantation" from Philip Whitehead Claiborne. Upon the
    death of Custis, one third of that land became part of Martha's widow's dowry;
    the remaining two thirds were legated to their surviving children, "Jacky" and
    "Patsy." "Patsy" would die in her teens in 1773. In 1774, George Washington, using
    Custis estate funds, purchased for Jacky a 1,683-acre parcel of land adjacent to
    the "Claiborne Plantation" property that was located on another Claiborne family
    plantation, the 5,000-acre "Romancoke." Jacky would also die prematurely (during
    the War of Independence). A third Claiborne plantation, called "Sweet Hall," was
    sold in 1769 to a man named Robert Ruffin.
4   The Great and Little Falls on the Potomac River are located about fourteen and five
    miles north of Washington, DC. The falls divide the Atlantic coastal tidewaters from
    the Piedmont and can be found by searching for Great Falls, Virginia, and Potomac
    or Bethesda, Maryland.
5   Flexner, 297.
6   Irving, *The Complete Works*, vol. 19, 205.
7   In a June 16, 1794, letter to Presley Neville, George Washington revealed that the
    parcel of land that Crawford had surveyed for the regiment abutted the rivers for
    about fifty-eight miles. Washington himself was eventually able to gain title to about
    30 percent of all of the acreage awarded his battalion.
8   In 1788, George Washington gave Lieutenant Colonel Henry Lee of Virginia
    an Arabian stud horse named Magnolio in exchange for 5,400 acres of land near
    the mouth of the Spring Fork River in Kentucky. Lee subsequently sold the same
    parcel of land to Alexander Spotswood, who was married to Washington's niece.
    Washington's nephew George Lewis learned of Lee's double-dealing and alerted
    his uncle. An incensed George Washington demanded better land from Lee in
    exchange for the horse and also offered to reimburse his niece's husband for the land.
    Spotswood, whose wife was an heiress to her childless uncle Washington's estate,
    graciously relinquished his claim to the property. It took Washington eleven years to
    gain clear title to the Kentucky land.
9   Over the decades, Washington would amass nearly 100,000 acres along the
    Potomac River. The United States Congressional Report No. 228, dated May 22,
    1826, contains an enormous bundle of letters, maps, and information gathered
    by Washington that date back to 1754, all on the topic of the development of the
    Potomac River as the gateway to the west.
10 His total net worth has been ascertained to equal about $600,000,000 in twenty-first
    century money.

CHAPTER 5: CURRENTS

1   "Bateau," a French word for "boat," refers to a flat-bottomed, double-pointed,
    cross-planked vessel specifically designed to transport people, products, and military
    supplies in shallow, narrow bodies of inland water and along the coastal shoreline.

2 Morgan Lewis to Harmanus Bleecker, May 26, 1828.

3 *Trekschuit*—a Dutch canal boat.

4 Carroll, pp. 34–35.

5 Ibid.

6 Ibid.

7 Despite a spate of books that place Alexander Hamilton at the Albany home of Philip Schuyler in the autumn of 1777, Hamilton neither stayed with nor met any member of the immediate family at that time. Hamilton arrived in Albany on November 5 after Philip and Catherine had departed for Saratoga to examine the charred remains of their beloved country estate. Betsey Schuyler, Hamilton's future wife, was with her sister, Angelica, in Boston.

8 Overwhelmed with emotion and gratitude, Burgoyne recounted that Schuyler welcomed him with every civility, stating to Burgoyne that, "he would have done the same." It is even more remarkable to note that Philip and Catherine Schuyler placed Burgoyne in the Schuylers' own master bedroom, as they would so honor George Washington and other illustrious visitors.

9 Chastellux on the Schuyler children: Peggy was animated, another daughter was charming and three sons were—"*les plus beaux enfans qu'on puisse voir*"—the most beautiful children one could ever see. Chastellux's appraisal in toto was that Philip Schuyler had an enviable life.

10 In the two years' time between their June 1775 march to arms and the September 1777 Battle of Saratoga, George Washington and Philip Schuyler exchanged 187 letters.

11 In attempt to prove loyal to the new United States of America while controlled by the British, New York surrendered its claim to a large parcel of land that included a good deal of Ohio, Indiana, and Illinois in 1782. Not to be outshone in dedication to the new union, Virginia ceded its claim to the Northwest Territory in 1784. (Virginia's transmontane lands south of the Ohio River would become the states of Kentucky in 1792 and later West Virginia.) Once again in competition with Virginia, New York surrendered its claims to the Northwest in 1785. Connecticut followed suit but continued to keep its claim on an area called the Western Reserve until 1795. Massachusetts claimed areas that today are parts of Michigan and Wisconsin, which she surrendered in 1786. A series of ordinances in 1784, 1785, and 1787 helped to clear a legal path for western states to join the union.

12 This political theory was articulated by Harvard University Kennedy School of Government professor Graham T. Allison in his 2017 book, *Destined for War*.

13 The spirited Angelica Schuyler had eloped with John Barker Church, a British-born businessman who traded in supplies to the Continental Army. Angelica would win the hearts of men like Thomas Jefferson, James Madison, and others. Mr. Church would return to England and serve in Parliament.

14 Hamilton was also the preferred choice of the Marquis de Lafayette, who not only volunteered to petition members of the Congress on Hamilton's behalf but also promised to "give you all public or private knowledge about Europe I am possessed of. Besides my private letters that may introduce you to my friends, I intend Giving

you *the* [sic] key of that Cabinet as well as of the societies which influence them. In a word, my good friend, Any thing [sic] in my power shall be entirely yours." (The Marquis de Lafayette to Alexander Hamilton, December 9, 1780.)

15 To New York representative and Schuyler cousin by marriage James Duane, May 14, 1780.

16 George Washington to Philip Schuyler, February 20, 1781.

17 Philip Schuyler to George Washington, July 6, 1781.

18 *The Continentalist* number 3, August 9, 1781.

19 Both Hamilton and his nemesis, Aaron Burr, made use of Philip Schuyler's library at The Pastures. Schuyler, whose library was the second largest in New York State, included copies of legal books by de Condorcet, Blackstone, Montesquieu, and Vattel, and titles including *Code Criminel de l'Empereur Charles V* and *The Parliamentary or Constitutional History of England, from the Earliest Times, to the Restoration of King Charles II*. The two-hundred-volume collection also housed many books on husbandry and ornithology, philosophy (Lord Shaftesbury, de la Rochefoucauld's maxims, Voltaire, Rousseau, and Scottish Enlightenment authors like Hutcheson and Hume), French and English poetry and novels, histories of European rulers like Peter the Great and James II, and ancient tomes in Greek and Latin (Homer, Cato, Virgil, Lucian, and Euclid), as well as contemporaneous mathematical textbooks.

CHAPTER 6: WANDERING IN EXILE

1 Aratus, an ancient Greek historical figure, lived in exile after the murder of his father in a military coup. As an adult, Aratus served as *strategos*—or military leader—of the Achaean League, a confederation of Greek states. The November 17, 1782, letter was posthumously attributed to George Lux, secretary of the Baltimore Committee of Correspondence.

2 The *Journals of the United States in Congress Assembled*, Saturday June 21, 1783, provides a moment-by-moment detailed account of the fracas. Other descriptions of the events include a letter sent "by express" from Elias Boudinot to George Washington on the same day as well as documentation by General Arthur St. Clair, who had been summoned to diffuse the armed mob.

3 August 30, 1783.

4 October 30, 1783.

5 Elias Boudinot to Thomas Willing, July 30, 1783.

6 George Washington to Robert Cary & Company, October 6, 1773.

7 A few members of these Sephardic Jewish families (with names like Barsimon, Seixas, Touro, and Levy), who arrived in North America in the seventeenth century notably fought for and won early and lasting legal equality and property rights for their diverse community that had been denied them in Europe. Men with names like Salomon, Bush, and Moses served gallantly under George Washington's command in the War of Independence. Daughters with surnames like Sarmiento and Franks integrated through marriage into prominent Christian families with familiar names like Biddle and De Lancey. Included amongst the many illustrious descendants of the early Sephardic Jewish American families is Emma Lazarus, whose poem, "The

New Colossus," etched into the base of the Statue of Liberty, serves as the welcoming anthem for those seeking refuge in the United States of America.

8   Dal Verme, Count Francesco, *Seeing America and Its Great Men, 1783–1784* (Charlottesville, VA: University of Virginia Press, 1969), 11–13.

9   October 12, 1783.

10 George Washington to New York Governor George Clinton, August 12, 1783.

11 Madison edited his notes after the decision was agreed to on October 7, so this insert is a reflection of the final vote.

12 George Washington's September 7, 1783 letter to James Duane, September 7, 1783.

13 Ibid.

14 Ibid.

CHAPTER 7: HADLEY'S QUADRANT & PARALLEL DREAMS

1   Lady Kitty's mother, Sarah Livingston, was the sister of signer of the Decleration of Independence Philip Livingston and Third Lord of the Manor Robert Livingston, and the daughter of Philip Livingston, the Second Lord of Livingston Manor. Kitty Livingston Duer was the great-granddaughter of Robert Livingston the Elder and Alida Schuyler van Rensselaer.

2   "Musicien, Dessinateur, Géomêtre, Astronome, Physicien, Jurisconsulte & Homme-d'État." (*Travels in North America*, 34).

3   Alice Hanson Jones, "Wealth and Growth of the Thirteen Colonies: Some Implications," 250–251.

4   His 2,500 acres on the Little Kanawha were situated about fifteen miles south of the mouth of the river. There was another tract at the fork of the Little Kanawha and the Ohio River that Washington was entitled to but the outbreak of war precluded Washington from the legal process of entering his claims at the surveyors' offices. While Washington was in service to his country, rival deeds were filed. Washington elected to forego some of his claims.

5   December 15–17, 1784.

6   George Washington to James Madison, December 28, 1784.

7   The New York delegates included Robert R. Livingston, whose great-grandparents, like those of Kitty Alexander Duer, were Robert Livingston the Elder and Alida Schuyler van Rensselaer; Walter Livingston, son of the Third Lord of Livingston Manor; Egbert Benson; and Charles De Witt.

CHAPTER 8: COUSINS AND CLIMBERS: NEW YORK

1   Mary Livingston Duane, Sally Livingston Jay, and "Lady Kitty" Alexander Duer were all the granddaughters of Philip Livingston, the Second Lord of Livingston Manor, whose mother was Alida Schuyler van Rensselaer. John Jay's mother was a van Cortlandt, as was Philip Schuyler's. Sarah Cornelia Clinton was also a member of the van Cortlandt family.

2   Hamilton and Sally Livingston Jay would enjoy a lifelong "brother-sister" kind of banter.

3   Sally Jay kept a list of her dinner guests for posterity. On January 10, 1788, for example, Spanish Ambassador Don Diego María de Gardoqui y Arriquibar, James

Madison, Ambassador van Bercek from the Netherlands, Baron von Steuben, and cousins William Duer, Chancellor Robert R. Livingston, and Alexander Hamilton were all present, as was Aaron Burr.

4   There were many firsts and historic events that occurred throughout the first year of the removal of the Congress of the Confederation to New York City in 1785: The first balloon flight across the English Channel would take place on January 7—four days before the opening session of the Congress of the Confederation in New York City; two days after the opening session of the Congress of the Confederation on January 11, the first issue of *The Times* of London would appear on January 13; on January 20, Samuel Ellis would advertise to sell his now storied eponymous island in New York Harbor but finds no buyer; on April 21, Tzarina Catherine II of Russia would end all privileges of nobility; on May 20, the United States Congress of the Confederation would adopt the Land Ordinance proposed by Thomas Jefferson in 1784 that provided for the division of the land west of the Appalachian Mountains, north of the Ohio River, and east of the Mississippi River into ten new states, enabling the federal government to sell lands and improve its coffers; on May 23, Benjamin Franklin would announce his invention of bifocals; on July 6, the Congress of the Confederation would adopt a United States currency called the "dollar," along with decimal coinage; on September 10, the United States would sign a trade agreement with Prussia; coal gas would be used for the first time for illumination; demonstrating a sign of complete divorce from the real needs of his people, Louis XVI of France would sign into law the regulation that all handkerchiefs must be square.

CHAPTER 9: POTOMAC FEVER

1   Watson, 246.

2   Watson, 267–277.

3   Watson, 297. Watson would share his diaries with Philip Schuyler. In 1792, the nearly sixty-year-old Philip Schuyler, still in the New York State Senate, effected the passage of an act that, like Washington's January 5, 1785, Virginia Act to develop the Potomac and James Rivers, chartered two companies, one for "opening a lock navigation from the navigable waters of the Hudson, to be extended to Lake Ontario and the Seneca Lake," and, the other intended to develop the waterways from the Hudson River to Lake Champlain, which Schuyler had begun during the War of Independence. Philip Schuyler would serve as the president of the Western Inland Lock Navigation Committee, the precursor to the Erie Canal, formed in 1792.

CHAPTER 10: DISUNITY

1   Delaware, New Jersey, Pennsylvania, New York, and Virginia. Representatives who attended were, from Delaware, former governor George Read, John Dickinson, and Richard Bassett; from New Jersey, Abraham Clark, William Houston, and James Schureman; from Pennsylvania, Tench Coxe; from New York, Egbert Benson and Alexander Hamilton; and, from Virginia, James Madison, Edmund Randolph, and St. George Tucker. To illustrate how disunified the United States of America was at

this point, even though the conference was held in Annapolis, Maryland, the state of Maryland had not even replied to the invitation nor did it send any delegates. Alexander Hamilton, whose Federalist sympathies contradicted New York Governor Clinton's own preferences, only received the nod to attend because his father-in-law, Philip Schuyler, was the most powerful member of the state assembly and arranged for Hamilton to join the delegation.

2 The November 8 Annual Report of that meeting recorded that "a small part only, has been received, & there are still considerable Ballances [sic] due of the sums formerly call'd for." The directors also approved a reimbursement payment of £34.10 to themselves, which included Washington, for expenses.

3 That meeting would conclude with a determination to make an even more aggressive effort to collect money due the corporation by its delinquent subscribers. Liens, foreclosures, and other hard-hitting measures were imposed on neighbors and friends not only with George Washington's approval, but often at his direction.

4 Rhode Island would not ratify until May 29, 1790.

CHAPTER 11: THE CALM BEFORE THE STORM

1 King's hometown would later be redistricted into the state of Maine.

2 Practically all physical evidence of the 1780s renaissance of New York City has been leveled. Number 3 Cherry Street is now rubble beneath the Manhattan side of the Brooklyn Bridge.

3 Included in attendance was New York City's Rabbi Gershom Mendes Seixas, a longtime friend of Washington. This hallowed site where men of all faiths gathered to observe Washington swear to uphold the Constitution, a building wherein groundbreaking historical moments had occurred, where Peter Zenger had been acquitted of libel, where the Stamp Act Congress sat, and where the Bill of Rights was written, would also be demolished (in 1812). The current Federal Hall on display for tourists was actually a Customs House built in 1842.

CHAPTER 12: TOWARD DUOPOLY

1 With adjustment for GDP, in 2021, that would be about $1.25 trillion.

2 Forrest McDonald, Alexander Hamilton: A Biography, p. 176.

3 In their 2010 biography, Madison and Jefferson, Andrew Burstein and Nancy Isenberg agree that Jefferson's claims are dubious: "There remains an aura of some mystery surrounding accounts of the so-called dinner-table bargain . . . [Hamilton, Madison, and Jefferson], as highly placed as they were, lacked the influence to determine by themselves the vote on two such controversial pieces of legislation." Burstein and Isenberg further assert that "there is no evidence whatsoever that Hamilton rounded up votes for the southern-based capital."

4 Hamilton Papers Publication Project, Columbia University, Box 262.

INDEX

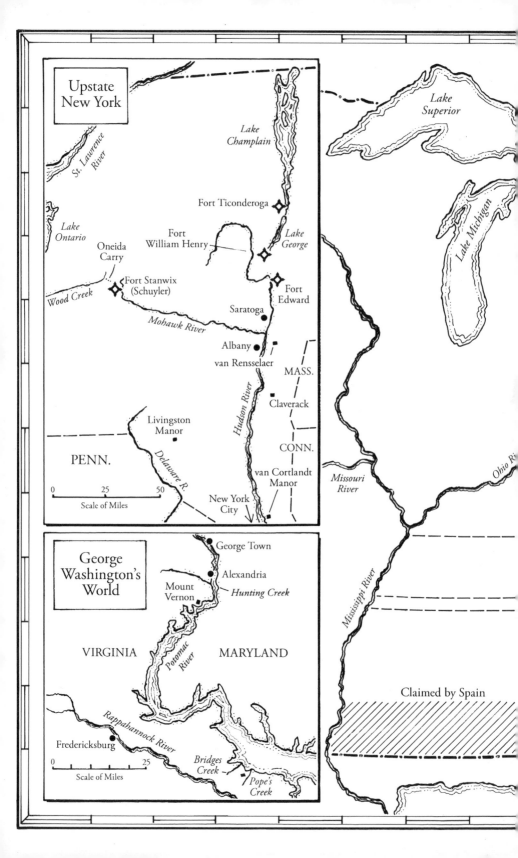

Upstate New York

Lake Superior

Lake Champlain

St. Lawrence River

Fort Ticonderoga

Lake Ontario

Lake Michigan

Fort William Henry

Lake George

Oneida Carry

Fort Stanwix (Schuyler)

Wood Creek

Saratoga

Fort Edward

Mohawk River

Albany

van Rensselaer

MASS.

Claverack

CONN.

Livingston Manor

Hudson River

Delaware R.

PENN.

van Cortlandt Manor

Missouri River

Ohio R.

New York City

0   25   50

Scale of Miles

George Washington's World

George Town

Alexandria

Mount Vernon

Hunting Creek

VIRGINIA

MARYLAND

Potomac River

Mississippi River

Rappahannock River

Fredericksburg

Claimed by Spain

0   25

Scale of Miles

Bridges Creek

Pope's Creek